Don't Give Up!

Left school at ten and a half
Wrote and published his own book

Patrick Flannery

Patrick Fla

ISBN: 978-1-905451-63-0

A CIP catalogue for this book is available from the National Library.

This book was published in cooperation with
Choice Publishing & Book Services Ltd, Drogheda, Co Louth, Ireland
Tel: 041 9841551 Email: info@choicepublishing.ie
www.choicepublishing.ie

To My Loving Mother

No day or hour passes that you're not on my mind. You listened when I talked to you in the hospital before you fell into a deep sleep. I said to you I couldn't wish for a better mother, with all the love and care you shared and gave to me. One lonely Christmas when I was all alone, I felt my life had fallen apart and all the people I thought would ring to wish me a happy new year and didn't. The phone rang, and it was you, my mother wishing me a happy new year. We talked and cried, and you were always there for me. It was so hard to let you go, but you taught me that when you love someone, you let them go with love. The loss of my mother, my best friend.

With love always, your son Patrick Flannery

My Life

This my life shall never be repeated,
it's no song that you can sing again.
So one day, since fate cannot be cheated,
I shall also pass to death's domain.
But whatever else I do while living,
This I beg of life before I'm done …
let me savour water, scent, rough weather
see the night stars, greet the rising sun.

I'd like happiness to call and see me,
And the finest feelings freely give.
If it's true that death will not release me,
How shall I unlearn to think and live.

Patrick Flannery
1994

Foreword

It has been said of Patrick Flannery that if he could read and write he would indeed be a very dangerous man. His first book gives a very unique insight into a man who has always shown passion and zest for everything he has done in his life, in his business as well as his interactions with others around him. Patrick is a man who sees the best in people but never suffers fools either. He is someone who has made a huge contribution to many people's lives and has put his own personal life experiences to good use in supporting others. This book is his life story to date and reading it will certainly have a impact on readers far and wide. Without Patrick's contribution to helping people and his own inputs and support, particularly to developing AA in the West of Ireland, many a person's life would have taken a totally different and probably worse direction. This book portrays how he grew up, completing his formal education at the age of 11, the strong and positive influence of his mother, where and how he made a difference to Erris and the many obstacles he encountered and overcame along the way. He provides lessons to people of all walks of life. His story is not only touching but tough. Patrick has walked through life standing up and fighting for his values, in particular for republicanism and his core inner belief in a united Ireland in control of and shaping its own future and destiny. In addition Patrick has always been an advocate of communities and has consistently fought for those same communities to take responsibility for themselves. His own life story is an example of this.

His relationship with alcohol as he describes in this book is probably now as much of an asset to him as it was a liability in the past. He can reach out to people, and today has a greater understanding of human beings resulting from the many, many events and adventures in his own life.

Patrick is still a young man and long may his life of experiences, adventures and good things continue. It is in itself a milestone in his life to publish this work and leave a legacy of advice, life's insights and experiences to others.

Gerard Mc Donnell

Chapter 1

<u>Back to My Teenage Years</u>

Growing up in Erris
Heritage Day / 15th August in Belmullet
Buzz in Erris / Banks / Borrowing
Palm Court / Dancing
Teresa
Younger happy days growing up in Porturlin
Telling my mother about the dances

Today is the 19th August 2005 and there is a big heritage day on in Belmullet. A day that the local people come with their stalls and sell their goods on the streets. It's absolutely beautiful, great sunshine today in Belmullet. There are people from all over the world here, people that came back on holidays and are still here visiting around Belmullet. It's a day like the 15th August again this year, 2005, and there is one of the biggest crowds that was ever seen. It's a traditional day as well, going back for hundreds of years, where people come to town and still keep the tradition up. On the 15th August there is live music on the streets.

When we were growing up as kids in Porturlin, we were always looking forward to the 15th August. It was a big thing for us all to come into Belmullet and we would spend the day in the town. Then as we were growing older, that night after the fair in the town, we would go out dancing to 'Palm Court' and would enjoy a great night of dancing. We used to look forward to it from year to year and it was one marvellous day, and still the tradition continues today. A lot of people are dressed up today in the old fashioned way and carrying on the tradition. It's great to see the people out enjoying themselves.

A lot of time in my life I would be around people that don't want to enjoy themselves, and when you are around people like that, they will pull you down. People in my life that I have seen getting up in the morning, always in bad humour, always complaining about something and I do not really want to be around them. They are not my type of people. When it is a genuine or serious concern, I will understand then that they have something to complain about. But I realise that there are people who go out of their way to find something to complain about. Earlier today I was listening to some of that complaining, and I just got dressed and left. I went into Belmullet to enjoy myself and that's where I was today. I always do, it's a special day, meeting people that are out on the town, and it's absolutely great to be able to do that, to have the health to do that. It's great to be able to get up in the morning and be healthy besides getting up in the morning complaining. I just cannot live around people like that who are moaning and groaning. I love positive people, people who are smiling and happy, it makes going through life a lot easier compared to people who don't do that.

When we were kids, the 15th of August was always a big day. We looked so forward to it. Our fathers would be fishing for the salmon for seven weeks and seven days a week. On the 12th of August they would make up the money that they had earned over those seven weeks, and it would be divided up among the crew and the skipper. Our fathers would give us so much money for the 15th August so that we could spend it and enjoy it on that day. I see it, even to this day, the kids spending their money on the 15th August at the fair. It's a great day, it's a family day and you are meeting people who are home on holidays. If you meet a fisherman you're talking about fishing, if you meet a farmer you're talking about farming and builders and so on. There is a great buzz in Erris.

Indeed there was always a buzz in Erris, but with the last ten years there is a massive buzz, with the new 72 bedroom hotel, so many restaurants in the town now. The whole town has completely changed, all new buildings, and it's great to see it. There are houses going up everywhere. People are thinking positively and it's great. They are moving forward and have better houses and homes now.

It's only with the last fifteen years in this country that people have started borrowing money from the banks and the banks have started lending money. When I was growing up, as a kid or even a teenager, there was no such thing as borrowing money from them. I believe that we didn't have to borrow money because we were fishing. Once we left the cradle, from eleven years old, I was fishing and so were my brothers. We were involved in making money from the sea. We wouldn't dream of borrowing money and indeed nobody would borrow money at that time. Whatever you had was your own. Like my father and mother, they didn't have a mortgage on their house, the little house that we had. Everybody was the same, what they had was their own. But today there are big houses with people borrowing up to one hundred per cent for their homes. People today are taking more chances; it's different times, totally different. The banks are encouraging people to borrow now; they are giving people cards now for the hole in the wall and the money will come out through the wall. It's all to tempt people, tempting students to borrow money as well. I think the banks are gangsters really; they are encouraging people to borrow more and more money. There is nothing wrong with borrowing money as long as you have a solid footing, that whatever you are borrowing for is fairly solid and you don't have to work all the hours God ever gives to pay back these banks. It's changed times and there are definitely better homes now. But it's a different way of life. There is more of a rush on this country today and the people than there was when we were growing up, and in my father and mother's time. But back then, we were looking forward to the 12th August and the money being made up. It would be divided up at my mother and father's house, on the table and all the kids would be around the table. We would all get money for the 15th August to have a good day out and to buy whatever we wanted. My mother would make food for my father and the crew and there would also be drink there for the crew, it was a celebration for the end of the salmon season and the money made. I remember the table being full with the money, an awful lot of money. It was nice to see it. And we were all a big happy family - that's the way that we were brought up. Whatever my father or mother earned would be all shared out and whatever they were thinking about, they would always share it with all the family. My father would always hand over the fishing money to my mother to buy the food for all of us and to look after us for the rest of the year. It was a nice experience to have this money on the 15th August to buy your clothes in Seamus Cafferkey's, clothes that would take you through the year. We looked so forward then to going out to 'Palm Court'. I loved going out there, dancing, I loved all the dance halls around Glenamoy, there was four nights that you could go out dancing if you wanted to.

We went dancing young too because we were out earning money at a young age, all we cared about was having enough money to get into the dance halls. We enjoyed the night, there was no such thing as drinking out in the few cars that were around at that time. Then the next night we would talk about the dance from the night before, people were happy then.

I used to get all the dances! The girls used to be mad for me to dance with them. I learned to dance when I was about twelve years old. My sisters taught me to jive, and we used to be practising the jiving in the house and waltzing as well. I turned out to be a fairly good jiver so I used to get all the dances. I went into the dance hall to dance, I would be out on the floor dancing. I wouldn't be standing around looking at people or be afraid to dance. I would be out for every jive and every waltz and I used to enjoy it to the last. I remember I had a habit when I was a young fella, I'd always say to a girl "Keep the last dance for me" and sometimes I might go back and dance with them and most times I wouldn't! But there was a time anyway, after Teresa and I was dating, my teenage love, that I would go to Palm Court that she would hold the dance for me. We'd be dancing and talking and chatting all night and then we'd go up to the mineral bar and have a minerals and I remember there was Club Milk's out. That's the sort of relationship that we had and then we'd meet every Sunday night. That went on for a while with that girl Teresa who was from Doohoma, Teresa Gaughan. We became good friends as well, she loved jiving and was a good jiver and I used to enjoy her company and we'd chat about everything - about our families and all that. Then when I would come home from the dance I would tell my mother about who I was with, but I used to tell her not to tell anyone else. And my mother used to say that she wouldn't tell anyone else but I realise that she used to tell all of the family! One night anyway, I thought that Teresa was going with somebody else behind my back, and there was a dance on in Aughoose, and she wanted to go to it. There used to be a dance in Aughoose on Wednesday nights, and I told her that I wasn't going. I went home and the weekend came and the following Wednesday came and it was time for the dance in Aughoose again and I remember going to the dance that night, thinking that she would be there. When I got to the dance her two friends, that knew me well, were there and they saw me out dancing and enjoying myself for the night. They came up to me and they were angry because they said that Teresa wouldn't go to the dance because she thought that I wouldn't be there. I felt like a real prick to have done that to her. She was a genuine young girl but my mind was thinking that she might have been going out with somebody else but she wasn't. But anyway her two friends reared up on me and I begged them not to tell her. At the end of the dance, I walked the last girl that I was dancing with to the car and the two friends saw me and they thought that I was with this girl, but I wasn't. But then the next night we went back to Palm Court in the car, a gang of us, and I had a date on with this Teresa again. I wouldn't dance with her until three or four dances from the end of the night, I had three dates for that night, I had told them to save the last dance for me. When the last dance came the three women must have got talking about 'Patrick' and saving the last dance for me but it was Teresa that I wanted to go dancing with. When I asked Teresa to dance she said

4

that she wouldn't dance with me. She said that I went to the dance in Aughoose without her and she was mad. But anyway we made up again after that and became friends again. It's a long story after that.

She went to England and I went to Scotland and we were supposed to meet up again in August but we never met up. Years went by and we never met each other but I always wondered what happened to her. When I did eventually meet up with her, it was when her father was dying and that was the first time that I had seen her in years. I was in the hospital in Belmullet, with my daughter Maria, visiting my father in law and there was a man in the next bed. Two ladies walked in to visit him and, after all those years that I never seen her, there was Theresa and her sister visiting their father. I walked out and as I passed her she said "Patrick" and we talked. We talked about both our lives all the way back to when were teenagers. I told her about my life as a fisherman and publican. I also told her that I started drinking when I was twenty and she couldn't believe it because in my young days she said "you always hated drink". I told her that today I counsel people to help them stop drinking. Then her father died and I went to the funeral. She could talk to me about anything, she knew that even when we were younger that we could talk and share anything that was in our lives - and we did. I always talked to her about my father and my mother. I hated drink at that time - I wouldn't look at drink. All I wanted was to go to the dances and enjoy myself. Years went by and I married and I had kids and she did as well. The only relationship that we had was when we met up and she shared her life with me. She talked to me for the first time about years ago in Palm Court . She is back in Manchester nursing, which is what she always wanted to do, even when she was young, she would tell me that she wanted to be nursing. And of course I wanted to be a fisherman and we used to share our dreams like that. But that was our life as teenager, it was all innocent. There was no harm in it and there was no love making or sex or that kind of thing going on, it was just that you would be going out to the dance with a girl, you wouldn't be going out with them for sex. You went out to enjoy yourself - the women and the men. The few that did go out to have sex, well they got their girlfriends pregnant and they ended up marrying them or the girls ended up marrying them. That was the way it was. But it was good times, I have good memories of going out dancing around Erris and enjoying myself. We went out to enjoy ourselves - we didn't go out to row or fight and even in them times you would see a lot of fighting. But the Porturlin lads wouldn't be into that type of thing - we used to work hard at the sea and then our reward was going out dancing with all the young girls and with our friends. We had good friends, I had a lot of good girl friends, as friends. We used to meet up in Palm Court and sit around the table with our 'Coke' or 'Orange' - them were the only two drinks that were available. Unlike today, there are all types of drinks going.

I'd come home and share the night with my mother and she would be delighted to hear all about it. She would love to hear who I had met at the dance, the girlfriend I had, and who I danced with, and she would know the mother and the father of these people and she would be delighted with me telling her all this. I shared everything with my mother in my young days. It was very easy to talk to my mother and I wouldn't talk to her until the rest of the family were all gone out of the house. She was a good, warm woman. I remember her telling me to always treat women the way that you would treat your mother, always show respect to women. And we did and they treated us with respect too.

There were thirteen in my family - my mother and father reared us to always look out for each other, and even our friends - boys or girls - we always looked out for each other. We made sure that we always looked out for each other, there was a great bond there as a family, as there was with the other families in Porturlin too. We made sure that everyone was ok.

Driving Sinn Fein politicians in Galway.

My father Tom Flannery
and mother Eileen Coyle
on their wedding day.
Married in
Bangor Erris Church in 1952.
Best man was
J.J O'Donnell (Porturlin)
Bridesmaid was Ita Corrigan (Dooyork).

Cow barn on
Flannery's farm
where cows are
housed in winter

Mary Deane's house in Graughill, our first home.

St Patrick's Day Parade, Pullathomas.

Curraghs used in Graughill
to fish in 1950's.

Cutting the hay with scythes before tractors came and saving it into cocks of hay for feeding the cattle.

Flannery Brothers & Sisters early 1960's in our home. Patrick on bottom left corner.

My Mother and Father around the table with some of my sisters and brothers taken in 1981

The cows are housed in the shed for winter

First Holy Communion 1983
Patrick (far left), Martin Joe McAndrew, Delia O'Malley, Brendan Flannery, Christy Flannery, Tony O'Donnell. Teachers Ann O'Donnell and Mrs Gardner

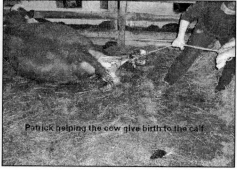

Patrick helping the cow give birth to the calf

Chapter 2

<u>Living in Erris</u>

4th November 2004
Gas getting go ahead from An Bord Pleanála
AA Meetings
My father / drinking
Working in Lincoln / Arguing with the English tractor driver
Scotland
Returning to Ireland / Asahi / Married
Caitriona being born / John standing for her / not paying me for the day
Back home to Ireland / Fishing / Dancing Mermaid
Us in the Talk of the Town
Violent Wife / Abuse
Walking out on my wife / Not on my kids
Returning home again at Christmas / Drink
Fighting with the Publican in Flannery's

Today is the 4th November 2004, a beautiful morning, nice wintry, frosty morning with no rain.

A couple of days ago the gas got the green light from An Bord Pleanála to come into the Pullathomas area where they will bring it in from thirty miles out in the Atlantic Ocean into Glengad. Then onto the peat land where they will build their plant there. I had a hearing against the gas, on the concerns on the environment, the water pollution and the tourism in the area, and how it would be bad and destroy the area. So the hearing went on for two weeks and the next hearing went for on for three weeks. There were two hearings set up on it. I had my concerns about it and so had about twenty other people and what it would do to the area. And finally, An Bord Pleanála checked it all out and gave a decision to give it the go ahead. Now it's going ahead so there is not much more that I think anyone can do with it. Just to try. Even it won't benefit the area that much, if somebody had something to offer the gas like places to stay or offices or maybe the pubs will gain so much out of the gas coming in. But there will be an awful lot of people that they won't. Listening to the people in the local area and how the gas will be good for us and how it will make this area and all that. But my belief in it is that there will be good work for two years but after that there will be nothing. It will not be an attraction for tourism. The local people called a meeting in the church the other night in Aughoose. To see what they could get out of the gas for the area, which I thought was a good idea. But they fell out amongst themselves. The meeting lasted two hours and they fought with each other for them two hours. Some of the people there sat there without opening their mouths. But a lot of the people did. Some of them came out with putting lorries and cars before the lorries coming in taking the stuff away – the bog away – towards the gas but it's too late for that now. When the people should have raised their voice and their concerns about the gas, they didn't. I remember picketing against the gas and Fahey back in Geesala a couple of years before that. I raised my concerns and the media, the television crowd was there and about twenty-eight people that was behind me picketing. The majority of them were women and kids. About two hundred of them went in just looking, listening to Fahey, to see what money they could get out of it. It's sad; it goes to show you that it's an area that never pulls together, to get anything for the area. I think that if they had pulled together, where the gas is coming in, that they would have got something worthwhile for the area. But they didn't agree amongst themselves and that's why the place is the way that it's going to be. My opinion on it now is that I am going to try and get some offices let to them and some houses and try and take some money off them when they're in. Because when they go in two years time they'll be no money. It'll be all lit up, a beautiful plant. They showed it on a screen to me when it's lit up, it'll be like a city in the middle of the bog. But it definitely won't be a tourist attraction. It's a pity that the Erris people wouldn't pull together and put a strong word into An Bord Pleanála that, if they were going to give them the go ahead that they would have put something into the area to benefit everyone. But the people in the local area, all that they are worried about is how much that they can get out of it. They're not worried about the area, they are worried about how much can "I" get out of it. And that is the reason why the meeting the other night ended up in arguments for two hours and had to be cancelled. Now there is another meeting called. It's sad but that's the way with the people in the local area. So I'll finish for now, I am going to a meeting in Glenamoy tonight – an AA meeting. I go to one or two every week and it's good. We don't talk about "gas" or business. We talk about how we are feeling amongst ourselves, sharing our experiences and hope with each other to stay sober, a day at a time.

The meetings are a good place to be. There are new members coming in and I can share my experience of being sober with them. A day at a time and help another suffering alcoholic, so that's what I'm doing tonight.

When I was growing at a young age, I started to hate drink; I hated the sight of it. I saw so much of it at home with my father. Back to when I was five years old I remember my father on some occasions coming home drunk. But he was quiet in the house; he was never a violent man. But I hated him for drinking. When he was off the drink then, as a kid, I was delighted to see him off the drink. I always hated drink; drink hurt me since I was five years old. In the village they would all work hard at the fishing and they drank hard. There were a lot of the houses in Porturlin at that time that used to make Poteen. They used to take it fishing with them too. My father always took a bottle of whiskey with him (when he was drinking) out on the boat fishing. I saw an awful lot of it from a young age and I grew up to hate it. I hated my father for drinking. As time went on in my life, when I was thirteen, I remember my father coming home and he used always bring a bottle of whiskey with him. I remember taking the bottle of whiskey off him and hitting him, which I am not that proud of now today and breaking the bottle of whiskey outside the door. I hated drink so much. My mother used to tell me not to do that, to stop doing that, that he was my father after all. He was the nicest man ever when he wasn't drinking even though he was never violent at home or anything like that. It wasn't my father that I hated all these years, it was the drink and and when my father took drink. I saw so much of it growing up in a village where people worked very hard and they drank very hard. Drink was very much accepted in them years and lots of poteen made. I used to fish all the time in the summer. But then I decided to leave home at fourteen and a half and I went to England after the salmon season and the lobster season; after the fishing season was over, in September. I remember going on Mickey McGrath's van. The van would be going along picking up young people, men and women, along the road, in Erris at that time. That van would go on to Longford and then Paddy McGrath, Mickey's brother, would have a van, he lived in Dublin, and he'd bring it to Dublin. All the way up to Dublin there was a big load on my heart, leaving Ireland, to go to England. I absolutely hated it but I knew for the winter that I wanted to make money and work and I was promised a job in Lincoln. So I went to Lincoln and the first job that I got was doing manholes and sewers with my aunt's husband. It was a dirty job, mucky old job. The money was very bad. I remember the first week out and when I had my food and my digs paid for I'd have about fifteen pounds or less left over.

The fear that I had was that I would never see Ireland again, that I wouldn't be able to save enough money to come home. After leaving a place where we were fishing, which we could make good money and I missed Ireland very much. I hated England; I hated the sight of it. That went on for me in Lincoln for the first month. I worked there in them manholes with this fella that wasn't paying me good money. I remember being in a pub one night and I didn't drink, but I was told that there were a lot of work lads in there and I might get a better job from one of them. That night was a Sunday night and I met these lads from Dooyork and Dohooma area from home, my own home in the Erris area. We started talking anyway and they realised that they knew my mother and my father. They told me that they were working out in Hornecastle and to come out with them and they would be able to get me the start out there picking potatoes. So we left there that night and we went out to Lincoln with the gang in a car. There were about twenty-five of them and they were staying in an air dome in Hornecastle, in caravans. There was a whole line of caravans lined up in this air dome. It was an army air dome years ago. There was a big canteen, about twenty showers and a big kitchen and there was an English woman in there cooking the dinners for them. But we were all around the table, and I was a stranger to these people. We were eating the dinner and I did meet somebody from home; from my own village, Peter McAndrew. He was over there working with them, that was his second year working with them. Peter told me that they were making good money picking potatoes. I didn't know these men and some of them had their sons with them. But they must have been out in the pub the night before and they had an argument in the pub. The next thing one of them let go the plate of dinner at the other one and the fight started within in the canteen, amongst themselves. One of them got cut, so they stopped the fighting and all sat down again and they started eating again. There was drink involved of course.

The next morning, we all got up and it was my first day out in the field and I'll never forget it – this massive field. You couldn't see from one end of it to the other and these potatoes and the machine that was digging out the potatoes for us. We had to pick them into big boxes, and the boxes were on to the tractors and the tractors were coming up behind them and the baskets. My first day working there I thought that I would never get the day over with, the pains in my back; it was cruel. I remember getting out the next morning and I had to roll out of the bed with the pain in my back.

We were well fed; they would give us a good breakfast and good dinners. So I started to get to know the men after that and their habits.

Every weekend they would go out to the pubs drinking and when they'd come home they'd be arguing amongst themselves. But I wouldn't go out and there was another fella there too and both of us wouldn't bother going out. We would watch the television in the canteen and then we would go into the caravans and go to bed. But we would hear the others coming in. They would be arguing and fighting and sometimes they would be the best of friends again the next day. That was with the drink. They would argue and fight but they'd get up the next morning and you'd never know that anything had happened, and it was back out to work again. Sometimes we worked six days and sometimes indeed we worked the seven days, Sundays as well. My first pay there was one hundred and forty pounds and I thought it was great money. So I worked there until Christmas, saving the money and bought all new clothes for myself, looking forward to coming home at Christmas. That was my first year in England, I came home and it was fine, everything was fine and I saved up money. Then I didn't go back again until after the salmon season was over again. But I hated it; I absolutely hated England, when I look back on it now it was slave work, we were slaves and I knew that too. But I did it because the weather was so bad in the wintertime back home that we couldn't fish.

The English farmer that we worked for had horses and I'd be looking at the horses outside the canteen on Sundays, our day off. It was fenced all the way around and he'd come out there and the first time that he came out he started talking to me. He said "You should be at school" - he had two daughters and they'd be about my age. He told Cathy, the English woman that was looking after everything, to look after me because I was the youngest in the squad at the time. But the daughters started to get to like me and they'd come down talking to me. One of them would be down talking to me and the age I was I started kind of fancying her a bit as she was fancying me! The English farmer, her father, seen that and he took her away, he said "Come on, let's go home". But I didn't see her out after that. I felt that he thought that I wasn't good enough for his daughter. I always felt like a second-class citizen in England anyway, especially if you were Irish.

Every day out on the farm, picking the potatoes the English tractor driver used to shout out of the window of the tractor "Come on Paddy's pick up them potatoes" and he kept shouting this at me. I told him that I wasn't Paddy, that I was Patrick. This went on for about three weeks and I told him "You fucking call me Patrick and you don't call me Paddy". He was very exact with his tractor and I knew that it would be covered over every evening so that there wouldn't be any scrapes on it and it would be well looked after and I hated him for it.

The last year that I picked potatoes over there, we used to have to bring a big spoon with us from the canteen. The ganger man told us to bring the spoon because the clay used to stick to the basket. Sometimes you'd hardly be able to pull up the basket through the muck and we'd have to clean them out with the spoon and try and get it clean to pick the potatoes again because the weather was so bad. The farmer started paying us extra money to pick the potatoes in the bad weather. It was cruel weather; coming up to Christmas, and every day there would be an argument between this English man that was driving the tractor and myself. He'd be a man in his fifties but at the time I thought he was very old, I thought he was ancient because I was only about fifteen and half. That was my second year picking the potatoes and I told him "You better call me my right name, you fucking English bastard, I'm not Paddy, I'm Patrick Flannery". One day he kept going on about it and I took a stone and I fired the stone at him and I broke the window of his tractor. I cracked the window of his tractor and the Irish ganger man came up and he gave out to me. I said, "I'm no fucking Paddy, I'm Patrick". The Englishman was awful disappointed with the tractor and the Irish ganger man sacked me. He said "You're fired, you can go back to Ireland and sit in the corner with no job" and I said "I would rather starve in Ireland than to slave in England picking yer fucking potatoes and you can stick your job up your arse". I left there and I came home for Christmas and the weather was still bad for fishing. Anyhow we wouldn't be starting the fishing until about April or May so I headed for Scotland after Christmas.

I remember going to Scotland at that time and started working with my aunt's husband. He was doing gas leaks all over Scotland. I never drank; I was always a teenager who never touched drink. I always tried to save my money and look after myself, have good clothes and try to do something for myself. Even though I could not read or write, I always made my way and I accepted that I would never be able to read or write properly but I had to stop being ashamed of it. I'd be proud of who I was, I was always proud of myself and I stick up for myself.

But the year before I went to Scotland, on our way home from Lincoln we were checked at Security before going on the boat. This fella wanted me to take a car back for him so we were taking a car back at the time. We were held up at security. The people that were with me at the time were local people. The Security man put me up against the wall, took my case and he turned all my clothes out on the floor and then he told me to put them back. I said, "No, I won't put them back, you threw my clothes out, you put them back". All the people that were with me from my local area walked back and were looking sideways and I seen them going on the boat while I was being held by security. He said, "Put them back you Irish bastard" and I said, "I'm not an Irish bastard and I won't put them back". With that he put me up against the wall and he said "I could throw you in Jail for the rest of your life, what are you doing over here". I replied, "I was over here working". He then said "taking our money and going back to Ireland with it, you put back them clothes, you Irish bastard". I said "I won't put them back" and I didn't. So one of the other security men said to this man "Leave him alone". He took the clothes and he put them back into my case. Then he called me an Irish bastard again and when I was going on the boat I said "Ye English fuckers" and I walked away from them. After that I hated England. I knew the history of Ireland and what they did to our country. How they raped and murdered before them and after them. How they put people out of their homes and shot them. The time of the Black and Tans - I followed all of the Irish history. So I knew then that with the torturing that they gave me in the three or four times of me going back and over to England in them years and that's a long time ago, thirty something years ago. At that time they used to give us a bad time going back and over. I know that I got a hard time from them and I grew to hate them. But the next time that I left Ireland, I was going to Scotland and there was no problem there. There was a difference because I felt at home in Scotland and I felt it was very much like Ireland. My job there was to go to the North of Scotland from Edinburgh, working on gas leaks for my aunt's husband. We would be travelling nearly all over Scotland. You might be a week in one place and then you'd be moving on to different parts. That gave me an opportunity to see Scotland and we stayed in good digs and good places in most of Scotland. But the drink was still there as well. I worked with Scotch fellas and Irish fellas and they all drank heavy. They lived for the high life of the pubs, drinking and partying. I didn't do that, I always came back home and I was very, very sensible when I look back on it now. I saved my money but I remember some of them, after them getting paid only a month would be broke and on Monday morning a few of them would ask me would I have ten pounds for their breakfast. I would say "no, sorry I send my money home, I have to send it home to Ireland" even though I would have money. But I was getting wise to these fellas and I couldn't understand them, because we were getting ninety-five pounds a week into our hand, which was good money. And if we worked overtime we would get extra. I couldn't understand that they would be broke on Monday morning. But of course they drank and partied at the weekend and they would have all their money spent. But as we were travelling in Scotland one time we stayed in this place where there was an Irish fella with us and the other boys used to leave him a lot of the time because all he ever done was drink. But when he worked he worked hard, very, very hard in the digging and doing the gas leaks. He was the best worker that they had but they would leave him alone because he was always drunk, God love him. He'd stay with me and we used to get the digs together. I felt sorry for him and I suppose that he reminded me of some of the people back at home and how they drank. But drink was always around me. It was like it was haunting me. Every place I went there was somebody there that was drinking heavy. Even in England and Scotland and I hated it but there was a part of me that felt sorry for them. I remember one room that we shared and we had to cook, eat and sleep in the same room. He'd come at all hours of the morning because he used to go out every night and drink. I hated it. I'd get up in the morning and make the breakfast and go off to work. Sometimes I used to say to him "What the fuck are you doing waking me at this hour of the night when you're coming in drunk? Can you at least be fucking quiet, I need to get up in the morning." And he used to say that he was sorry. He was a gentleman except the drink had his life taken when I look back on it now. The next time we travelled, we travelled to Cameltown and we went searching for digs, which we found hard to get. Anyhow we got digs eventually in this house in Cameltown that is the nearest point to Ireland. You can see Ireland on a clear day across to Belfast in Northern Ireland. I remember it was coming up towards Christmas and we stayed with this fella and there was about eight fellas in the house. It was a big house and there were about eight bedrooms in the house. There were Northern Ireland lads and I got to know them. We talked about the troubles, even back then in Northern Ireland we thought that there were there. They were strong Irish republicans at the time. When we'd be gone in the day working they would be sleeping and they would be gone in the night working or wherever they were going. I got to know them. They told me not to give any information to my friend that was with me that was drinking because in the pub they talk. They said also not to tell him too much as we were discussing things that were happening in Northern Ireland at that time. But they turned out to be great lads. We had the finest of grub. The fridge and the freezer were full with chickens, steak and everything. And they were charging very little rent. When I finally left there and said goodbye to them lads we moved to another place in Scotland. It was one room again that we were staying in. I remember working in Scotland – down around Edinburgh – the vans would be sent off to this large hostel or whatever it was in Edinburgh city that time. And we would be sent in many a time to pick out lads that wanted work. And you would want to see the state of the house. They used to call it the Doss House where there were an awful lot of men and women staying there that were bad with drink and drugs I suppose at the time. We'd ask them, "Who wants to go to work today?" Maybe twenty of them would go into the vans and they'd work hard for the day and in the evening all they were paid was a fiver. Five pounds for the day. I found it awful sad that this was happening to these people and they'd work like a slave for that fiver.... for drink the next night. You might not see them again the next day. It might be different ones. But that's the way the contractors that time - the Irish contractors - slaved their own Irish people over there for them to get rich. I thought that it was awful sad the way that they were treating their own people, while they sat down in their big houses, with the ganger men working for them. The Irish ganger man that time was treating his own people very, very bad. They worked the hell out of them. The next time that we were moved on again to another part of Scotland we stayed in this room, in digs and the man that used to travel with me all the time was with me. The other lads would have booked into hotels or somewhere else because they'd have partying and they'd have women and everything. We stayed in one room together and I was getting sickened of it. It was coming close to Christmas and one night he came in late and wakened me. In the morning I used to cook the breakfast for both of us and he'd be singing in the night and he'd be dreaming in the night. I said to myself "Fuck this" and in the morning anyway I reared up on him and I told him that I was going back to Ireland. I said, "I'm going back to Ireland, I'm not going to be going around fucking travelling the North of Scotland with a cunt like you". He started crying and he advised me to go back to Ireland. And I said, "I'll find myself an Irish woman and marry an Irish woman and settle down". That time I was very strong. I wouldn't even go with an English woman or a Scotch woman. I was very strong Irish in them years. He advised me to do that, to go back to Ireland and to settle down and not to do what he had done. I asked him what he had done. He told me that his father and mother died in Ireland and that he didn't go home for their funerals. And I asked him why and he told me that he never had the money to go home. He said again "Go back to Ireland, Patrick, you're a sensible young fella, you don't drink or smoke and don't ever drink". And that's exactly what I done. I came back to Ireland and I started out fishing again. The fishing was good in them years as well.

I was married on my twentieth birthday. I did marry an Irish woman. After the fishing season of that year of being married when I came back that first time when I said that I was going coming back to Ireland to marry an Irish woman. I remember on my way back, I flew into Dublin, I got the train down. I came down into Killala and at that time in Killala Asahi was going on – a Japanese plant that was put up there which had a lot of work going on. Killala town was booming at the time. The pubs then of course were booming in the town because there were a lot of work people at the time. I remember coming into a pub in Killala where my sister was working and I got talking to her. I asked her if there was any work in Asahi because I didn't want to go back again to Scotland. She told me that they were looking for steel directors. And I asked her to introduce me to the boss who would be looking for them type of workers. He was in the bar drinking. He was another man that drank heavy. My sister Kathleen introduced me to him. He asked me what did I do. I told him that I was in Scotland. And he said, "What do you do in Scotland?" and of course I was very fast with the tongue and I said, "steel directing". He told me that he had a lot of names down so I told him that if I got that work that I would stay. There was another fella that came back with me from Scotland and he was from Killala and he was looking for work as well. So that was on the Friday and he told me if we were steel directors that he wanted steel directors. He had a lot of lads on to do steel directing and that we could start work on Monday morning. So I got started on steel directing in Killala. I stayed in a flat in Killala, in Hannick's flat there and shared with my sister. I worked in Asahi. I remember the first day going up there as a steel director. We got a white helmet, which made you look important that time if you had a white helmet. We got straps around us. We had to go up three stories high of steel and you'd have to crawl out on the steel. You'd have the tips of your boots on one end of the steel and your hands on the other end. All you'd see underneath you was two stories if you fell down or three stories and you had straps if you were in a dangerous area. You'd clip it on. We had to learn fast how to crawl out on that steel. I remember the first day that we were up there, lucky enough that there was a lad that was very professionally trainer at the job, and he saw that I was a bit nervous. He said, "You didn't do this before did you?" and I said, "No but Christ don't tell the boss, I need the job, I don't want to go back to Scotland or England again, I need to stay at home now". Because I had met my wife at that time, I had started going out with her that time and I wanted the job and to stay at home. Then he said, "Alright, I'll train you". So he showed me what to do and after five days I was flying it. I was crawling in and out and back on the steel. These big massive cranes would drop down the steel and it would hit into lots. Then we'd have the bolts and nuts, which was our job, steel directing them down into that and bolting up this steel. So I turned out to be a good steel director. But drink always followed me. The boss there would ask us down to the pub every weekend with him and he'd always be playing cards. We'd play 25 sometimes with him because he was our boss and then he would tell us to go up to the counter to buy drink. We bought drink but I still didn't drink – it wasn't my life, I still hated the sight of drink. I stuck there in Asahi and I got married when I was in Asahi. I was married a short while after meeting my wife, Marian, engaged probably within four or five months, married within just seven months, I was married on my twentieth birthday. I remember Asahi gave me two or three weeks off for going off getting married and I had the job back again. I liked the job. I always worked, I hated being idle, I was brought up to work and to be always able to earn and to survive and that is what I done. I worked up in Asahi for just about the year and after getting married I decided that I would go back to Scotland again. I wanted to save up for my fishing boat. I wanted all the money I could get to buy my boat because at this stage I had my own fishing boat ordered, to be newly built for me. It was to be built in Monygold in Sligo and I needed all the money that I could get. So I decided after getting married that we'd go back to Scotland. So I went back to Scotland again and I was sent up to the North of Scotland again by my aunt's husband John. I worked on the gas leaks again. But I just couldn't wait to meet up with my friend that I used travel Scotland with before to tell him what I had done. That I married that Irish girl and we were going to have a baby. I travelled up the North of Scotland and saved all the money we could. We stayed with my aunt in Scotland – Anna. At the time she had three kids, it was awkward, it was a three-bedroom house. I worked there from the end of August up until Christmas and I wasn't getting the breaks that I wanted with John Keane at the time. He wasn't giving me any break to better myself and make more money. He used to always send me up to the North of Scotland and I would have to come home at the weekends down to Edinburgh. It wasn't easy leaving a wife who was expecting our first child. But I decided then that we would leave it and we would go to London. And it was the last pay before Christmas and I remember that my daughter Caitriona was born in Scotland. John stood for the child, John that I was working for and my aunt stood for her also. We bought the food and the drink and we had a party in my aunt's house for the Christening and it went very well. And that was the only day that I took off work. John was supplying us to the Gas Board at the time; we were supplied so he'd be paid for us anyway. It was my last pay and I was done for the day that I took off for the Christening even though he was standing for the child. I thought it was the meanest thing that he could ever do. I needed all the money I could get and the one day that I took off for the Christening, and he stood for the child, our last pay before Christmas and he done me out of the day's pay. Anyway I licked my wounds and I headed for London, the South end with my wife and beautiful baby daughter. We stayed there at Christmas with her family and her brother had a lot of work on and he asked me would I stay. He said he would pay well – it was demolition work. So I started working right after Christmas for Vincent and worked hard at the demolition work. And he finally started to give me the houses on price. He'd price them at maybe two fifty, two hundred maybe sometimes up to three hundred a house and I would have a house done in a week. I worked all the time that I could possibly do on them, whereas the other lads would go off to the pub and a lot of the lads would drink, although they did work hard too. Any money that I could get I made and then saved it. Finally I had enough money to put a deposit on my boat, the boat that was being made at the time back in Sligo. So I had to leave out so much money until I would come home. We came home in May of that year and my boat was being made. I went back out fishing with my father, fishing with my father while I waited on my own boat. At the age of twenty-one I had my own fishing boat and my own crew as well. I hired new lads to work for me and we started fishing very, very hard. My boat was made just about two weeks when the salmon season started and some of the lads were doing good fishing. I was up and down to the boat builder every day saying, "get this boat out, get it out of the boat yard, I need to go fishing". He called me then one day when he had it ready and I went back down in the evening with my crew to Monygold in Sligo and he had the boat taken out of the boat yard and she was tied up to the pier. It was blowing a strong North West wind and it was getting dark. The boat builder begged me not to take the boat out that the weather was too bad that night. I said, "We're going out, sink or swim, I am not going to lose another hour's fishing". I left Monygold in Sligo that night, that bad night with heavy seas and we landed - after I don't know how many hours that it took us, a good lot of hours - at dawn in Porturlin. We started fishing out of Porturlin and worked all the hours that God gave us. At that time you could fish seven days a week while the salmon season was on. I started a new thing by fishing at one o'clock in the night and fishing straight through the night. I took all the breaks that I could get and all the chances that I could get and we made good money, very good money at the fishing. My second year fishing salmon on my boat, which I called the 'Dancing Mermaid', I remember us getting three pound a pound for salmon and that's twenty-six years ago now to this date. The salmon was very plentiful. On the last nine days that we fished we had over one hundred salmon every night. We worked hard, we were young fellas, we slept very little, two or three hours a night and back out fishing again. My crew at that time were Tommy McGuire, a young fella and Joe Mills from Glenamoy, a hard worker and they were greedy for money and that's what I wanted. Our second year fishing for seven weeks, after paying the crew and all the other expenses, I had eleven thousand clear profits. And that's twenty-six years ago. But I liked the fishing because I was brought up with it. I was fishing since I was eleven years old. My father had trained me since I was eleven to fish. He trained me to respect the sea and he trained me everything to do with the sea. My father was not a greedy man, he would never take the last fish in the sea but I wanted to make money for my home and family. I wanted the family life and my own home. I didn't want any government house but I wanted my own home for my kids and my family and that's what I worked for. That year that I made the eleven thousand profits from the fishing I went to Ballina with my wife Marian and I put that money in the bank.

We were both delighted. We had the plans got to build our house. We were going to build a four-bedroom house. In Ballina we went into Howard's pub – my wife always took a drink. She always liked her drink. I remember taking a pint even though drink wasn't my scene at all but that's when I started really taking a drink. When I got married first I started to take a drink and the taste for it. When I look back now I never liked the taste of drink but it looked like everyone that was around me was doing it. I had to try it out. My wife's brother Vincent that I worked for in London, had the pub bought in Bangor – 'The Talk of the Town'. He came up to me and he said, "I have a pub bought off PJ Carey in Bangor and I want you to run it". I said, "no, I don't want the pub, it's a thing that I don't really want, a pub". I was quite happy with my life, my house was ready to be built, I had a new fishing boat, I had my dreams that I wanted. All I ever wanted was my own fishing boat, my own home and my family life. I think when I look back on it now that I started life very young, I don't remember my childhood. I was a man when I should have been a child but I have no regret of that up bringing. I can only recall the while that I went to school and I left school at about ten and a half. He asked me again and again if I would take the pub. But I kept telling him that I wouldn't take it. He called Marian my wife and his sister down to the back beside him. She came back up to me and she said, "You've never seen a poor publican, we should take the pub". That's how I got into the 'Talk of the Town' in Bangor. I was over at the pub at the age of twenty-two and I changed it. There were brown tiles on the floor and the pub wasn't doing good business when we went in there. But we didn't know, we hadn't a clue! But it wasn't doing business. I bought all the stock that went into the pub and it cost me eleven and a half thousand pounds to stock out the pub. Vincent wanted one hundred and fifty pounds a week for rent at that time – twenty-six years ago. I had to run the pub and all the costs then on top of that. I went into the pub and Marian worked in behind the bar. I learned how to pull pints, to change the taps, to put on the barrels. We took on staff, I always wanted young staff, young girls to work there. We put down all new carpets. There wouldn't have been too many pubs that had carpets at that time. It was an expensive carpet that we put down. We painted up the pub and gave it a different look and that's when the pub took off. The business started. Then we started doing weddings. We had staff coming in helping to do the weddings and Marian did the cooking for them and the pub took off big time. We worked all hours of the night. It might be three o'clock when you would get to bed at night. We had one child at that time, Caitriona. Marian was expecting our second child while we were in the pub. Patrick, our son, was born while we were in the pub. I started taking drink and that was my biggest downfall. I can never remember falling with drink. But when I took over the pub I realised then that everybody drank. While running the pub I took drink. Then I was a binge drinker. I'd go off and work again in the pub and it was making a lot of money then – or so I thought. When we went into the pub we had no loans, no borrowings and I owned my own car. We were three or four years in the pub. My wife always took her holidays. She would go to England or to America and she would spend a lot of time at her home place, in and out to her family. I felt lonely and a lot of the time left out. I remember our first Christmas in the pub everybody asked me to open the pub on Christmas Day. It would be packed. But of course the staff told me that they wouldn't work for me and my wife wouldn't work for me on the day that I opened the pub for the first Christmas. And it was packed. They used to tell me how bad the police were in Bangor but I didn't care. I ran that pub all day on my own and I was flat out all day. One fella - Paddy Meenaghan - a friend of mine, a publican in Dublin, came in and helped me out. The pub was very busy all day. They were buying bottles of whiskey and everything because the taps weren't being pulled fast enough because I was trying to do the whole thing myself. It was coming up to ten o'clock at night when I was thinking how would I get all these people out. At that time there would be a lot of rows at the weekends in the pubs. And that was the only fear that I had that there was going to be a row and it was Christmas Day. Anyway I cooled them all down and I told them to be quiet that I had something to tell them. I said, "The police are outside the door and they are giving me fifteen minutes to clear the pub". Within fifteen minutes of me saying that the pub was clear. But the police were not outside. I just lied. They left

22

pints after them and bottles of whiskey. The pub went on running like that doing good business. I had lost my beliefs; they were starting to get away from me, my dream of my fishing and my work that I had built up. But the pub was a different scene, a scene that I never wanted really. It went on and my drinking was getting heavier and heavier. I became an alcoholic while in the pub. I could drink thirty pints a day. It changed me completely. I was a different person when I took drink. I was never violent at home when I would came home to my wife and kids. But I suffered a lot of violence. My wife was very violent. She often hit me with the pan down on the head and threw teapots at me and fired cups at me. There was many an occasion where she threatened me with a knife so with that I suffered abuse. When I look back on it now there were times she was very abusive towards me but there were times also that she was very good to me. She always got her own way. She was strong headed and hyper. I saw that there was something going wrong here and started to get unhappy but I didn't know what was wrong with me. And the unhappier that I got the more I drank. So we decided to leave the pub. I think it was after four years that we decided to leave the pub. Everyone thought that I had done so well in the pub, that I had made millions in the pub and I agreed with them. But it wasn't. It was the worst thing that I ever done – for me to go into the pub, even though it was a good business. Even though a lot of the people had a lot of respect for me, the people liked me and they came from all over to the pub. I went all over the place with teams playing darts. I loved the darts and I'd have the team playing darts in different places and we drank.

We got out of the pub but I could never get myself back. I had lost all my dreams at a young age – they were shattered. I tried to go back out fishing again but I could never get it back right again. The whole scene wasn't great. I was very unhappy at home. There were many times when I was going to walk out on my marriage but I could never walk out on my kids. I just couldn't walk out on my kids. When I got things right there would be something wrong anyway. No matter what I done there was always something wrong with my wife. I couldn't do anything right. I think she was jealous of me. There was a lot of jealousy in her. I remember six months before her mother died, she told her out in the house that she always worked hard. She had this attitude that she worked hard. She was a good worker but so were we all. The mother said to her "You never worked hard in your life, you were born into a new house, you got married and you never had a bad time when you were married, so don't be talking about hard work. My family that left and went to America at a young age now they worked hard". She was the second youngest in her family and I believe she was spoilt in one sense and she was never wrong. She was always right. It didn't matter what I done or said I was wrong. But that went on in my life until I decided I'd leave and go away to America to work. I went over to her brother that was in New York and when I mentioned it to her she was all for it. Because I just couldn't get it right again. I lost everything that I dreamed of through the pub, by going to the pub. I remember going to Dublin for my visa and passport when I decided to go to America. When I went to America my young girl was very young at the time, she was barely walking I'd say at the time that I left. When I landed in New York airport I felt that I was there all my life. I felt a great feeling to be in America. I loved it there. I really took to it. On my first day working there, a man asked me "what do you do?" I said "Anything". He told me that they were doing painting and decorating. I said, "No problem". So we started doing shingles on a roof, roofing. The next day we were painting and decorating. That's what I done out there and I loved it. I was earning seven hundred and fifty dollars a week at that time which is nineteen years ago. The first five or six weeks that I was there I never opened a pay package. I have ten dollars with me, not a big lot, but we drank that weekend. I went out with the lads, with her brother, he used to drink too. Drink was always around me. The only thing was that I was working and starting to get my balance back again. I remember sending them first pay packages home and I worked there up until Christmas but I was missing the wife kids at home. But I didn't want to come home; I had started a new life away from the scene at home, the unhappiness. I was happy in America and I didn't want to leave there. So I asked Marian would she come to America but she said that she wouldn't leave her father and mother. I remember one day her calling me up where she had started working in the Talk of the Town for her brother. Somebody else was looking after the kids at the time. I couldn't believe it because I didn't want that and I wanted her to be with the kids. Them things used to make me unhappy but she never understood or she never wanted to understand. She was right all the time. But coming up to that Christmas I decided that I would go home. In one way I hated it to be going home. I was quite happy there. I was making money again and saving money. I remember one time when we were working out in New Jersey. There were a lot of houses in that place. At the house that we were working on the lads were whistling on this young lady. She told the boss and he came out and he reared up on us. I said, "I didn't whistle on her" and she said, "No, no he didn't whistle on me, he's a gentleman". The next day after that I was working on her house and she came out talking to me. She was a young woman only about twenty-one and her husband had left her. I think that they were just married when the husband left her. She used to bring out drinks to me, bottles of Budweiser and it was great! The first time that I tasted Budweiser I thought that it was beautiful! A lovely drink! I used to get sandwiches and teas from her. Everyday we would have a chat, she was a nice woman, and her mother used to come out chatting as well, and her brother and uncle. The uncle used to be doing houses as well and he offered me work to go away and work the painting and decorating. I even got an opportunity to start out on my own as well when I was out there. I told him that I had a family at home and that I would have to go back. I remember the day that I was leaving this lady said "goodbye" and cried after me. Herself and her relations brought me around all the houses to show me all the Christmas trees. I always made friends wherever I went. I always met great people as well but indeed I met some bad people but I always hung around with good people. I always hung around with positive people, people that thought positively. I used say "If you hang around with positive people, you'll think positive, if you hang around with negative people you'll think negatively". I would never be with the ones that thought negative. I left there and I came back home into Shannon that Christmas. Marian was waiting for me. The tree was lit up in the house and the house was lovely done up, the four-bedroom house we had. I started that house when I was twenty-two and I had my own home at twenty-three and we didn't move into to it until I was about twenty-four. My little girl, Maria was sleeping on the couch and my other two kids were there and I was delighted to see them. I woke Maria and she said "Daddy" and she recognised me God love her. My mother, God love her, was there looking after the kids. That night there was a party at our house and a few people came around and we done a bit of drinking. Of course there was drink. But I was like a stranger in my own house. I felt like the odd one out. It was the worst feeling that I ever got. I felt an absolute stranger in my own house. I was wondering what in the hell was wrong with me. When I was leaving America I swore to God that I would never drink again. I knew myself that drink would bring me down again. I was very positive when I was leaving America and there was a pub up the road that I used to drink in. It was called 'Flannery's' where I said that I would be back again to America. The only ways that I won't come back is if I would get the opportunity to run 'Flannery's' pub. There was a sixty-five foot trawler in Killala. There was a skipper – a French fella – whom I knew that owned the boat – or if I got skipper on that trawler that I wouldn't go back until I get running the pub, otherwise I'll be back to America and that will be it. So that was my intention. The day after I came back I went down to Porturlin to see my friends in the pub. My drinking buddies the fishermen. And I went into the pub and I drank and drank and I got home at one o'clock that night. The drink was taking me over again. It was starting to be my number one again. Even when I was binge drinking I would go off it for maybe a couple of weeks but I'd always go back on it. It was always there in my head. It had me absolutely haunted. When I'd think of something good I'd be delighted with the positive thinking but the drink would come into my head again and I'd think negative again. I was home about five or six weeks and one day I was looking across the sea and thought that I would never see America again. I thought the drink was going to beat me, going to destroy me. I was torn apart with unhappiness.

I always worked through all my drinking, binge drinking or not I always worked. I worked on the sea and fished. I was starting to work very hard at the end, working harder than years before that. I used to feel that for somebody who was totally against alcohol and all I seen with it and all the unhappiness that I seen with it as a teenager growing up and then I find myself drinking. I was very good when I'd go into a pub. I wouldn't be a downer. I would always be laughing and smiling and happy if there was a country and western singing on in a pub I would stay there and enjoy the music. I was always a happy go lucky person. Everybody saw me as a happy go lucky person. But inside I was torn apart. Inside I was hurting. My drinking was to start to get worse. I never drank until I was twenty. Now I'm twenty-seven and twenty-eight and I just couldn't go into a pub and take one drink and walk away. If I took one drink I could stay until I got drunk. I could drink twenty or thirty pints a day but I never fell with drink. But it changed me. I wouldn't run away from fights if somebody said something to me in a pub. I got into some fighting with drink as well. I was one of these people who wouldn't walk away and I always found that I never went into a pub to start a row either. But there would always be some ass hole in the pub that would pick on me and I would never run away from a fight. I could handle myself. I remember some people down in the local pub that hated me for some reason or another. I used to go in there drinking and he never liked me and he used to always be trying to knock me and saying smart comments.

There was a fella up the road that used to be drinking very heavy. The publican used to take him home. That man fell over the bridge outside his house one night and he was found dead two days later with drink. This publican that used to leave him at home used to always stop outside my door and hoot the horn in the car, just to annoy me. That went on for years. But one night I went out to his red van and I fired at him. I emptied the automatic rifle over the van and that stopped him hooting outside my house. There were a lot of people that were very hard to mix in with . And he was one of them. One time I was drinking in Belmullet and I hadn't much sheep, I always loved sheep, but I hadn't much land here at that time. I had about only five or six sheep because I was fishing I didn't have much heed on farming. And the sheep went all over the place into people's fields. Neighbours used to come to the door. I remember two or three neighbours at different times coming to the door giving out about the sheep. One fella came to my door this night that I was just in from fishing the night before and came knocking at my door. This is the fella that was always in the pub, and he used to be listening to the publican giving out about me, for no reason at the time. He was giving out about my sheep and I told "Hold on until I get my shoes on". I went in and got them on and when he saw me coming, he ran. I got a hold of him by the neck and I told him that if he ever came near my door again that I would fucking kill him. But some of the neighbours were very funny. They were very jealous type of people. I felt that I was different that I was brought up different than that. But that time in Belmullet was after a party in our house, we'd used to have parties in our house for Christenings and invite people around. Myself and my brother and a young Ginty lad that was with me, Martin Ginty and he used to be a good friend of mine. We were in Belmullet and this publican was after hunting my few sheep, tore the side out of the sheep. We took the sheep into the vet that day but the sheep died in the car. He hunted the dog after them and he tore the whole side off the sheep just because it was my sheep. That hurt me. The only mistake that we made was that we started drinking in Belmullet and we landed down to Flannery's and we had a few more. Finally, I ended up in a row. I took brandy and drink changed me completely. If somebody done something on me I would track them down no matter where and have it out with him. We went into this man's pub that tore up the sheep with the dogs and he served us the pints. We had three pints. I asked for the third round of drink. There were about eight or nine in the bar, locals that would always be in telling him all the news. They thought that that was good to be going in telling the news to this publican! He said to me "I don't serve tinkers". The pub went very quiet. I had a fair bit of drink at this stage and I said, "Who are you calling a tinker"? And he said again "I don't server tinkers". He looked down to the boys in the corner and they started laughing. He had one hand pulling a pint and with that I struck him. I put him flying behind the counter, then I jumped the counter and I nearly killed him. I wrecked the pub and I asked if anyone wanted to come and fight me. They all ran out of the pub. The boys that were laughing were soon running for the doors when they seen me in action. I smashed up the pub. I went out to my car and I had an automatic rifle in the boot of my car. I used to always carry it in my car. Three or four of the lads sat on the car and they begged me not to do it. I would have shot him dead. But we left then and we went to another pub and I was cool again five minutes later. But he drove me to do it. He was years picking.

Interview 1 Mid-West Radio

The Problems with Drinking

Tommy

Some parents have this theory that if they introduce alcohol in the house at an early age, 15 or 16, that and say to the children "Look alcohol is fine, we're not saying that you shouldn't have it, but we're saying that you should have it in moderation". This is one road that a lot of parents have gone down but it hasn't always worked. Of course we are hearing lots of stories from parents over many years, of where people are raiding wine cellars and drinks cabinets and so on from different locations across this country.

Good morning to you Patrick.

Patrick

Good morning Tommy. How are you?

Tommy

I am very well. We spoke before Christmas and we were raising the issue of the high rate of teenage drinking that is going on here. I was speaking about those two articles that appeared in the papers this morning. To try and get rid of, what is now becoming a clogging situation, where most of the people in hospitals - one in five - are there because of an illness that is alcohol related. One consultant said that we need to free up our hospitals and a physiatrist made the point that every hospital should have in-house alcohol counsellors, that unless alcohol abuse detection rates improve, he says that such patients would continue to clog up the health system. So certainly in middle or later life scenarios things aren't improving. But you are doing your bit to try to get young people aware of the rights and wrongs of alcohol. You have sponsored a particular booklet called "Safety Awareness Journal". How did this all come about?

Patrick

That's right Tommy. It was after listening to your show and thanks to your show. I've been highlighting the issue of alcohol because I am a victim of alcohol myself. I was brought up to hate drink and all I had seen of it and then in later years I went bad on the drink and I became an alcoholic. I have listened to a lot of people discussing the drink and what should be done, and blaming the pub and blaming this and that.

My belief is that we all have a part to play. Thanks to your show before Christmas for bringing up that and I figured after that show that I should go out and do something. I remember here fourteen or fifteen years ago there was never a word about an alcoholic around Erris, or that it was a problem or that it would damage your liver or damage other parts of your body. I started a meeting in Belmullet which is fifteen years running now. An AA meeting and that was the first time that people knew that there was such a sickness of alcoholism, that if you took too much drink that you could become an alcoholic and abuse your system with it. Now there are four meetings going on in Erris over that one meeting that I started up fifteen years ago. A lot of people have come in that never realised that they had a problem and have done something about it, thanks be to God, and have got sober and are going down the right road. That was the first thing that I thought of then. That we should be encouraging the kids at school, we have good kids out there and instead of blaming the publicans we all have a part to play in it. So have the publicans, the priests, the police and so have the parents - they have a big part to play to protect their children from becoming abused by alcohol.

Tommy
You run a knitwear factory near Belmullet?

Patrick
That's right, I have a knitwear factory in Pullathomas.

Tommy
And you have sponsored this booklet?

Patrick
That's right Tommy. It's all about alcohol and the abuse of alcohol, drugs and abuse of drugs and abuse of smoking. It's a good book so I sponsored five schools in Erris - Bangor, Barnatra, Inver, Pullathomas and today this booklet is going into Rossport National School.

Tommy
And who actually designed and who wrote the book?

Patrick
A guy called Pat from Dublin that I got in contact with first. I told him that I wanted to get a book that would be encouragement to put into schools, that would encourage the teachers to teach the kids about alcohol and the abuse on your body. He came back to me then and he

told me that they had done up a book and it was him that done it and I sponsored it.

Tommy
Now it's not just solely about alcohol, it deals with a whole range of issues from smoking, your body, illegal drugs, how to say no, what help lines are available for the different problems, medicines and so on, so it's wide ranging.

Patrick
That's right Tommy. It's a very good book, on the back pages a way to get help. An awful lot of people I find, between youngsters and grown ups too, that have a problem with alcohol and they don't think that they have a problem and they don't know where to turn to sometimes. We were brought up not to let the neighbour know if we had a problem but I think that we are more open now and I think the kids today are more intelligent than we were growing up with alcohol. I think that if they are taught in school, by the teachers, and made aware that if you abuse drink or drugs that you will end up destroying your life, your body and everything.

Tommy
Now did this book have to get clarification or anything from the Department of Education before it could be put into schools or is it up to the relevant teachers themselves?

Patrick
It's up to the teachers. I called around to the teachers and I told them that I was sponsoring this book and told them that it was about alcohol and drug abuse and would they teach the kids from six years of age onwards. The teachers were more than delighted and they wanted to pay for them but I told them that I was sponsoring them. So it's in the hands of the teachers now to teach it.

Tommy
What about any parent now? Teachers are now in their class merrily teaching pupils, this is aimed by the way at primary schools isn't it?

Patrick
Well it is but I am also putting them into secondary schools as well. I intend to do, in time, all the schools in Erris.

Tommy

But what is your own view as to what age group it would appeal to most?

Patrick

Well I think the younger that you start teaching the better, from six years old up. Whatever you tell a kid when he is five or six he will always remember and if he is taught up until he leaves school. I have been asked by teachers over the years to come and talk to Leaving Cert students about alcohol abuse and what it can do to you before the kids were leaving the school. I was in Belmullet one year, in Castlebar and several schools just when the kids were leaving the school. That made me aware that it wasn't much good talking to these kids that were leaving the school, that they should be taught from a young age.

Tommy

So here you are, just an ordinary business man from Belmullet, and your input into trying to elevate the alcohol problem is to sponsor a safety awareness journal for children to read and to at least understand the dangers of alcohol and smoking and drugs?

Patrick

That's right, Tommy. When I was growing up, I was never taught that - I was taught that Guinness was good for you, that if you had a cold to take a hot whiskey and poteen and that it was good for you! I'm a victim of all that and now I can give something back now to try to save a kid from going down the road that I went down.

Tommy

Ok but to any parents out there, I would suggest to you that this is a fantastic read. The only problem of course would be now that you would get snowed under with people looking for this booklet and that it would cost you more money.

Patrick

Well Tommy if I have to mortgage any property that I have, I intend to get these books into all the schools. I also told the teachers that maybe they could give the book to, we'll say that there is four or five kids in one school that they could bring it home to their mother and the mother could teach it to them kids and bring back the book when they would be finished. There is more than one book gone into the schools.

Tommy
Thank you for your time Patrick

Chapter 3

Selling and Promoting Flannery's Knitwear

Promoting Flannery Knitwear
Building up the business
Providing local employment

It was in the nineties that I took to the road to promote and sell the knitwear on the road to knitwear shops. When I would be leaving Flannery's Village and I would fill up the boot of the car with sweaters and I would fill up the back and front seats of the car also with sweaters. It was all packed with sweaters. I'd hit the road and my first stop would be Newport. I was supplying two shops in Newport that I had got into. I would continue on then to Westport to supply another shop or two there and then I would continue on to Leenane, where I had another two shops to supply. I built up friends all over the place and then I'd go on to Cleggan for another shop, and on the way there was another shop between Clifton and Leenane. From there I went onto Miller's in Clifton. I used to be very nervous travelling to Miller's because when I used to try to get into the shops for them to buy my sweaters, they all opened their door for me, it took a lot of time and a lot to promote my knitwear - and to promote it as quality knitwear, that I was selling a good garment at a good wholesale price. It took a lot of time to convince them to do that and I didn't just run in and out, I built up time with these people. I remember that for three days before I would go travelling that I would be nervous as hell of Mrs. Miller because she was a very strict business woman. It was an honour to get into any shop but if you got into Miller's it was a big thing because most of the big companies were supplying Millers. So the first time that I went in there selling my quality Flannery knitwear, she said 'show me the quality that you are doing'. She was very exact but my stuff was quality and she bought it. She was very sharp, she wouldn't let anything go with me at all, if I was trying to explain to her about how good my knitwear was, she'd tell me that she knew knitwear, that she was in the business a long time " and you are only starting off." So she would always cut me off but as time went on, and even though I was nervous around her because of the way she used to be in the shop, I built up a good relationship with her too. She turned out to be a good lady and we used to talk. One day I was in the shop and when I was going around that time I always wore denim, denim jackets, shirts, I used to wear very eye catching shirts, I was more like an American - dressed with a lot of American clothes - and they were very eye catching. One day I was in the shop and I was repeating orders with Mrs. Miller and the shop was packed out, and while she was doing business, you wouldn't go up to her and say "excuse me, can I talk to you, I have some nice samples to show you". It wouldn't be that, you'd have to make an appointment. I often waited two hours in the shop for her to see me. But I would wait, I had the patience. So one day I waited and she gave me the order for the sweaters, a big order and when I had finished, she was on about the shop and how the business was going. And she said "by the way, when you come into my shop again, you are no different than a tourist, the way you dress with your jeans and your bright eye catching shirts, and your denim jackets, when you come into my shop in future as a salesman, you dress up in a suit". So I said "yes, Mrs. Miller". And I left, when I went outside I said in my own mind "Fuck you". And I went off down the road to Roundstone. It was the late nineties when I got into the market in Roundstone and the first shop that I went into there was 'Kings'. When I went into the shop, of course I was dressed the same way with the denims and the eye catching bright shirt, and I did look like a tourist, so when I went into Kings there was a beautiful lady called Eileen in the shop. It was a very friendly shop, you could see that. I said "I'm from the tax office, I'm a tax inspector", just to break the talk and chat. The look that she gave me first and then she looked at my clothes and then she realised that I wasn't a tax inspector with the way that I was dressed! We got chatting and she ended up buying my knitwear, so I supplied knitwear - scarves, caps and socks - to the Kings family and we sat down and we had a cup of tea. Her mother came out and I got to meet all the family over time. That was the type of business that I was running. I built up a relationship with friendliness and I wasn't out to rip them off or they weren't out to rip me off either. We became good business friends and friends.

Then I would travel out to Joyce's in Recess - another family that had great time and respect for me. Then I would go on into Moycullen, into Tressa Garavan and they were the same way. We built up strong relationships as they were buying my knitwear. They would wait each year to give me orders and then I would go onto Tressa's sister in Galway city. And I would then travel all the way down through Tuam, all hours of the night travelling. But I realise today, in 2005, when I went back and visited all these shops and the people are still there, thanks be to God, and the shops are still open. But they never forgot the warmness, the minute that I walk into their shops, it's all 'Mr. Flannery, it's so good to see you'. The Kings in Roundstone had a great welcome for me, the big hug and the sit down and we had the tea and the brown bread and the chatting - we shared everything. They shared their lives with me. How their business was going, how their families were doing, if somebody was sick, that was shared and that's the type of relationship that I had with these people. I love Connemara, I loved everyone that I dealt with, between Galway, Connemara and the whole island, which I travelled selling and promoting Flannery Knitwear. Today, in 2005, they still want me back with the knitwear. I have been in the shop and they want me back early next year and they will give me orders again. And even though I don't supply them now, we still have the great relationships. The door is always open for me to go back into any of them shops, the respect they have and show for me and the respect that I show for them. They are able to tell me today too that Eileen in Kings in Roundstone is married and has three little kids now, showing me the pictures of them and the mother and the father were there. It's amazing, I'm so proud that I have done this with the knitwear, that I have travelled the whole country, meeting such lovely people like the Kings in Roundstone, like all the people that I dealt with. It's an education in life that will stick with me for the rest of my life - the warmness and the kindness - and yet we done business together.

I stayed in Roundstone last night, travelling with my partner Teresa, we are on a four day's tour. Most of the places that we are travelling to are shops, I'm looking up the shops that I used to supply.

When I started the knitwear first, I started out the knitwear in my garage onto my house, producing the knitwear, I had two knitting machines. When I was trying to get into the shops, they would ask me where my factory was. I would tell them that I had it in Pullathomas, but it was just a room onto my own house, a garage that I was working off. But at the time I couldn't go saying that I was working off a garage, it wouldn't look the part and I knew that I had to sell myself, to sell my products. You had to look the part. That's what I done and even one man said to me today "Jesus, all them years you had a Mercedes". I remember buying a Mercedes especially to sell the knitwear. It was a white Mercedes, the first one that I had back in the early nineties. They remember me coming up to their doors with the white Mercedes and it packed to the top with the sweaters. Them were great days that I remember. And the girls that I gave the work to at home, my ex wife at the time, was working with the knitwear as well, pressing and labelling. It gave jobs to all them people. It was hard going though the travelling. I went into the shops and they might never have seen me before but within two hours I would have sold the knitwear.

I remember one time between Tuam and Galway there was a flower shop and I went in there talking and they were sorting the flowers out. It was just after starting up for a few years and within an hour and a half of talking to the lady there about how good she was doing, I started telling her that she would need something extra to boost her business and she asked me what. I told her that she would need something on the other side of her shelves to attract people in and when they come in to buy the something else, they will buy your flowers. In that time I had encouraged the woman to sell the Flannery Knitwear sweaters on those shelves. We turned out to be great friends after that and the knitwear and the flowers sold and she always told me that she couldn't believe that the sweaters and the flowers would sell together in the one shop because it was the last thing in her head. She was only into plants and flowers but that's the kind of educated business salesman that I became. I could sell anything! I loved people and I loved the road.

Then I was thinking about the machines going from half nine in the morning until one o clock at night in the garage down at home - it was booming. The pressing then was done in our own house and it was hard work but it was enjoyable - the workers enjoyed it.

Well we're still travelling, we stayed in Clifden last night and travelled around to all the people that I used to deal with throughout the years with the knitwear. We are still touring around now and we got the ferry to Kerry. We're going on to Tralee. We left home on Friday and we are gone into four counties already, just seeing the places that I used to travel with the knitwear. It's nice and the ferry coming across to Kerry is great, we saved two hours off the journey. So we will be travelling around for another few days. It's great to see all the houses going up everywhere in Kerry, the county that sees a lot of houses going up and the changes that's landed to Ireland in every county everywhere you go. It's the 26th August 2005 and it's great that we can do this - get away for a few days.

I built my factory in 1996 - the Knitwear factory - with the coffee shop and there used to be over one thousand in stock at all times there. And then after opening the factory I wasn't afraid to be telling the customers in the shops that I had a new factory for the sweaters. I invited them all down to visit us in the shop and pick out any design of a sweater that they wanted. That was a great achievement in itself, and then of course I built the holiday homes and then it all became Flannery's Village. When I travelled to America as well to sell the knitwear I invited the people that bought the knitwear to come and stay with me at the holiday homes for free. People were buying our stock from Chicago that time and it was the same way in Germany - I marketed the sweaters there as well and invited the people to stay again in the holiday homes. The people that came and stayed would order goods from me and we would send them on directly to them then.

Theresa and I stayed in Tralee last night. She enjoyed visiting the shops I used to supply. The highlight of the trip was this morning when I went to the Sinn Fein office in Tralee where I meet with my old comrade Martin Ferris, a person I know for a long time, a good Irish republican, and we sat down in the office and chatted about things and the way the government is handling things now and up above the door of the office was 'Release the Rossport Five'. We discussed their case and what would be the best way to get justice for them. He showed me some old pictures of troubled times and things that happened away back. We are now moving on again with our tour, trying to cover as many counties in Ireland as we can. We have already been in four on this trip in August 2005. It's great to see the country booming, with building going on everywhere and there are beautiful towns in Ireland. We certainly have a country that we can be proud of and I'm listening to the radio this morning about Florida where they have a hurricane - hurricane Katrina they are calling it - where it's over two hundred miles per hour. How people are afraid for their lives there and here the sun is beating down on us today. That's the way the world is. We are lucky to be living in this country of Ireland and our climate is not bad when you hear about these hurricanes that other countries get.

We are now in Dingle, a beautiful town - a fishing town - in Kerry. I was off to see my Twinship - the trawler that I used to own - the Twinship. We are just leaving Dingle now and we are going on Terbet Ferry then we will be heading back to Flannery's Village again, to our own base.

I also visited the McMullans in Sligo where they used to buy my knitwear as well. Annie Kate and her husband used to give me the first order around Easter time, and her order could be anything up to one thousand sweaters, it would take six weeks to get them ready and as soon as they were done, I would deliver them to her. She was a great customer and we turned out to be great friends as well. I still do business with them and we have the chat and the tea and the knitwear and she always says that I make quality sweaters - indeed I learned a lot from her and her designs too. Also Donegal town, I have friends there and in Killybegs and indeed all over Ireland and Northern Ireland that I used to supply with knitwear - I sold a lot of sweaters up there too and made good friends up there. It is a part of Ireland that I liked visiting and still do today.

Chapter 4

Summer of 2005 – Conflict in Erris

June 2005 - watching Tideway dredging at sea for Shell
Friend & cousin going through a break up of a marriage
Drinking to solve problems
Another girl going to AA meeting
Lodging 20,000 in credit union / time I looked for loan with them
June 2005 - Martin Ferris meeting Rossport 5/Shell/Sinn Féin's support
Gerry Adams into America
Shell to Sea Parade in Belmullet - Sinn Fein support
Division in Erris over Gas / Low support for me in 2001
People jealous of each other in Erris
Our picket of Frank Fahey meeting in Teach Iorrais in 2001
Contacting ministers trying to get Rossport 5 out of jail

Today is the 19th June 2005 and it's a beautiful day, absolutely beautiful. I'm watching Tideway who are here dredging for the gas pipeline out in the bay and their big ships that they have for dredging. I suppose it's a day that you can enjoy summer. And then on the other side, I was talking to a friend of mine, who is very, very down. He feels that nobody wants him, not even his family. He's a man that's going through a break up of a marriage which will be dragged through the courts. Everything is getting to him but he's handling it the wrong way. He's turning to drink. He has turned to the drink. He drinks most days now. I've been talking to him several times, twice a day sometimes, trying to get him away from the drink. Trying to get him to see that it's not the way. I told him today that by drowning himself in alcohol will not solve his problem. But he said that the drink is his only friend. But I tried to explain to him that it was not a friend. It's the worst enemy to have when you have problems. It makes things worse. It also makes you depressed. Alcohol can keep you up on a high and then you can be depressed because of it. And that's what I said to him today. He is a relation of my own, good friend and I have good time for him. And I will be here for him. But by the way he was talking today, he is really down. He thinks that his life is not worth living. And I was able to tell him that life is worth living. Life is very short anyway without making it shorter. But I hope and pray that he will come to the AA meeting with me some day and get sober and get the gift of sobriety. It teaches you to stay sober one day at a time. It also helps you to live life one day at a time. And to learn to cope with everyday life one day at a time. But this friend of mine that I'm talking about cannot see that today but I hope and pray to God that some day he will.

Another person asked me to help him. He has a high job in the government and I went to see him and saw how down and out he was, his marriage was breaking up. He was going through hell in his own home and he had to leave it. After being talking to him, he came into AA with me and he got sober. So he called me today to thank me for helping him out and he was away up at home, out of Mayo, in the Sligo area. He was telling me very sad news that his first cousin's son is after committing suicide and he was only sixteen years old.

Today is the 23rd June 2005 and last night I was at a meeting with another girl that came and asked for my help with her drinking. Her husband called me and asked me if I could help her out. And I took her to a meeting last night in Ballycroy. She just called me today. She hasn't drank today. She called me to thank me for going to the meeting. She said that she would continue to go to the meetings. That will help her to stay sober one day at a time and I feel good when I achieve something like that. I always look forward and reach out and help people out, which I did last night. I then got to stay as well and call her husband to tell him that she is OK. Alcohol does a lot of damage to families too. Most families, when there is an alcoholic in the home, don't understand them. They don't understand the sickness of alcohol and they just shout at them, roar at them, fight with them. A lot of times they are called tramps and useless and good for nothings. Those people that call an alcoholic those names don't understand the sickness and disease of an alcoholic. That poor woman doesn't want to be the way she is but alcohol is more powerful than she is and took her life over. Once again I will pray to God for her and I will help her get sober and get her life back one day at a time.

Today I am going into the credit union. I went in the other day and I remember when everything went wrong for me, when the banks closed down on me, so did the credit union. And I was able to lodge twenty thousand euros in the account and when I was lodging it she said "Jesus, that's a lot of money". And I said "some day I'll own this credit union. Not like when I came looking for a loan, I hope you were telling me right before but from now on I won't be looking for loans." It's good to see that there's always a bright light up ahead for me and that I'm able to do things. I'm not one that lies down and plays dead in self pity. I don't wallow in self pity.

Today is the 23rd June and I am being brought back into court again by my ex wife and my solicitors and barristers. This time for the right of way around the two houses - the four bedroom house and the two bedroom one, that I signed over to her. When the Judge decided on that agreement, he decided that both parties would agree on boundaries. But once again I didn't get justice in court. She said that there was a court order ruled by the Judge, to say that the boundaries that they had drawn up, not the boundaries that my engineer drew up, it was their engineer. All around my property they have sixteen or seventeen foot taken in around the street that they were supposed to take in only ten foot. And once again they have got away with it. There is no justice for men in court and I am definitely one that didn't get justice. I explained this to my solicitor and barrister there before we went before the Judge. They told me to sign the court order which I don't trust them at all. I don't think that it was a court order at all, because it was in writing that both parties would agree on boundary rights and that isn't agreed on. Because the plans that my engineer drew up is not accepted at all. They haven't them in court. It looks as if the solicitors and barristers are all the one in this case again. And this is the second solicitor and barrister that I've had to get. I signed over their rights, that is what they said. The boundaries that they wanted - just to get rid of it and to get a peace of mind back in my life. When I signed that, she said that that was it now. So we brought it to the Judge and he said that if I didn't sign it that it would cost me five thousand euros, that the Judge would rule for costs. I would have to pay these costs. When I thought about that, I thought that I had enough spent so I signed it over. Twenty minutes later, before we went before the Judge, my solicitor and barrister came back again to me. This time to tell me that my wife said that the AIB had a charge on the land rights around the house, which they haven't. My ex wife knows that but it's just another thing to keep dragging and dragging. At this stage, I couldn't take any more. My solicitor, was not advising me, but TELLING me, again and going by what my wife was saying. In the building of the wall, the Judge told me to build the wall around the house, which is what I was going to do. Now Marian's solicitor and my solicitor came over again telling me that she wanted to build the wall and that she didn't trust me to build the wall, which was ruled by the Judge for me to do it. Again, my solicitor ruled that maybe we should let her build the wall which is terrible. It's going on since twenty past ten this morning and it's just after two o 'clock now. We're still not gone before the Judge. I just couldn't take it any more. I told my solicitor that I wasn't getting any justice there and told him to do what he wanted. And I walked out. That's the way it is now, I won't be going back into court again without getting justice in court. I see several men in court here without getting justice. They are losing their houses. Mary Robinson has an awful lot to answer for. She went to all the governments for the rights for women and she over abused it. She didn't know what she was doing at the time but she definitely over abused it. All these women are abusing it, they are in there to get as much as they can from the man. They have the right to bring it back into court even after there's been a settlement. My settlement was done years ago. My solicitor told me that she wouldn't bring me back into court if I signed the settlement. I signed all the agreements but she brought me back into court again. She's been bringing me in and out of court since 1999. I just couldn't take any more today and I walked out. They can go to hell because I am not going to lose any more nights sleep over my ex wife, her meanness and her hatred or the solicitors and barristers. It's like being in a cattle mart before you go before the Judge. They are all out there wheeling and dealing again today. If there's a Heaven and they are going to it then there's definitely no Heaven! There are people terrorised in there, going back and over, men and women and especially the men. The women are there because they are getting everything free anyway. It was the men's hard work that built up over the years. And they don't only want half - they want it all. And the Judge is ruling really for the women today. It's a very sad life that the men are living today especially in Ireland. I suppose this goes on all over the world. The Irish women today have so much rights and the Judge is ruling for them. There's a war going on in a marriage between men and women today, it's like a civil war. Until the Judge sees justice for both parties the man will never get justice in court. It's a very sad way that things have turned out and a hateful way. But the women seem to be smiling all the way to the bank and definitely in these cases it is not the men. So as I said again about Mary Robinson she has a lot to answer for. She went and she bent the rules and twisted the rules that make sure that the man will suffer in courts if they break up. There was a man in there that I know very well. His wife worked for me and he is going through the same thing. He told me that he can't sleep at night, that he's torn apart. He gave her a site which is worth one hundred thousand and a settlement out of court and she still brought him back into court. She wants half of everything that he owns, again on top of what she has got already. Until the day that the law in this country, the solicitors, barristers and the Judges will look at the mental affect that these women have. A lot of these women I believe, seventy per cent, are suffering from some form of depression in this country. And someone should send these women away to hospitals to be tested out because they are definitely off their rocker! Of course there are women that go and get help for depression and them women lives normal lives. Any man that I have spoken to about their women, they are suffering from depression or they have taken an over dose of tablets. And these are the women that are dragging their men into the courts. There's no Judge, solicitor or barrister looking at this aspect. And this should be the number one issue when you are taking a case that the woman and the man should be tested out for mental illness. Because definitely in Ireland today these women are very mentally effected and the courts are not looking at this. I wish to God that they would look at this because I was married to a very mixed up woman and there are an awful lot of men married to very mixed up women. They drag them through the courts and the solicitors and the barristers will fatten it out. The agreement that I signed the last day, my solicitor and barrister said that it was a court order, agreement on right of ways, which I didn't dispute any right of ways. But the right away around the house that she's taking in seventeen foot, half of a street, that's leading into three of my properties. I'm just after investigating that and there was no court order on that right of way. I had no problem in giving her right of ways. I wanted her to drive in between her own house, a driveway around the gable of her own house, but she wouldn't. She wanted instead ten foot to seventeen foot out into the street. This would block off at one end that she could drive right around the front of my property - again just to cause trouble. And the Judge, both solicitors and barristers agreed and said that it was a court order agreement. It never was as I'm just after finding out from the Court itself. The agreement was on right of ways. The agreement that Marian's solicitor had drawn up was a map that she stuck into the court order on the day of the court which lied again that this agreement would stand. That's the crookedness again of my solicitors and her solicitors and herself. She won the right to put up the wall and never did.

Today is the 1st of June 2005 and my daughter in Naas, who has been sick for the past four or five days before the court case came off, and I couldn't go up to see her. She went into hospital for an operation. She wanted me to go up and look after her when she comes out because she won't be able to do anything for herself for a while. I drove up last night and I stayed at a bed and breakfast across from the hospital. I spent the night up at the hospital until I had to leave. So I'm back outside the hospital again to visit my daughter and to take her out to the house that she stays in. I want to spend time with her until she gets strong. Thank God it's nothing that endangers her life and that's all that matters even though the operation was serious enough. Right of way to lands doesn't make any difference as long as my daughter is ok, Maria. Today is a beautiful day, the sun is shining. Last night when I came up to Naas, everywhere was booked up, there was no place to stay. Hotels were booked out because the Curragh Races were on and U2 were playing in the city so you couldn't get a bed and breakfast. I must have gone to about twenty places for a place to stay, I even thought at one time that I might have to sleep in the car. I stopped at this lady that does B&B and she was so saddened that she didn't have a place for me and she said "You'll never get a place to stay now". So anyway, we started talking and she said "are you up for the races?" I said "no, I'm up to be with me daughter, she is in hospital for an operation and I came up to spend some time with her". The lady picked up the phone and she said "hold on for a second, I have a friend near the hospital in an ordinary family house". She told me to go out there and that woman would put me up. I stayed with a lovely lady and she only charged thirty euros for the night and I gave her forty euros and I had a beautiful breakfast. There's some great, good hearted people out there too. The welcome that was made for me in their own home was second to none. I would do the same thing too. So there are good people out there too. I'm glad to be back at the hospital again this morning now. I'm looking forward to bringing Maria home, please God, to her own house in Naas, spending some time with her, and taking care of her. She is one daughter that was always there for me. I just have to say that it's good to be here, to be able to do it, to have the health to do it, to be there for my daughter.

Well thank God Maria is out of hospital now. We went back to the house that she's staying at. She wasn't that anxious to go home but I thought that it was the best thing for her to come home to Mayo and to rest and I'll take this week off now. And I've told her that whatever she wants to do or wherever she wants to go that I will look after her and drive her around. We are on our way home now from Naas to Mayo.

It's June 2005, today I'm meeting with Martin Ferris of Sinn Fein who is coming down to see the five farmers that's protesting against the gas by not letting the pipe through their land. They are holding out down in

Rossport. So I am heading down there to meet Martin Ferris today.

I got down there and met with Martin Ferris and the farmers. They were in the Shell compound and looking at where Shell put in a sewer without planning permission and Shell were denying it. And to see the people there, their families and their kids and the stress of the whole lot and these farmers wanting the people to support them. We waited there for about two hours. Martin listened to their concerns about the safety of their families and their kids if this pipeline went through. After that we left there. Two days later, there was a high court case in Dublin on these five men. Because they broke a court order on stopping the pipeline going through their fields, the Judge sentenced them to jail until they let the pipeline through their lands. Ever since I have been on to Sinn Fein, Martin Ferris is highlighting the issue of the wrongs that were done on these people of the local area. On the first day of the lads being in jail, I was down in Rossport where there was all media. There was about five or six hundred people gathered there. We decided that we would all move to where the lorries were coming out on the peat land, taking out the bog. We would picket the gate there. I led the picket there that day, all that day, and there was about seven hundred people there. There was nothing but media and cameras and everything. The first lorry driver that I went up to was one of the lads brother-in-law that was in prison. We were carrying the banner and we said "If you go in, you won't come out". The lorry driver said that they wouldn't go in past the picket. The picket went on all day. The Bord na Mona workers that work with Shell, stopped their work and the driving of the lorries and joined the picket. It was a day of encouragement and a day to be remembered. The Irish flag was flying that day. I said to the people to unite in force and that was the only way that you can over rule high up power companies like Shell. We spent all that day picketing and it was on television that night and it was on the papers and everything. It was a day that I'll never forget and be proud to be Irish. I made a speech on how our people fought and died for this land that we have here. How our people died in prison in the hands of the British. One time I used to say, I shouted "Brit's out" but today I'm shouting "Shell out".

The picket is still carrying on, there's people there twenty-four hours on Shell's gates. The whole place is closed down now for at least two weeks and they put the locks on the gates as well. But the five men are in prison all the time. The people are standing united all the time. On Saturday next there will be a big parade in Belmullet. There is expected to be anything up to five thousand people at it. A lot of people from outside Erris are coming in to support it. There's a lot of anger too around, that people's rights are been taking away from them. Like the rights of your land, people are questioning if they own our land or has the government sold the rights of our land out. On the gate as well, one of Shell's men knocked down one of the lads that was outside the gate and he's in hospital at the minute. He's not too bad but afterwards Shell wanted to speak to me to negotiate to let the men out, the thirty five men inside that couldn't get out. We told him that the only way that we would let them out was for them to give us in writing that they were closing the place down, and the five men to be let out of jail. Some of the lads got brave then and they came out with their jeeps and they blocked the road side to get their lads and there was nearly blood shed. I pulled one fella out of the jeep because he nearly ran into a woman and her kids on the road. There was about three hundred people around this man. He was an English man, I told him to go back to his own fucking country. He nearly got killed before there was a citizen's arrest made. Me and Máire Harrington made the arrest but only for that he would have been killed with these angry people. There was a lot shouting "Brit's out, ye shouldn't be here". There is an awful lot of British working for Shell. This is making the people angrier. The fear that I have is that there will be more trouble, and that some one will get killed here, if the five men are not let out of prison. That's the sad thing about it. There's an awful lot of brave people around. The police in Belmullet are coming and going there all the time too. But they seem to be on Shell's side too, not the people's side, even though the police in Belmullet are here to protect the people of Erris, and to protect the law and their rights. But the police are corrupt as well and they are very easy bought and Shell probably have them bought out as well.

I have spoke to Shell several times on this issue since the men went into jail. I had spoken to them even before that, to come in and speak to the people properly. Andy Pyle, of Shell, was on Mid West Radio and he didn't want anybody else to go on apart from him so he did the whole show. It was like that the people weren't good enough to talk to. I have spoken to Ministers on the phone, several Ministers in Dublin, mostly Fianna Fáil and Sinn Féin. Sinn Féin has always stuck by the people out here since this started. I know that because I have been involved with them. Martin Ferris and other Sinn Féin members have told Fianna Fáil that they should go to their Taoiseach in Dublin and immediately release these five men out of prison. They shouldn't be in prison, they are innocent men. Sweetman and the solicitor, came up with something on the last day in the court, to say that Shell had no authority to go through these people's lands, because they hadn't their paper work in place properly. So the government gave them an undertaking to go through. They took a court order on these farmers to go through their land which KC, a good solicitor that works for Sweetman, and he had a case and a hearing in Ballina as well. He was there to fight the case for the people. In court he turned the court around again that's coming back up that they didn't have one hundred per cent of right to go through these people's land. This is a thing that I'm hoping that KC will turn this case around. That these five men will be let out of prison and that Shell will have to negotiate with these people again. And that they will change the pipeline because these people shouldn't be in jail. They are not getting justice. This morning on the news here I heard that the Judge said that even if they sign for the pipeline to go through the land now that it's not to say that they will release them because they broke a court order. The justice is very wrong in this case I think. It's not too long ago that there was scandal up in Donegal and they speak about the law and these five men broke the law and the law is so corrupt in this country. It's not too long ago, it went on for a year or a couple of years up in Donegal where the police was involved - four, five or maybe six police - and an awful lot more of them that weren't caught, on a case where they destroyed a couple of families up there with their lies and corruption. They were finally caught out. What happened was that the police that were involved were promoted and some of them got early retirement. What they done there was so wrong. They destroyed people's lives, two families lives that was destroyed in this. And when I think of the five men who are in prison only to protect the rights of their lands and the rights of their families, their heritage that was handed down from father to son because that is the way that it is out here. These men, the five farmers, that are in jail got their land from their fathers and the father's before them got it from their fathers and that's the way it is to raise their family. And to think of the corruption that is happening here. Tomorrow there is another protest in Belmullet, which I expect will have up to three thousand people at it. I will be there to support these people. It's only yesterday (Today is the 8th July 2005) that a bomb went off in England and there was an awful lot of people killed. They still don't know how many innocent people were killed. Four or five bombs went off blowing these people to pieces. While Bush and Tony Blair were down in Scotland celebrating or coming to some agreement, these people were being blown to pieces. The sad thing about it all is that it's innocent people that got killed. But again they should look at their government. They have brought this upon themselves because them people - the suicide bombers - that planted them bombs, have seen their own people being destroyed. Being bombed and shot by Tony Blair's government for years and the Bush government out in Iraq. They have killed thousands and thousands of innocent women and kids and this a war that cannot ever be stopped. It's a war that when you come into somebody else's country and kill innocent people, these people come back and do the same thing to them and it never ends. It's sad that it's innocent people that are getting killed. The targets should be these governments that caused these wars, like Tony Blair. Going back to our people that are in jail now. The reason that Shell are here, and these other massive companies that are coming in here, is because our government is letting them. It's always the head of the governments that causes these wars and bombs and the killing of innocent people and that's what happens all over the world. George Bush, two days before the bombs went off, came to England and it was headlined on the English news where he went out cycling on a bike and ran into a policeman who is now in hospital. He knocked him down on the street. And this is the intelligent man that America has head of their country, to lead the country, Bush is stone mad in the head. He has disgraced the American people. Everybody says that. However if this is what education does, to put a lunatic like him as head of the country, it is no wonder that the world is the way it is. He has targeted the whole world as terrorists - anyone who sticks up for their rights - and all this is causing is more wars and more trouble and encouraging more people to take up arms.

When Clinton was in power in America everything was going well. He was a man who won the heart of all the people in the world indeed. He was a great man, his party was the Kennedy's party and stuck up for the rights of the people. He was a very intelligent man, he played a big part, indeed all the part, on the peace in this country in Ireland. He played the part of letting Gerry Adams into America where he let him speak. Before that they wouldn't let the Sinn Fein papers or any papers, or anything that had to do with the likes of Gerry Adams or Martin McGuinness or any member of the Sinn Féin party speak - they didn't want the truth. He was the first person to give a visa to Gerry Adams to come in. Today that is why we have peace on our island. The truth came out when Gerry Adams and Martin McGuinness spoke and the Sinn Fein party, about what was happening up in the North. Before that it was controlled. The media was controlled by the British because they didn't want the truth to come out. Clinton was a great leader for America and I think that a lot of the Americans know that now. It was sad that he could not run again, he ran for so many years, so he couldn't take over leadership again. Today we owe him for peace. When he was in I always flew the American flag beside the Irish flag. When Bush got in and went to war with Iraq and killed innocent people, without listening to anybody but himself and his government, I didn't fly the American flag since. I do respect America, it was very good to this country. After all up to sixty nine million people claim that they are Irish in America, so that's very, very strong. In the White House I have a relation of mine working there, that is one of the head of the Security Men for years and years. I got to know him when he came and traced back the Flannery family and it was me he came to. We've turned out to be good friends and we stay in contact. He comes every year now to see me. Also I get a Christmas card from the White House every year and have with the last seven or eight years. I also have the number for the White House, both numbers of the Secretary in the White House, so my connection with America and the White House is big. I do respect and love America. But it saddens me to see leaders like Bush, Margaret Thatcher and people like that, that cause trouble and war all over the world. Margaret Thatcher has a lot of blood on her hands, so has George Bush and Tony Blair, heeding George Bush to go to war in Iraq. They left a lot of sad homes and families by the killing that was done on the streets like in our country. I remember one time Margaret Thatcher saying that she would back the IRA up against the wall and shoot them down like dogs. The next thing the bombing started in London. She brought in a shoot to kill policy where if you were seen talking to an IRA person or you were thought to be an IRA person or an Irish republican, you would be shot down on the street. Even outside Ireland where the three IRA men were shot out abroad. People fought and stood up for their rights in Northern Ireland and in this country. They went out to fight for their rights by peaceful marching. For their rights to vote in their country, the rights for jobs for their families. Britain sent over troops on Bloody Sunday and shot Catholics like dogs on the street. Then they created another war. When that happened there were people signing up to join the IRA all over this island. And the war started and it lasted up to thirty to thirty five years. Thank God today that there is peace in Northern Ireland. The British made out, before the truth came out, that it was a religious war, that it was a Catholic and Protestant war. That was never the case. Paisley, as an orange man, never recognised a lot of the Protestants in this country. If you weren't an orange Protestant you weren't a Protestant because he was British. He was saying that he was British - if you were orange you were British, and the British made it out to be a religious war. Catholics and Protestants in the twenty six counties and indeed this whole island agree and work together. So there's no dispute between the Catholics and Protestants. Going back eight hundred years there was a big dispute between the British invading this country and the Irish and that is still here today in a lot of people. It's sad that innocent people have lost their lives over all this. That people were put into jail, died on hunger strike - lots of people lost their lives in jail on the hunger strikes. They were speaking for their rights and for freedom. The right to freedom of speech, the rights to jobs and the rights to vote. And the governments stood back and let it happen and that includes the Dublin government. Clinton did a very good thing for this country.

Today is the 9th July 2005 and we went to this big parade in Belmullet showing our concerns for the five farmers that are in jail and talking about Shell's pipeline. There was about one thousand people gathered there and I had the tricolour flying through the town. There were speeches made that was already made, that we heard in 2002. There were some of them that were very interesting speakers who spoke about the concerns of the people and there were others who just wanted to be heard. They made big strong speeches. Gerry Crowley was leading the parade and organised the parade. The wives of the five farmers in jail thanked him. But Sinn Fein's spokesman for Mayo, Gerry Murray was there and spoke of the concerns of the pipeline in the local area. The majority of the people want to see the pipeline done at sea and the gas to be pumped in, not the raw material coming in. I would agree with them on that. But Sinn Féin were not even mentioned at that parade, and since 2002 Sinn Féin have been behind the people of this area. I've been in contact with Sinn Féin all along regarding the concerns for the local area. But the parade went off very well. There was some people that are involved in this too and you would have to laugh at them. I could see that the picketing started off as a peaceful picket. I could see that they are picking on the employees that are working in the plant and the locals. You don't win like that because anyone that is working and getting money out of them my heart goes out to them. The people are right when a big company comes into the area and upset the area then to get as much money out of them as they can. But there are some of them that are leading the picket, or so called leaders, who are not in it for the issue and the sake of the area. That's why I looked very carefully at this parade yesterday. There was one thousand people at the picket, they said that there was fifteen hundred. Erris has a population of eight and a half thousand people, three to four hundred people would be from outside the area, so the majority of the people that are concerned about the local area was very small. I believe it's because some of them that are involved in this picket that a lot of Irish people realise that they are not in it for the good of the people in Erris. They are in it just to cause trouble and tell lies - some of them. And some of them have their hearts in the right place. It's starting to get divided. The people once again in Erris are starting to become divided and that's when the war weakens. I always said that when the army spreads then you loose the war, when the army stays together, a tight line together, you will win the war. There are a couple of them there that are teachers or retired teachers that can afford to be out shouting and roaring. They are coming up with, and what they cannot come up with, they are making up but we all clap for them. But the reality is that the majority of them don't know a thing about this pipeline. In 2001 I said that there should be an independent investigation and research on this pipeline to tell the people and show the people whether it is right or wrong, which the way Shell has done it so far, has been wrong. An investigation did take place but it was by one of Shell's companies. And if they go down the road of taking in somebody outside this country, that is genuine, to come in to do the research on it, it would be better. There was some engineer that spoke out there too. I know the engineer, most of the engineers in this country, and any project yet that they have done was from a computer, and was all a disaster. When I look at the disasters that these engineers have tightened up on cleanness and environment issues, which I would be all for in this country, and local areas. How they have put people through hell to get planning permission for a septic tank on their own land. This is pollution into the rivers. They fear that it wil leak into the rivers. They make people put in maybe ten thousand or eight thousand euros worth of a treatment plant. And it doesn't treat properly because it still leaks into the land, and they are so strict on this. Then when I look at these engineers, that's so called qualified, and we were in Belmullet yesterday, and all that sewer from all these buildings in the town are going into the sea. Belmullet has grown so fast, and I'm so delighted about that, houses going up everywhere. We have a new hotel, which is a great thing for the area. A local man that built it and I do support him. But with all this building that is going on, Mayo County Council and indeed the government are talking about the environment and cleanness. The town is built right on the bay and going into the sea. Along the shores is starting to get dirty. It's getting more dirty along the shores now. One of the most clean environments, Erris' shores are very clean and the people indeed are starting to clean up very much with their bins. There's not as much rubbish thrown around as there used to be, say ten years ago. And people are obeying. But then again Mayo County Council and engineers that are qualified are letting the people down and that is a big issue, the pollution going into the sea. We were out yesterday and rightly so, protecting the rights and the heritage of the people of Erris. But then I see all that sewage going into the tide polluting the bay and the fish and our beautiful beaches. Then you listen to an engineer that goes up on the stage and he says that he knows what he's talking about because he's a qualified engineer. I don't buy that. I was listening very carefully yesterday and have been listening since 2000. There was only one good speaker that spoke yesterday that made any sense. He said that he was going to bring it up in Brussels for the rights of the people. The politician only goes up there and he will speak so high and so good for the people and we'll all follow him. When he'll come off that stage and he'll go away down and go into a big hotel and have a big dinner and that's the end of him. It's not the Shell or the Tideway's that are to blame but we are to blame. It's our own government that gave Shell the right to go through these people's lands anyway. So I hope people, this time in Erris for once in their lives, stay together because it's starting already, people are starting to divide and scatter. There's an awful lot of pub talk on the gas and talking about each other as usual what they do. They are nice to your face and behind your back they would put the knife in you. It's a sad way but it's the way of life for them. Seventy per cent of Erris people are jealous of each other, it isn't that they are bad it just became a way of life with them. And then it's very hard for a community to build a strong bond to stay together for the rights of the community. I hope this time that they will stay together. If they don't there won't be any justice for them five men that went to jail for the concerns of letting the pipeline go through their lands. It's only when it hurts your own foot, most times in Erris, that they come out against these things. But in 2001 if people backed me and backed a few more people that had big concerns on this pipeline, it wouldn't have gone as far as it has today. There's a lot of work done today in 2005. There's an awful lot of work carried out by Shell and an awful lot of money pumped into this area, which they will find harder to walk away from. Shell are not going away, losing millions and millions, out of the Erris area without a fight. So people that are concerned about the five farmers in jail should be getting the government around the table now and getting Shell around the table. And not to be saying, which some of the teachers are saying, that they'll be no negotiations. Well if you have no negotiations then you'll have these men staying in jail for long enough. My thing would be to sit down around a table, not to get into Shell, not to get into the government, but sit and talk because if you don't sit and talk you're going nowhere. An awful lot of them instead of doing this are talking from one to the other. And talking in the pubs of how good they are. I hope this issue will be resolved and these men will be released out of jail to their families. I have stuck up for them since 2001 and I still stick up for them and for my own concerns in the Erris area.

It isn't that Erris people are bad in a way. These people that are jealous of each other, it has become a way of life for them, I suppose, hundreds of years of this way of life. It's an old saying that a man told me one time 'you could be a tramp in Crossmolina and you could be a gentleman in Belmullet'. As long as you're not doing well in the local area if you're a local it's ok, you'll fit in. But if you're an outsider that comes in to start a business, they'll support you, but if it's a local business person they won't support you as much. It's rare but it's true.

In 2001 Enterprise Oil and Shell called a big meeting in Teach Iorrais Hotel in Geesala. Before the meeting I had highlighted the concerns of this gas coming in and what damage it could do. I had experience about it by travelling to America and by working with the gas in Scotland. I had experience by listening to people and what they went through in Scotland. The gas was coming in and the oil coming in, and it was taken out of their area and went to England and left the area in a disaster. And more so in America, it was the same thing. I had all that experience and I had highlighted that in the media, on television in 2001. I had come out and spoke to the people in the Erris area and had called up a lot of these people that's just speaking out now about the gas. And the big concerns on the area and if we didn't put a good fight against this gas that we would live to regret it. Our grand kids and our future generations would regret this gas being let in the way that it was coming in at that time. I organised a picket. I called a lot of people. I called some of these people that are in jail today to make sure that they would support the picket in Geesala. It was highlighted by the media, it was on Mid West Radio, it was on the television that there was going to be a big picket against the gas in Geesala against Enterprise Oil and Frank Fahey and other government ministers. Because I knew that Frank Fahey had sold out the rights before that anyway. It saddened me that the media were on me there from ten o'clock and there were only thirty people that picketed behind me. We had placards up there and we went around with them. There were twelve police standing outside to ensure it would be peaceful and these people in Erris walked past and through the picket - which if they knew anything about a picket - you're not supposed to do that. And they walked in and they sat down with Enterprise Oil and with Frank Fahey. I was watching them through the windows as we stayed picketing in the rain and shouting. Frank Fahey and Enterprise Oil sent out five or six messages with a minister, Tom Moffett, to sit down and discuss this issue that we had with them. And I told him that we were not going to sit down with Frank Fahey because he had the rights of the people sold out. There were Erris people looking out the window laughing at me because I was putting up such a strong case with Enterprise Oil and Shell. And it saddened me.

I was there for four hours and picketed against them before the meeting was over and they all sat down and listened to them. We got all the television and media coverage outside. After the picket, I sat on the wall in Geesala and it saddened me that people didn't support the picket outside. It saddened me that these Erris people, over two hundred of them, walked through the picket and didn't back the picket. They wanted to see what was coming out of it. The majority of them wanted to see how much money they would make out of it. But that's what happened that time. Ninety nine per cent of the Erris people wanted this gas. They wanted the wealth, the money. And it's only now that a few people have stood up and said that they won't let the pipe through their land. The reason the people are out now is because the five farmers are gone to jail. Otherwise, there would be no picketing. Erris people are funny. They are very hard to weigh up. I love Erris and I still love living here. I'm here now sitting on a rock as I talk today down in Rinroe not far from where I was brought up. I visited my mother and my father's grave on the way down and said my prayers. It's an absolutely beautiful day, the clean air, the clean beaches, kids screaming and walking out in the water in Rinroe. They have a picnic here today. I'm here with Teresa and it's absolutely gorgeous. But it saddened me that time. On the 'Farmers Journal' as well there was a big write up on me at that time. They came down to me and I done an interview with them and they took it down and it was highlighted on the 'Farmers Journal'. We got big coverage on the papers about my concerns on the gas. Yesterday I was cutting out the write up. Teresa photocopied fifty copies of them and we handed them out to people that I told in 2001 which is the same thing that they are trying to say today. So I guess I was five years ahead of them at that time. I knew by me going against the gas that I had more to lose than them. I knew that I had a business and holiday homes. With the gas coming in I was going to gain money anyway. But I knew the risk was too high to pay for the future of the Erris people, not just for myself, but for the kids. The sad thing about this today in Erris is an awful lot of people just think about themselves, 'as long as my foot doesn't burn it's ok'. So that's a bad attitude for the future, for the area, for the county and for the country. We're supposed to look after this place, keep it clean, keep it pollution free, keep the air and the water clean and purified, for the future generations to come. That is what we are supposed to be doing because as the old saying goes 'we'll go out the same way that we came in anyway'. But it would be nice to leave and think that we have left everything clean and helpful behind for the next person.

The Tideway boss came to me today. He told me how Shell have been on to him about how I have got so heavily involved in the picketing against the gas and to release the five men in prison. They wanted him to pull out from my offices. I told him that I would leave that up to him. If he wanted to pull out I would respect him and that I would break the contract that was made. That means that I lose twenty thousand euros. I also told him that if Shell wanted to pull out that they should pull out too, because while these men are in prison, I will be standing by my word, standing by the people and the release of these five men in jail. He respected that and he told me that he would come back to me within a few days to see what they could do. This is my commitment to the thing, money doesn't buy me. Although I am a businessman and I do try and do business to keep my property and my banks paid up, because I have paying back to do, I am a tax payer so I have to do that. As I said I left school when I was eleven years old, I don't get a retirement pension from the government. I do pay my taxes as good as I can. So I have a lot to lose and a lot to gain, but I wouldn't turn my back on the people either. I would stand by my principles as much as I can. I am one to go on the front line if I see it's right and that's the way I am. I know an awful lot of them that are picketing who won't stand in the front line. Or if there are any arrests to be made that it won't be the teachers, or these people who are talking in the pub. It'll be someone like me who stands up for what I believe in. Like the five farmers that are already in jail.

Today is the 10th of July 2005 and I am going doing a talk. I am just after meeting one of the sisters of the husband's who are in jail. She has been into the prison to visit her brother-in-law and she told me that the five are finding it hard to be in there and I know that too. It's very easy for the people here that are not going to go to jail, to go up on the stages and make big speeches and get a big clap, but when it's going to jail, a lot of them won't go into jail. My aim is to get them lads out of jail because I know when you spend a long time, or too long in jail, you don't come out of it as the same person. It doesn't make a better person out of you and they are innocent people. Five innocent people really that are sticking up for their rights. But I have been on to the Ministers, to Sinn Féin - Martin McGuinness, and everyone that I could think of that could help. I am trying to keep away from the ones with the big mouths that are doing all the shouting, but I am doing the work behind that. They are trying to keep them in jail as long as they can so these five men look like they are scapegoats now. Get them out of jail and get justice for them is my aim of the game.

Well it's been three or four days since I was talking to one of the five's sister's in law and I've been on to Sinn Féin Ministers - Martin McGuinness and Martin Ferris, to Eamon Ó Cuiv and every minister that I could get in Dublin. I spoke to them over the phone to tell them that it was awful important to release these five men from jail and give them justice. I told them that it didn't look good for our country in the way that the people of the Erris area are been treated. They are treated like dirt. I kept pressing on and pressing on. Three evenings after that I was on a direct line to the prison that I could negotiate through somebody else in the prison, with the five men. They came back into negotiations with me and they thanked me for all the help that I had given them by getting the Ministers into the prison. And thank God after two days of negotiations that there was a break through. A Fianna Fáil Minister agrees to take a whole new independent research on the project again, on the safety aspect of the pipeline coming in. Not Shell, it was Shell who took the last couple of 'independent' safety evaluations on the pipeline coming in. With the pressure that has been put on them to carry out this independent research on the safety of the pipeline, at four o'clock, I got the word from Dublin that there was going to be an announcement made by the nine o'clock news. So I have good inside contacts and good inside calls made to the Ministers in the right places. Martin McGuinness is also involved in this. I'm proud that they are involved in the negotiations at least. Today I thought the lads would be freed with Shell closing down until this is sorted out, and I'm glad of that.

I do welcome an independent evaluation into the safety of the pipeline. At least then they'll be able to tell the people that this pipeline is safe because up to date, Shell or the government indeed, wouldn't guarantee the safety of it. Myself and an awful lot of other people asked for this a long time ago. So this is a step in the right direction. And there has to be negotiations. I know an awful lot of them now on the picket line that are shouting for no negotiations. I want these men to get out of prison and I want these men to get justice because this is justice for everybody. This is the only way forward. So I'm glad now that I played the part of helping to get this around the table. I have good inside information even with Shell. I have people in amongst Shell that they don't even know about, and they are feeding back information to me. I have information even on the government that is said back to me. I know the five men are in good hands but being in prison is not easy for the likes of these men because they are not criminals. They are innocent people, they are only sticking up for their rights. Like I would be doing myself for the rights and the safety of families and indeed the pipeline. So there's a good break through. The court case came off today. Because Shell hadn't their paperwork done properly, that they had the rights to go through their lands the first time, the solicitors brought this up so the men will have to stay in jail for another eight or nine days and the court will hear the case again. So I'm looking forward to these men being released right away and that the independent research will be carried out to show that the pipeline is safe for the people of Erris.

It's the 16th of July 2005 and there was another picket on in Ballina yesterday and one thousand people showed up to support the Shell to Sea campaign. And there were a lot of speakers there who spoke on the gas being processed at sea. The five men are still in jail. I have a lot of concerns for these men and their families and I'm hoping to God that they will be released as soon as possible as they are innocent men.

But the battle is still going on today. Teresa, my partner, went out to Ballina and brought two big box loads of food for the people who are camping down at the shores at Glengad. There are four people camping down at the shore. She brought water, food, milk and everything they could eat. I also did the same thing with the Eco Warriors. In the back ground I am still pushing the politicians. I am calling them up at all hours of the day and night to try to get justice for these five men and get them out of prison. Sometimes it is working and I hope and I'll keep pushing all the time, that they will get justice. Not just for the jailed five men but for all of us in this country for the government selling us out.

Well it's the 28th of July 2005 and this Saturday we are preparing to go to Dublin. Busloads are leaving Erris to parade the streets of Dublin for the release of the five men. The fight and the battle is still going on and the picketing in the gates. And now, the politicians, the local politicians, are starting to talk. They are about five years too late. But they are starting to come out now and talk. They are bringing it up in the County Council offices and Shell are willing to talk to the local people now. Before that we weren't good enough to talk to. And now they are just after coming out that they want to talk to the local politicians and the local people, which it took them so long to do. I see the local politicians now speaking out that they should put the gas to sea and when the planning permission went in for the gas the same local politicians sat around the table with the Mayo County Council and gave the planning permission for the gas to come through.

Rock fishing off Graughill in 1950.

Grandfather Sonny Flannery
taken at his farm
in Porturlin in 1956

At Sinn Fein meeting I organized in Geesala. 1997

Maria with her pet lamb.

At Teach Iorrais August 2003, from L: Tom & Patricia Gaughan,
Martin & Bernie McGuinness, Brendan Grace, Patrick & Theresa.

Bellanaboy standoff against Shell.

My daughter Katrina, linking the sweaters.

At Stillwate, Minnesota, during tour of USA in 1993.

Campsite at Stillwater, Minnesota during USA tour in 1993.

Brother TJ Flannery with grandson TJ.

My first fishing boat: The Dancing Mermaid

Chapter 5

Confusion of the Gas in Erris

Corrib Gas again - concerns - parade in Dublin
Singing songs on the bus home
Picketing in Glengad
Ministers
Sinn Fein

Them same politicians now that are speaking out about the concerns of the people in the local area, are five years too late. Those same politicians sat around the table when the planning permission was given to Enterprise Oil at the start, at the early stages, five years ago. The same way with the Council, they didn't say one word on behalf of the people, the safety of the area or the pollution going into the sea. Or the concerns of the Carrowmore Lake. They never said one word. They were all for the gas including every single one of them. All the Fianna Fáil, Fine Gael and independent politicians backed this gas plant coming in here. They all said that it would be the best thing that ever happened to this country. They boosted the people up so much that they would get loads of money out of it, which didn't happen. And the same politicians are speaking out now. The second time that it went around was because four of us had hearings in with An Bord Pleanála for the concerns of the local area. Some of them the concerns of their own area, and their own benefits of their houses that the plant was too close to them. The only thing we got out of those hearings at that time was that they were forced to close down the whole project and apply again for planning permission. These hearings went on for two weeks in 2002. it was found that Enterprise Oil hadn't got the proper planning permission. It went before Mayo County Council again for planning permission. Those same politicians that are jumping on the band wagon and speaking out now and they know well that they cannot change it. They are the ones that gave the planning permission to Enterprise Oil again, the second time. Then they are making out that they didn't know how dangerous this gas plant was to the local area. They knew very well how dangerous it was. I wonder, and we know that the government has taken brown envelopes in the past, was the

61

brown envelope passed around to Mayo County Council and indeed the politicians in Erris that were elected. These people that are supposed to be representing the people, and haven't represented the people. I always said that out here in Erris you would be better without any politician but local people to look to the government for things for the local area themselves. I think that we would gain more. A strong voice from the local people would be better than the politicians that are elected here over the years. So the thing goes on. As I said before I am going off on Saturday, a bus load of us are going, to Dublin to take part in the parade in Dublin, to show a strong united front to get these men out of jail. Even yet an awful lot of the Erris people are not taking part in this and an awful lot of the Erris people are still for the gas to come in. Then the rest of them don't give a shit whether it comes in or not. But there's more for the gas in Erris, at this stage, with the five men in jail, than is against the gas. It's a very small minority that have spoken out strongly against this gas, indeed I am one of them. I have offices rented out to Tideway, an offshore subcontractor to Shell. There about a week ago or two weeks ago Tideway's boss came to me and told me that Shell wanted them to move out of my offices. They said that I was the ring leader for the picketing, because I led the picket for the first couple of days over there. I have good respect for Tideway because they are men that you could talk to, they are proper business men not like Shell. I told him that I have nothing against him if he decided to pull out, that I would respect him. I'm going to lose out on a lot of money on it. But I just couldn't sit back and let this gas, without my say, to come into the area because I still have a hearing with An Bord Pleanala. It still sits there with my concerns about the water supply to Carrowmore Lake, that supplies all Erris, the concerns about the fishermen, the pipe going into the sea and the pollution of the bay and the danger of the pipeline itself. Indeed the plant will pollute the area, I said that in 2001 when I raised all these issues. But sadly I didn't get the backing at the time. So my issues, I told him, still stand. And in the contract with Tideway for renting my offices, says that my hearing still stands against the concerns of the gas coming in and the dangers that it could cause to the local area, to tourism and pollution. They respect that and they did sign at the bottom of that to say that they had no concerns and that I had every right to picket against the gas. So they really were gentlemen, the Tideway employees. They are a very respectable company and Shell were too big to sit down with the people, they thought that they were above the people. But they have paid the price for not doing this. It has cost them millions and millions, even though they can afford it.

The picketing is still going on, today the picketing is on in Glengad. I told some of the picketers that there was no need to picket now because the Tideway company are pulling away. They wanted to get in to take their gear out and some of the picketers stopped them, a small minority of them. But the most of the people know that they shouldn't do that, that the workers should be let out. Tideway should be let in to take their gear out. I also had a meeting with Shell today. They came along here to talk to me and the concerns again on the local area against the gas. They told me that if the gas pulls out of here now that they will never come back again and they won't be putting it back to sea. Also that there will be nothing here and I told them that it wouldn't be benefiting the Erris area anyway. The Erris area didn't benefit much from them and not to blame the people who are only sticking up for their rights. It was Shell who made the mistakes, Enterprise Oil made the mistakes when they came in first. One of Tideway's bosses, who I do respect agreed with me and he told me that people say Shell are ruthless and it's how they are stupid. They were stupid more than ruthless because they didn't have their paper work in order. Even as we speak to them today, I had already found out that they were still going to lay the pipe off the Broadhaven Bay, out to the gas well anyway in a week's time. And he tried to bluff me, to say that they weren't and that the gas wouldn't go out to sea. If they pulled out of here that this country would lose so much money on it. I was trying to tell him that the country sold it out. They sold the rights for this gas out anyway and that we are all going to lose money on it, business, but they didn't give the business to the Erris area. He still tried to tell me that he did. He didn't. Most of the business was outside Erris, and it was only a handful of Erris people that would have gained anything on it anyway. He asked me would I stop picketing when this independent research would be completed, which I wanted in 2001. But the two independent reports that were carried out before were by Shell so the people have lost their faith in Shell. The people don't trust Shell anymore because of their lies and the way that they handled this gas plant coming in. They weren't open or honest with the people. By putting the five men to jail was the wrong thing to do anyway. They denied that they put the men in jail, that it wasn't them but we know that it was. That's why I said I will picket while the men are in jail. He asked me if the independent report showed that the gas was safe, that the pipeline was safe, would I still picket against the gas. I told him that if the independent report was taken out honestly and that it is safe to come in that I would not picket against the gas, there would be need. But so far, there's no guarantees of safety for the people. While there isn't a guarantee, the Erris people will always be wary of this. He went away with that and I did tell him that they didn't benefit the area. He agreed on that but said that they tender for all the work and I did state about the catering. There was a local man here, Healy's, that cater for food, and he didn't get the tender. The person that got the catering tender was a son of the boss on Mayo County Council. I said that it was like it was fiddled from the word go. It was unfair that the local people couldn't benefit from it when you had deals made behind their backs, like that with Mayo County Council. I asked him how could you expect the people to trust you then when there are things like this. But they always have the answers, saying that it had nothing to do with Shell, we put it out for tender. It had a lot to do with Shell. The way that they handled this project caused them problems. They thought that the people in Erris were stupid but they've found out that we are not that stupid after all. And I did say what they should have done when they were coming in here was to give shares to every household in Erris. That they would have a share in the company at least. That they'd have so much shares for the hassle that Shell are giving the people of Erris. But he said that they couldn't do that. I asked him how can some Irish companies do it, like banks, they can give you so many shares. They could have done that, but it has cost them a lot of money, millions and millions, wasted with the hold up with this gas. Then he tells me that they cannot give shares to the people in Erris. The Erris people are divided now too. It has put bad feelings between people, people who are against the gas because of the safety issues and the people that want the gas. A lot of Erris people want the business. Then there's a few that are unreasonable as well in the picket line. They won't negotiate, they won't listen to anyone but themselves and you cannot work with people like that anyway. There has to be negotiations to get justice, if there isn't any negotiation you cannot get justice. I have spoken to a few of them on the picket line that are very head strong and told them to do it the proper way. I hope that they will listen because most of them have genuine concerns.

We went on a bus to Dublin on Saturday as well to picket against the five men again in jail. There were three to four buses. About one hundred and forty people left Erris to raise their concerns about the five jailed men and to highlight it. I went on the bus with my partner Teresa. There were fifty people on the bus and the first thing that I noticed about the people on the bus was that if we weren't going grey, we were going bald. It was then that I realised that it is only our generation that cares about the environment and the danger of the gas coming into our area. There were no younger ones. When we got to Dublin and saw all the people that were there, I was very disappointed, there were only about one hundred and forty people. I was hoping that more would have showed up. But we were lucky because around the corner was a lot of Sinn Féin members, about thirteen to fourteen hundred of them. There was over two thousand people altogether and we led the march to express our concerns through the city of Dublin. I was delighted to see Gerry Adams there and Mitchell McLoughlin supporting the people of the Erris area and the five men in prison. I was delighted to shake hands with Gerry Adams, an old friend of mine, and a good Irish republican. We marched through the city, over two thousand people and the speeches were made and the politicians. Sinn Féin played a big part on the rights for the people for Erris. They didn't go on the stage. They worked on the ground which I respected them for. On the way back that night we had the sing songs. There was a microphone on the bus and we all sung the Irish republican songs. Paddy McGuire and his cousin sang, I sang and a lot more people sang. It was great sing song and a cheer coming home. It was lovely on our bus. There were fifty of us on it and we were all happy and united after the march went well in Dublin. Our hearts were lifted when a lot of people were saying that the gas wouldn't come in now and that the government got the message for selling the rights of the people out. We travelled all the way down, stopped and had a big meal. We went on there to Paddy McGuire's pub where the people there welcomed us coming back. It is an experience that I will never forget. There was such happiness on that bus and the pride that we were doing something for the Erris area. And we didn't forget the five men in jail. It was all about 'Shell to Sea'. But of course Shell knew well that they wouldn't be going to sea because they had the government behind them. I realised that too. There were days that I thought that they would put the gas to sea. Especially after the five men were put to jail over the pipeline going through their land. And when people raised their voices strongly. When we picketed the gates, and we showed the government up for what they were. That they would have to put Shell to sea, but they never intended to. It's only today after meeting with Shell that I realised that they never had an intention of going to sea. They were going to bull dose their way in anyway. So it looks like it is going to go ahead in the next year, 2006. More than likely. It will hurt a lot of people and it will definitely not do the area any good. But when you are against the government and a powerful company like Shell, the people's concerns aren't heard. Nobody's listening to them. If some of the ministers don't stand up against their own government then we won't win this battle with Shell.

Any day that I speak with a minister on the concerns of the five men in jail and to try and help them out, I've been on to Martin McGuinness and I have a direct line into the five men in prison so that they are getting the messages, I have been on to Eamon Ó Cuiv, Martin Ferris and a lot of other ministers to get involved and try to get justice for these five men and get them out of jail. Any breakthrough that I get, I get the message to the men in jail and another message telling them that we are all strongly behind them. It's sad to see five men in jail. It is wrong. It proves to everyone in this country that they don't have the rights of their lands. I thought that we owned our lands but we don't. Those people in prison didn't want Shell to go through their lands but the government gave them the go ahead to go through them regardless. I always believed in this country. Twenty years ago we had a good country and a good government. They would stick up for the rights of the people but this government is selling us out every year. Every second year, there is something else sold out in this country. This government has a lot to answer for and it's history repeating itself. I always believed that this country was freed. The IRA fought and died for the freedom of this country. They were hung in prisons; they died on the hunger strikes in prisons, for the rights and freedom of people in this country. That no man, woman or country had the right to invade us, like the way the English invaded us. The only one that you couldn't stop was the ESB, by putting electric poles on your land. But they were giving a service to the village, or a water scheme, you couldn't stop that either. But I know in my heart that Shell had no right to go through any one's land because this is not giving any service to Erris or indeed to Mayo. This pipeline is going to Galway and Dublin. It is not giving any benefit to this area at all. I know that if this case was taken to Europe and fought as hard as we fought here that we would win. There was something put in when the State was founded, and the freedom of this country, that no man would have the rights to invade our country again or invade our lands. Our people that came before us fought and died for this country for our freedom now. The IRA had to take up arms because we were invaded. Us, Irish people, as Irish republicans, never invaded any other country's lands or to try to take over another country. The British invaded our country for eight hundred years. They never defeated us. The IRA won this war. Even Tony Blair said it that they could never beat us or they never will. England never won a war in their whole history, they never invaded a country and won. They always had to bring in another country, or two to help them. That's one thing that we didn't have to do. We stood and fought them as Irish republicans in this country and proud of it. I'm proud of being an Irish republican. I was sympathising with the IRA when I was eighteen years old. I admired them for what they done, to fight against the British. It was sad that a lot of innocent people got killed and it was all because the British invaded our country. But they always wanted to blame the IRA for everything that was done. They refused to tell the truth. It was only when Gerry Adams was let into America by Clinton that the truth was told. About what the English had done to this country in the North, they raped and murdered and blackmailed the Irish people. That is the reason that the IRA had to take up arms and fight them. I know that there will never be peace on this island while there are British soldiers on this soil. History will repeat itself again and we will fight the British again until the day that we have a United Ireland. But I'm glad to see the peace today and Sinn Féin are going down the political road. The orange protestant in the North, the British don't want them. We never said that we didn't want them because they are Irish people too. They are on our island. The day will come that the orange politician in the north will be looking for votes all over Ireland, because he will be living as an Irish man in an all Irish country as Ireland and that day will come. We never had any hate for the Protestants in this country. They were the first people to fight against the British. May all the people who died for this country rest in peace and the innocent people that died also. It was terrible what happened in Northern Ireland where our Dublin government sat back and let it happen. They did nothing about it and today the IRA and Sinn Féin have to go into politics to fight around the table for a United Ireland.

When you have people like Martin McGuinness, a man that I admire and have the highest respect for, sitting around that table, I know he won't sell out our country. He will fight for the benefits of Ireland and for an all Ireland country. When you have the likes of him, Gerry Adams, Pat Doherty, Mitchell McLoughlin, Caoimhín O Caoileáin and several more good Sinn Féin Irish republicans around the table, I know they won't sell out the rights of this country. I do trust them men to do the right thing for the benefit of all of Ireland. They will always have to watch the Dublin government. Indeed there are people in Sinn Féin as well who are jumping on the band wagon now, that will have to be watched as well. Because some of these people I wouldn't trust either. It's down the road of politics for Sinn Féin. I know that when the next election comes up that Sinn Féin will gain an awful lot of seats on this island, because a lot of people have lost their trust in this government. It's a rich mans government, the Dublin government of today. The rich get richer and the poor get forgotten. It's the old story of once I have enough I will forget about my neighbour. But I know that the leaders of Sinn Féin will speak for equal rights in this country and that's what the party is all about. I'm happy enough to see these men heading up Sinn Féin. Martin McGuinness is a long term friend of mine. We get on very well. We speak the same language and we know that we will always speak out for the good of our country. Over the years I got to know Martin and his family very well and he is a good family man. He's all for his wife and his kids and his heart is in the right place. We were up in Letterkenny at Martin's daughter's wedding and it was a big wedding there. It was an honour to be asked up by Martin and his wife Bernie to attend the wedding. The nature that is in his wife and his family is the way that I was brought up - full of nature, full of goodness. Gerry Adams and all the party members were there from the six counties and some from the twenty six counties. I was one of the people that was there from the twenty six counties at the time and we were all re-united around the table. It was a beautiful weekend away for this wedding and an honour for me to be there. Martin and his wife were delighted to see that I could make it. Over the years, even before I met Martin, I always followed his path. I always knew that he was the right man in the right place and he was a strong voice for this country. He risked his life and risked his family's life during the troubles and I know that they didn't have it easy. That's why I know that his heart is in the right place and that he will do good for this country. I also know that I will see the day Martin and Gerry Adams in the Dublin government, and the day will come that he will be the Taoiseach of this country. That's when Irish people will trust their government again. We were brought up like my father, trusting Fianna Fáil to do the right things for this country. Over the years this country has changed so much but it is forgetting about its roots and where we came from. That's the sad thing. Fianna Fáil are getting too rich, too fast. They are forgetting about the rights of this country. The nature, the roots which Martin McGuinness will never forget. We know where his heart lies and that's with the people of this island, an all Ireland.

This is the 1st August 2005 and I'm looking forward to Martin and some of his family coming down again this year to meet up. They will have a couple of days chatting and I'll be showing him around Erris. He loves that. Going into Inis Gé islands, visiting businesses in the town that are growing and maybe a day fishing and eating the wild salmon from the sea. That's Martin, he loves doing things like that and we'll be catching up on old times.

The sheep are fed in the shed in the winter.

My father Tom Flannery fixing my fishing net just a few weeks before he died at age 59.

Successful delivery of a bull calf born on Flannery's Farm

32 County Farm Development Award Presented by Lord Debs in Belfast, 1997.

Fishing in Killybegs age 28 in 1984

Off Porturlin.

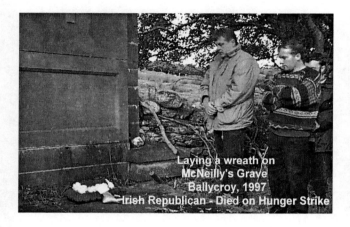

Laying a wreath on
McNeilly's Grave
Ballycroy, 1997
Irish Republican - Died on Hunger Strike

Visiting Flannery graves
in Lincolnshire, England
with brother-in-law Dick, 1996

Gerry Adams being chauffered
in my car outside my home in 1997.

97 MO 3157

Another win for Flannery Knitwear
in local horse race in Geesala, Aug 2001.

Interview 2

Michael Burke,

Experiences of Growing Up & Fishing in Porturlin

Well I'm down here with Michael Burke from Porturlin, a second cousin of mine. We'll be doing a talk about the fishing and the way times were

Patrick
Your father fished with my father, Tom Flannery?

Michael
That's right

Patrick
And were there boats that time?

Michael
Ah there wasn't, that was in the late fifties, in 1957, lobster fishing, salmon fishing and lobster fishing

Patrick
And was it currachs then ye used?

Michel
Yes twenty two foot currachs for the salmon fishing, eighteen foot currachs for the lobster fishing

Patrick
And it was hard work I believe at that time?

Michael
It was, cruel

Patrick
And would ye go far out fishing that time Michael?

Michael
We would go out six to eight miles if it was calm. It would depend on the weather

Patrick
And was the salmon plentiful that time?

Michael
The salmon was plentiful that time but there wasn't much gear to catch them with. Five nets to each currach and five men in each and five oars

Patrick
That would be like one hundred and fifty yards would it be?

Michael
It would work out at about eight hundred yards, I think for the five nets and the way that they had them mounted

Patrick
Eight hundred yards. And how much would salmon be making that time in prices?

Michael
Well I don't know. My father when he was young was getting three to pound

Patrick
Three to the pound?

Michael
That would be the 1920's now, it's going back a long way

Patrick
And what was Porturlin like as a village that time? Was it all fishermen?

Michael
Yes all fishermen

Patrick
They wouldn't be but small farmers

Michael
A few acres each. There was only twenty one houses in it

Patrick
And what year then did the first fishing boat come?

Michael
In 1961, the first boat came to Porturlin and in 1962 then six more boats came and it went on then till well I remember thirty four being in it, fishing salmon in Porturlin

Patrick
And was it twenty six foot boats that came first?

Michael
Yes

Patrick
Would they have been grant aided then?

Michael
They were grant aided by BIM

Patrick
So did they catch more fish then

Michael
Of course they did indeed, twice more than they were getting in the currachs

Patrick
And they brought in more money of course too

Michael
Yes but then again the market wasn't great either. They had to do with whatever they got, so for one and six pence a pound

Patrick
Was it in the currachs that our fathers fished together?

Michael

Yes it was of course. Well they didn't fish together but they fished they used to fish lobster together alright

Patrick

And what kind of pots did they use for the lobster that time?

Michael

Pots made from heather off the mountains and the cliffs

Patrick

They were hand made?

Michael

They used to weave them like the way the baskets are made now, they were made in a different shape, round with a pipe in one end of them

Patrick

And how many would they use in each currach then for fishing the lobster?

Michael

They'd use twenty to thirty pots, some forty, or fifty

Patrick

And tell me Michael, Porturlin as a village, was it a poor village or was it because we were fishermen that we were better off than the villages that didn't fish?

Michael

I don't know, I guess we were better off because we had the fish from the sea but only had the summer months back then. The fishing gave us extra money for the year and kept us going.

Patrick

But lads like ourselves that were brought up in Porturlin, we didn't have to go to England like other villages

Michael

Well we didn't have to go in the summer months, but maybe at the back end some of them might go for the winter

Patrick
And they'd work the winter over there

Michael
Yes and come back again for the fishing.

Patrick
The fishing always brought them home again. How old were you yourself when you started fishing?

Michael
I was thirteen years old

Patrick
And how old were you when you left school?

Michael
I left the same year

Patrick
So you left school at thirteen and went fishing at thirteen. And did you find it hard?

Michael
No it wasn't, we had engines in the boats and there was no rowing. And we didn't mind hauling in the fishing gear by hand. Each man would give you a hand and we would take turns to make the work easier

Patrick
But the hands would be sore for a while

Michael
Oh they would but you would get used to it, they would harder up and get stronger. When you'd weigh the fish in the morning you would have a good glass of whiskey and two bottles of Guinness. You'd go home then and eat a good breakfast and sleep like a pig!

Patrick
And you would go back out fishing again?

Michael
Back out again then in the evening

Patrick
And tell me about the drink Michael. Was it the men that were buying the fish at the time

Michael
They would buy the drink, but no one would go too far with the drink. Every man would have a drink in the morning

Patrick
A couple of whiskeys?

Michael
Each man would have a glass of whiskey in the morning and the two bottles of Guinness. They would be sober and they'd go home

Patrick
So do you have good memories of Porturlin growing up Michael?

Michael
Oh I have

Patrick
You were happy growing up in Porturlin?

Michael
Oh I was, it was a great life with the fishing. There were summers here that there would be over one hundred men fishing there.

Patrick
That was amazing

Michael
And maybe up to one hundred and fifty some summers there.

Patrick
And people from outside the village would come in and fish there?

Michael
Yes the outside villages, around locally

Patrick
Michael what year was it then when the bigger boats again came?

Michael
I would say in the 1970's, in the 1960's it was all the twenty-six footers, then in the seventies a few thirty footers came, and thirty six foot and up to forty. Well it didn't make things any better then because the fish started getting scarce then. The salmon was getting scarce then. The bigger trawlers started fishing the salmon out in the deep so they weren't letting them in where the small boats used to fish them. The Donegal trawlers had it fenced off

Patrick
So they didn't help the fishing around here?

Michael
No, no they robbed it of all kinds of fish. It's like their own out there and now the fish are scarce.

Patrick
The fish is gone out of it now

Michael
It is the fish is gone scarce. Then the super trawlers took them as well. The coastline of Sligo, Mayo and Galway the fish has gone scarce.

Patrick
It's sad though because there was a lot of money to be made here

Michael
You would have to go one hundred miles now to get a fish. One hundred miles west, out in the deep

Patrick
Tell me Michael when did the boats got bigger, the fish was getting more scarce so I'm sure the crews started go get smaller

Michael
They did, they started out with four men, this was reduced to three men, some of them are fishing now with only two. And even a few trying to fish with just one person

Patrick
They couldn't afford to pay a full crew

Michael
No they couldn't afford it because if they are not getting any fish they are not making enough money

Patrick
So do you think that Porturlin is worse off now than it was?

Michael
It is for the fishing because the fish is so scarce. It's almost finished there now. There's only a few boats fishing crabs left now but its harder to make money. There are more pots in it now than crabs!

Patrick
It's sad. Tell me about the poteen. Do you remember it?

Michael
Oh the poteen was a good old crack. People used to make an odd drop for themselves

Patrick
So they always had their own drink?

Michael
Some would have. They didn't make the poteen for sale or money, they would just made a drop for themselves

Patrick
So it is a changed village now

Michael
It is, it's not as lively as it used to be when the fishing was good, it put great life in the place. Everyone had extra money to spend then sure

Patrick
That's right. Do you remember the first car coming into Porturlin?

Michael
I do.

Patrick
And what year was that Michael?

Michael
Well I don't remember the first car because the first car was here before I was born. I think that it was in the 1960's that they started coming in

Patrick
Then everyone had a car? And would that be because the fishing was good then?

Michael
Oh it was, yes

Patrick
And the road going into Porturlin, what year was it tarred first? I think I remember the tarring of that road. Would it have been in the sixties too?

Michael
It would be in the late sixties, about 1967 or 1968. I worked on it.

Patrick
Did you work on the road too? In the winter time?

Michael
Yes I did. It went on for two years I think

Patrick
And who was buying the salmon in them years?

Michael
When I started Eamon Munnelly, Geesala, used to buy them, and the O'Donnell's would buy them too

Patrick
And Brendan Doherty?

Michael
Yes and Doherty's from Carrowteige

Patrick
They would be the three main buyers

Michael
They were. Sure they were paying as well as they could and as good

as what was going at the time. Things were very cheap in the 1960's anyway. When you went into a shop, you would get an awful lot of stuff for five pounds or ten

Patrick
So food was cheap. Do you think that when the fishing was good that there should have been fish factories put in at Porturlin to keep the fishermen there? Do you think that would have worked?

Michael
I suppose it would have helped for a while surely. The way it would be that the factory would only last as long as the fish would last

Patrick
But it would have been better do you think?

Michael
It would have been better in them years for the village. They were the days that there was big money made in Killybegs, back in the sixties and there was a market for the herring and white fish. I remember when we were out fishing and when you'd look down in the water, you could see the herring under you. They were so plentiful. Schools of them, playing near the top of the water on a warm day

Patrick
So you believe that the super trawlers did take the fish?

Michael
I do, they cleaned it

Patrick
Does it sadden you when you think of that too?

Michael
It does of course. It was nice when we went fishing, for sure. And you were sure back then that you were going to get fish. But now you're not so sure. It's not worth while going out and coming back in again empty, most of the time

Patrick
But that time the fish was the main food that we ate, that there wasn't much meat

Michael
Not a lot of meat

Patrick
And then in the winter you'd salt the fish like ourselves and you'd   have the supply for the winter

Michael
We used to salt the mackerel. And a glass of poteen before the dinner and you'd eat a good dinner then! Salty mackerel and ten or twelve good potatoes and a raw onion. And you wouldn't want anymore food for the day

Patrick
Healthy food Michael?

Michael
It was healthy and you would sleep

Patrick
Do you think the people were stronger then than now and there wouldn't be too many with flues or sickness

Michael
The people were stronger and no sickness

Patrick
Tell me how the people in the village got on, did they agree with each other

Michael
They did, agreed with each other very well

Patrick
Was there jealousy amongst them?

Michael
Oh no jealousy or I never saw any trouble or any fight. They were great neighbours altogether, all running to help each other.

Patrick
Do you think that this generation has changed a bit?

Michael
They haven't I don't think, they are alright yet, they are much the same way

Patrick
But there are lots of younger people now

Michael
They are growing up, finishing school and going away to Galway and all the cities and those that don't, work around. There aren't as many going to England now as there used to be. When I was young people were going to England and America and all the girls went and never came back, only for holidays

Patrick
It's different times now Michael. When you look back at them times and the fishing, were we better off then than we are now? Were we happier then than we are

Michael
I suppose we were younger then anyway and it's alright all the same

Patrick
There is no one starving here

Michael
Oh no, and if there is anyone, its their own fault

Patrick
The houses now have changed and everything. Bigger houses now

Michael
Visiting was a great crack in winter time - the 'rambling houses'. And you had the card playing in the houses, twenty five

Patrick
Would that be five nights a week?

Michael
It would be. Then Saturday night and Sunday night we would go to the pub and to the dances

Patrick
How many dances would you go to?

Michael
There used to be dances on Saturday nights and Sunday nights one time when the Palm Court opened up in the 1970's where the Web is now

Patrick
So there were more things happening in Erris at that time

Michael
I don't know because there seems to be good crack all the time around Belmullet. Of course we are twenty two miles out from Belmullet. And the drink driving is playing hell. The police have stopped the crack, everyone is afraid to have a drink

Patrick
But do you remember PJ Garvin's hall?

Michael
I do indeed, it used to be good

Patrick
Would there be one dance a week there?

Michael
No there might be two dances a month. All the big nights then around the Christmas time, St. Patrick's Day and Easter and all them

Patrick
And big crowds?

Michael
Yes and big bands, good bands, good ceilí bands

Patrick
Did he run pictures in it then as well?

Michael
He did in the winter time and the priest used to have socials there as well

Patrick

What do you remember about going to school Michael? Was it Porturlin school that you went to? Who was teaching at that time?

Michael

Yes Porturlin school. When I went to school first I think it was Peggy Doherty of Carrowteige. And then a Mrs. McGuire and Mrs Garner from Crossmolina. Ms. Gardiner then from Ballycastle way as well

Patrick

And were they qualified teachers?

Michael

They were supposed to be. The education back then was just to read and write

Patrick

But when you left school you were able to do that?

Michael

Well not great at it. The girls had a bit more heed on the education but the boys were fishing

Patrick

So when you left school, was there any of your class mates that couldn't read or write

Michael

I suppose that there would be a few

Patrick

But they didn't mind because they were fishermen

Michael

But they taught themselves again after that. The papers, the newspapers, the Western People was a great paper for learning how to read. If you kept reading it every week you would be learning new things every week. It was slow but sure! You would get some help with it

Patrick

But in them times there wouldn't be as much worry on people as   there is now though. There was less pressure then

Michael
Ah not as much worry and less pressure.

Patrick
The schooling is a big thing now in Ireland

Michael
It is, education is the main thing. If you don't have your education now you have nothing. Worse than an ass

Patrick
Remembering back to them days again, was there two shops in Porturlin?

Michael
There was

Patrick
So you could get everything that you wanted there?

Michael
Oh yes, everything was in them

Patrick
Do you remember dealing with the shop keeper at the start of the salmon season, and everything would be put in the book until the end of the season?

Michael
If you didn't have the money, they would give you what you wanted until the fishing season was over

Patrick
And everything was cleared up again?

Michael
Oh yes, the fishermen would clear the books then

Patrick
It was a way of life then that way?

Michael
It was, things were scarce back in the sixties. An awful lot of places had

to close up for the summer and go to England or Scotland picking potatoes to gather up a few pounds for the winter

Patrick
I'm sure you put in some bad nights at sea too?

Michael
There was some bad nights alright. And bad days. Rough seas

Patrick
Was there anytime that you thought that you wouldn't make it back into shore?

Michael
No there wasn't

Patrick
You always keep the faith?

Michael
I did and we were used to it. You would know when it would be too rough and you would haul up the gear and go home. It was better

Patrick
Do you think that Porturlin was lucky in the line of deaths at sea?

Michael
It was thank God, there was no drowning. I suppose they used to look for it because they took chances when it wouldn't be fit

Patrick
Would they have a drop of whiskey with them in the boats?

Michael
No, I never seen whiskey on the boats or anyone drunk going out either. They were careful like that now. And if they had a small drop in self they wouldn't abuse it

Patrick
So any other memory of Porturlin Michael?

Michael
No not really, just going to school and coming from school and that's all.

Going to school with a sod of turf under your arm for the open fire at school, for the teachers. That small school down in Porturlin I remember eighty two kids going to it, which was a lot for a small school and there was only the two villages really, Porturlin and Shrataggle

Patrick
That was a lot of kids

Michael
It was

Patrick
I remember walking in the feet in the summertime. Did you?

Michael
We would be in the feet in the summertime. They'd be no shoes

Patrick
But you would have the shoes if you wanted them

Michael
You would but once one person were in their feet everyone went in their feet in the summertime

Patrick
Then in the summer, when you would come home from school, there would be the saving of the turf

Michael
Yes everyone went to the bog that time and saved the hay. Everyone had their own supply. Everyone had their own potatoes, their own vegetables, their own fish, their own cowsand milk sure

Patrick
Every house in Porturlin?

Michael
Yes
Patrick
Do you remember them killing the sheep?

Michael
I do indeed

Patrick
You wouldn't be buying from butchers then?

Michael
No

Patrick
So with the fishing and the small bit of farming in Porturlin they were able to survive

Michael
They were, yes. They survived in the winter times. And according to what we are told not one died the time of the famine in Porturlin with hunger. The cause of the hunger was that no potato grew during the famine years and the same thing happened in Porturlin with the potatoes but the fishermen survived on the fish.

Patrick
Amazing. Would you say that you had a happy childhood?

Michael
It was. I would do it all over again!

Patrick
Do you mind me asking you how old you are?

Michael
I am fifty five

End of Interview

In 1970 the Porturlin school closed down. The Porturlin parents wanted to send their children to the Carrowteige school. But the teachers and the community in Carrowteige at the time objected. They gave the excuse that the Porturlin children did not know any Irish. Finally the Rossport school accepted the Porturlin children. And even in the Rossport school certain teachers used to make fun of the Porturlin children joking that they smelled of fish. When a Porturlin child had a problem with sums the teacher would say that if it was fish you'd be able to do it. The Porturlin children were abused by being not accepted in the Carrowteige school and they were verbally abused at Rossport by certain teachers. However they all ended up doing OK because their parents and the sea had educated them.

I left Killala on the 25th of April to go to Dublin with my friend Joey Greene and it was the fastest time ever that I was driven to Dublin. He's a car racer. It took us just over two hours to get to Naas. The reason for my visit to Nass is to see my daughter and she was entered into a beauty concert representing Naas at the Punchestown Festival. So we came to see Maria interviewed and the contest and she won it. I was so proud to be her father and to be there with her and my friend Joey Greene from Belfast. We had a good night. We stayed in the Naas Court.

I am just waiting for Maria to come down now to show me her prize. She's going to be taken around Naas and to the Racecourse for the whole week as the Queen of the Currach. So that was my journey to Dublin. Seeing Maria with the media around her, taking pictures of her, she will be on the papers. She is eighteen years old. A girl that knows what she wants from life. And she will achieve it. And my advice to her last night, when I hugged her for winning, was "Maria, you are going places and you will get places, but just keep your head cool". So it's a big celebration again today.

I'm just interviewing my daughter Maria about the night that she won the Ms. Punchestown Competition.

Patrick
Maria, how did you feel when you won?

Maria
At the beginning of the night I felt nervous but I had my family and friends there to support me. So when I went up there on the stage I was good and I just acted naturally. And I think that is how I won

Patrick
So what are you going to do for the rest of the week? You are going to be involved with the Festival for the whole week
Maria
I will. I will be in Naas to meet people and I will be introduced to Ms. Punchestown 2004.

Patrick
Ok and what was the pub you represented?

Maria
The Cavness Pub

Patrick
That's the pub that you work in part-time?

Maria
Yes, it is

Patrick
And can you tell me how you got the job in the Bank of Ireland?

Maria
I met Kieran Redmond, the Manager of the bank through the pub and I asked him would he be able to help out in getting a job in the Bank of Ireland. So he told me to send in my CV, and he would help me out and he did, I got the job that day

Patrick
And how long were you waiting?

Maria
Two hours

Patrick
Are you happy working in the bank?

Maria
I am delighted

Patrick
So you have the brains of your father!

Maria
I don't know!

Patrick
So what are you going doing today?

Maria
Today I'm going over to the boss to see what I have to do for the week

End of Interview

I'm landed in Knock and I have to get a way to Charlestown because I left my car there on my way up to Naas. I was looking around and I couldn't get any lift. I seen these two fellas in a small van and I went over and I asked them would they give me a lift. He said "Fucking walk it" and then he called me back and he said "You seem to be a character". He was very drunk but he was very funny. I got in the back of the van and he asked me what my name was. I said "Patrick" and he said "Mine is Padraig and who gives a fuck?" He saw the funny side of the story but the other fella was very weird. The fella that was drunk said to him "Come on, I have to get home to Achill" and he tried to start the van. But there was no keys in it! Then he started looking for his keys and that was another half an hour of a delay. He said "I should have left the keys where I left them before, on the seat". The other fella was coming out with funny stories about his drinking and he was after coming back from Germany. He told me that the other fella was very weird and he said "I think it's him that's drunk instead of me". So anyway we couldn't get the keys and the man didn't know what to do. The drunk fella said "I think I'll stretch my legs because it's pointless hiring a taxi like you" and he started laughing. He said "no fucking keys to drive it!" So he got out and he looked in the driver's seat and he said "sure the keys are stuck in the ignition, what in the fuck is wrong with you?" They were there all the time and the other man couldn't see them! But anyway I got to Charlestown to pick up my car.

MOUNTAIN OF MUD

Big clean-up as villagers survive horror avalanche

I ESCAPED MUD SLIDE TOMB

Paddy saves family after 4hr ordeal

Nobody mess with my kitchen!

With Martin McGuinnes and sons at Ceide Fields in 1995

My fishing boat beached in Belmullet in 1989.

I took Martin McGuinness to meet my mother at her home in Porturlin. August 2001.

Myracehorse, Nordic Oak, running in Naas in 2001.

Playing with the Molloy Brothers
at the
Flannery Village Annual Christmas Party 2001

Ready to go out dancing
at Palm Court 1974

Taken at Porturlin Pier
fishing for lobster, 1977.

A Pat Doherty, Vice-President, Sinn Fein, and M. P. for West Tyrone, cutting the tape to officially open Sinn Fein's new constituency office (Clarke, Duleman and Healy) at the SMA Arcade, King Street, Ballina, last week. Also included are from left: Searoid O Seuille, (Mayo Organiser, Sinn Fein); Cllr. Gerry Murray, Charlestown, (Mayo County Council); Mrs. Mary Doherty (nee Conroy, Belmullet); Vincent Woods, Mayo Sinn Fein candidate in forthcoming general election); Pat Flannery, P.R.O., North Western Delf. Fishermen's Association; and Bobby Cawley, Secretary, Gaughan/Stagg Cumann, Ballina. "Western People" pictures.

With grandson Nathan in August 2001
in my knitwear shop.

1997 when I brought Sinn Fein to Geesala

Chapter 6

<u>2003 Landslides & Support for Irish Republicans</u>

Wolfe Tones in Geesala / Sinn Fein
Tax Inspectors
Michael Gaughan's Anniversary / Sinn Fein / Republicism
Hatred for the English Government
Liam O'Donnell / Sickness / Money
Sunbathing in Rinroe / Beautiful Erris / Money
(Post) Landslide at Glengad

On the 19th August 2004 I had the Wolfe Tones in Geesala, which there was a good crowd at it. And we took in about €4,000 but the band was very expensive so we didn't make much profit on the night, myself and Paddy McGuire. There was a good crowd at it and people enjoyed it, the Wolfe Tones are a very, very good band. And on the night I had Michael Flannery my friend that looks after the horse that we call Flannery Knitwear 2 and his partner from Belfast and we had a few people there from the North and from all over and holiday makers and that and there was singing about Bobby Sands and the people that died for the freedom of this country today and people that I admired that gave their lives for our freedom and he mentioned my name and called me up to do a speech on the night, well I went up and I done a speech and I thanked them all for buying the tickets all the time that I had the Wolfe Tones and ran dances back in Geesala supporting fundraising like for the Columbian Three, for Sinn Féin the fundraising I done, myself and Paddy McGuire for Sinn Féin and the help I got from Teresa and many more people like them and the support we got and how I got Sinn Féin recognised in Erris in bringing Sinn Féin's whole party down to Geesala to the old hotel in '96 where Martin McGuinness, Gerry Adams, all the parties from Monaghan, from Dublin of Sinn Féin at the time, which we held in Geesala organised by myself and Eoghan who lives in Galway now, who was in prison for being involved in the IRA for fighting for the freedom of speech in this country and who done his time in jail with the hunger strikers at the time and that's when Sinn Féin took off. I became Chairman of Sinn Féin in Erris I think many years before that. and brought the word of Sinn Féin to Erris which there was only

Fianna Fáil and Fine Gael here and I'm proud of that and I talked a bit on that and thanked again the people and many people was from England here and people shouted up and I welcomed the people from England to Ireland to our country as we always did but I said I didn't welcome their government and I never will in Ireland and that I didn't want their government in this country and I spoke of the people of the hunger strikes and the people that gave their lives for this country and I did state wherever you go in the world be proud to be Irish because Irish is recognised all over the world today for their goodness, their kindness how they fought back and how they worked all over the world. We have a lot to be proud of being Irish we have a lot to be proud of, and as I said I couldn't say that about the English government. But after finishing the speech I came back down and the night went on and everyone enjoyed themselves and there was a big clap and a big support for my speech and then there was two English girls that are married to Irish fellows and they, after the dance, came up and they felt they were insulted that I didn't like the English and I explained that I have nothing against the ordinary English people but I have against their government to be in our country, to have invaded our country and I explained it to them and they agreed with me that the English shouldn't be in Ireland. And they were English people and they apologised to me for taking me up wrong and I thanked them for coming along and enjoying the night and then about a half an hour later there was an Irish fella came up and he went off the head that I insulted the English and that he worked in England and that he was proud to work in England and he just lost the cool and he said that the IRA would put a bullet in my head for what I said there about the English so anyway I told him to go away and I didn't want to explain to him. He got very, very cheeky, you know, and he said that he didn't give a fuck for me and my friend Michael Flannery jumped up and he wanted to fight him outside the door or anyone of his mates and then he got very, very, very scared then and I knew he was only a bollocks so I told him that as well and I said all he was, was a piece of shit anyway and I said it's Irish people like ye that sold out our country, that wouldn't stand up for what they believed in and their Irishness and he was put out.

And the night anyway finished up and it was very, very good and we had a good night away from that. I still stand for what I say for being Irish and I'll be always an Irish Republican, I would give my life for my country and always will and I don't like seeing it being sold out by the Irish people either, we have to stick up for that, always, and then on the next morning at half eight I was woke up by two men at the door – tax inspectors – at my door and they came in and they said that they were here to collect taxes that I don't know whether I owe them or not it's going away back three years of PRSI and stuff like that and all the hell I went through in the last five or six years trying to hold my place here, refused - well I would never draw Social Welfare – and all through my sickness I wouldn't even draw sick money – I would eat grass with the hens like I told them before I would go back on Social Welfare but just to think all the people that is drawing everything off the Government in this country and all around Erris – and all people that get Social Welfare and some sick money and me paying taxes and I don't mind paying my due and I told them that and so anyway. I owed them €6,000 and they would not leave till they got their €6,000 and lucky enough I got cheques borrowed from my partner to post date them and I'd honour them, the cheques, and I honoured 2,000 that morning on one cheque and they walked away and they thanked me and they were sorry for coming to my door but it makes me wonder "is our country sold out" when you have this thing coming to people's door and collecting taxes so I know that the taxes have to be paid but I think that it's very unfair the way the country is ran. You know, you have people drawing Social Welfare, some farmers, some fishermen, they're involved in anything going – they're impossible to live around because they think they are due everything that they can get and they never pay taxes. But today I have it done and it's a week down the road and I'm proud that I paid my dues. I paid the taxes and I'm paid up to date, just one's year's accounts to go in, I can keep my head high on that and I know I will come out trumps on that and I called the tax people yesterday and I told them that I don't know whether I owe them or not but ye have the cheques now and I'll honour the cheques.

So that's my story, you know, some days it's good, all me day is good except the only hour we get bad is sometimes when the tax man comes to my door but away from that it's good, it's nice to be able to hold my head in the air as well, no matter what.

On next Sunday coming up is Michael Gaughan's anniversary - on the death of Michael Gaughan and I intend to be there to honour Michael Gaughan that gave his life on hunger strike for the freedom of this country and the freedom of speech in Ireland and died to give freedom to millions of people in Ireland and I'll be there to honour him and a lot more – but there's an awful lot more that should be there that won't be there but my belief still today is United Ireland and the sad thing about it now is that I don't hear it mentioned as often as it used to be – I don't hear the words "United Ireland" coming out of a lot of Sinn Féin people who are now selected into Sinn Féin and elected as politicians. I hope that they are not just there because they are elected to Sinn Féin and everything is alright – the Agreement was signed up for a United Ireland and that's what I hope will come for the good of all people in the Island, Catholic and Protestants alike. It was never a war with Catholics and Protestants and I always said that – I never had anything against Protestants in this country – they have every right to live in this island the same as anyone – me or anybody else as Irish people -but I have learned so much of getting to know Protestants over the last few years that call themselves Irish – they never said they were "orange" "English" – they were Irish Protestants that lived on this island of Ireland and proud of it. I remember one person I met there lately – a whole family called Gardners – she's protestant, she lives in Dublin and she says to me one day, which I thought was nice, "I'm an Irish Republican, every bit as good as you Patrick", you know I thought that that was very good and nice because then I explained to her that all the times since, I was 19 years old, I was a strong Irish Republican for a United Ireland – I hated the English Government and what they done to this country and I told her that and I said that I always, never once, thought it was a Protestant and Catholic War – it wasn't. It was the English invading our country and the Irish had to fight back. We had fought the English, back to our history, 800 years and the last 30 something years in the 6 Counties and when I explained my belief – she respected me for that so did her father and mother and what I believe in Irishness and they are Irish too. Our country will be united as one island with Irish Catholics and Protestants alike but it suited the British to blackmail, to refuse any paper of truth to go out about Northern Ireland – they put out black mail and propaganda all over the world for twenty something, twenty five, thirty years of the War. About how bad the IRA was and it suited them to say it was a Religious War – it suited their propaganda all over the world which I knew and a lot more people than the Irish knew it wasn't a Catholic and a Protestant War – it was an Irish and the English invading Ireland and that's what the war was about. So I'm learning an awful lot about Church of Ireland Protestants living in this country and they say that they are Irish and proud of it the same as I am proud of being Irish – they never said they were English – they are proud of being Irish and I'll finish this story with or I'll continue this story with learning more about the Protestants in this country of Irish Protestants – the Wolfe Tones were freedom fighters that fought for the freedom of Ireland and they were Protestants and a lot more of them that fought and gave their lives for the freedom of this country and they were Protestants.

Today is the 29th August 2004 and about an hour ago a lady ran up to my Knitwear Factory and she was out of breath and she was trying to tell me to come quick – her partner had fell on the floor and she thinks he's dead, an English woman, and I ran down. His name was Liam O'Donnell, he originally came from this village, left here years ago and returned back and built himself a holiday home. So I ran down as quick as I could, jumped in the car and we got down, I jumped the gate and I got in there and he was fell over the radiator and there was some water coming from his mouth and there was no movement out of him so I acted fairly fast and all I could do was, I straightened him up and I told her to get me Lucozade because I remember him telling me that he had sugar diabetes and I kind of forced the Lucozade down on his neck and, after about a few minutes I told them just to keep his head up, not to let his head down and I dialled 999 and the Ambulance replied right away and the Ambulance from Belmullet was here in 15 minutes and the doctor was here in 20 minutes and it is about 8 miles from Flannery's Holiday Village to Belmullet and before the ambulance came out anyway I gave him some more Lucozade and I got him around a bit and I was able to, after 10 minutes, get him up on the bed and the Ambulance came and they took the blood pressure and everything and they rushed him away to the hospital and the doctor checked him before he left and he's gone to Castlebar and I just hope he'll be alright and I was glad to be there to do some help with Liam O'Donnell and his wife and to calm down his wife because she was panicking at what was happening to her partner – I just feel that I have done a good day's work today to help somebody and I know that he would do it for me too so I just hope to God and pray that he'll be ok and I'll be able to talk to him one of the days about this and God bless him.

It's only the other day that Liam O'Donnell was up here at me and talking about his life – he lived a very busy life – he worked hard and made a lot of money, made millions over his life time and was taken over by work too. His life was taken over by his businesses and everything and he never gave much time for himself – he has built a home here in Graughill that he could come home and spend time with himself and his partner and it's only the other day that we were talking about that – life is so short and he said the same to me, you know you can get carried away with your work and the power of money as well, you know the power of money is very, very strong and when you get in that fast lane, which Liam did, it's very hard to come off it you know, he's in there and the work is so demanding and he had a couple of hotels and a house out in Spain and you know it makes me wonder too, always life is worth living and we can live with a lot less and a lot more happiness. So I would rather to be a multi millionaire in happiness and less money and it doesn't take any awful lot of money to live a happy life, in fact I think it takes less money to have a happy life. I see people just making enough to do, getting by and they seem to be more happy than the ones that are making the millions. I've nothing against money, it's a good thing, but when it takes your life over and it leads you instead of you leading it and it's only now that that man could be relaxing, it's only now that he has realised that he's taking it easy, he told me that the other day, he told me he sold his hotel and his pubs in England and "I'm not going to kill myself anymore" he said. Sometimes it can be too late, we can push them few years with work and couldn't come off the fast lane and sometimes it could be too late. I hope it's not late for Liam, he's got a lot of living to do but when I seen him there today, I thought he wouldn't make it when I seen him the first day when I ran into the house I thought he was dead, he was in a bad shape, didn't seem to be breathing there for a while, I hope he'll make it because it's only now, he told me, he realises what life is all about and the nature, loves the nature, the sea, the birds, the freedom, the things that God has given us, each and every one of us, man, woman and child, free, is the most important thing in life, he gave us the freedom of life, the nice things we can enjoy, we cannot buy these things, you cannot buy happiness, a person was telling me once that after you have money you can buy anything, no you cannot, the simple things in life are the rich things in life, hopefully God will leave him around to enjoy the things that he realised that he missed out on.

Well it's been 3 weeks since that happened to Liam O'Donnell when I was involved to see if he was ok, that he's doing ok now and he just called me from England to thank me for saving his life that the Lucozade brought the sugar levels back up and he was in a coma before that and he send me a card – a thank you card with 50 Pounds Sterling to get myself a meal and to treat myself and I think that that's very nice, he recognised that and he is doing well since. Liam thanked me for saving his life, it was good that I was there when he needed me, it's important to be there for your friends when you're needed.

I'm sitting out here getting sunbathing on the 20th September 2004 in Rinroe and it's a beautiful day, Rinroe Beach in Erris and I'd say the heat is in the 80's and you're looking out here to the beautiful beaches that we have out in Belmullet area down Rinroe, Inver area. We have the finest beaches in the world and I'm just looking at a fella here out swimming on the 20th September and how the weather is such beautiful weather that we get here at this time of year, and to hear the sea blowing on in against the rocks, it's absolutely gorgeous, I see a family there having a picnic on the beach and you know often people talk about Florida and all this where they go where the sun is, we get the sun here in Erris in Ireland too, in Erris, especially in Erris out here, it's absolutely gorgeous, people ask me out here what's it like out here in the Winter, very mild, we don't get any bad Winter, and then I hear – it's only a couple of nights ago – where these hurricanes are coming in and homes are being lost and three and a half million people moved out of their homes for safety, every time it makes me realise how lucky I am to be out here, living out here, brought up out here, the beauty of nature, the freedom we have out here, it's absolutely gorgeous to think that I can be in my shorts getting sunbathing out here on a rock, looking out on Rinroe beautiful Beach and how peaceful, it's marvellous and you know it's like hidden away out here in a world of her own, like nobody knows only ourselves that are out here, and the few tourists that come out here think that it is absolutely gorgeous. To be living along the sea is a gift, close to the ocean, at the weekend I can go down to Porturlin and pick up some fresh fish for my dinner, from my brothers that are fishing. I'm lucky, very rich in that line, so today is a good day for me, you know with all the hell that I went through, and all the money that I have lost through courts and investments and stuff. I got a phone call today that I never thought I had and God works in funny ways and she says there's 10,000 waiting here for you, an investment I put away in 1999 that I didn't even know I had. That's good news for me today, I can pay a few bills with it, but I don't, money was never my mission in life, it always comes and goes, the health and the beauty to be able to go to the beach and switch off and realise what life is all about. I was talking to a friend of mine also today – they are very, very rich and how she feels left out because her partner is too busy with his life, he's worth a lot of millions and he has a lot of business, he has a lot of clients, he's seven days a week nearly at his business and I listened to her today how she feels left out and her kids and she talked to me and I gave her the best advice I can, you know he's in the fast lane that he couldn't see no way out, and that's a part of him, and when you get in that deep there's no back, his work and his businesses – he makes me wonder - he's worth millions that he could just stop and enjoy his millions with his kids and his partner but no that's not the way it works for some people – they can never see beyond that and that's sad – very sad, but today for me I'm worth millions in happiness and freedom and sitting out here on the beach – I'm not chasing that gold and I always get enough. I remember one time a man telling me that God always provides and gives you enough – and I believe that God was a worker too, but you can work for a living without leaving your family out, your kids out, like that woman talking today how she felt left out, she makes the dinner for him at seven o'clock in the evening and he doesn't come home until 10 or 11 o'clock and she told me that this has being going on for years now and it's sad for her. We were talking on history, how this Protestant lady that I'm talking about, we were on about history and how the Protestants were the first to fight for the freedom of this country and she didn't know that so that's why she called me and I'm still working on that part of my book but some day with the help of God that this book will be published. That Protestant lady and I turned out to be good friends. Someday the book will come out and people will read it and I hope that what I'm talking about will help people along the way. In my life I was always a giver, I always felt that I was more of a giver than a taker and when you are a giver sometimes you're soft hearted and you'll always get hurt along the way and life hardens you up to be able to cope with things that comes your path and it opens your eyes when you start looking for things and wanting things – that's not saying that you are going to get these things! But life today is always a challenge, I'm lucky to be able to come and enjoy the beauty of this beach here today on the 20th September and to see that the sun is beating down. I'm looking over at where the landslide was in Glengad and the sun beating down like nothing did ever happen. To me its sometimes it's like a nightmare, it now and again crosses my mind, how we were stuck in that landslide that night and to look today you wouldn't think that nothing ever happened. It's shortly coming up – the anniversary now – the anniversary of the landslide – it's almost a year and just to think back a year ago and how we were stuck out on that landslide from half nine at night until five o'clock in the morning, fighting for our lives, and how different it is now, a year later, so nature moves on and we have to move on with it and today I'm out sunbathing, a year later. So God is leaving me my life for another while, around, and Anthony, Siobhán and Teresa that was in the landslide and that I helped out that night as much as I could, and I was told I'm very cool and I'll always remember anyway that when excitement happens, or danger happens, I always get cool, I don't loose my head, I always think fast in the right things because when you are in a situation like we were in the landslide and you don't get chances to make up your mind, you do the right things with a cool head and you'll survive, you lose the head, you don't do the right things and you die. I learned that probably through my fishing at sea and things in life that you don't get a second chance, one little mistake and you're gone when you're in danger but hold the head, keep the cool, make the right decisions and you'll live.

Well it's the 20th September 2004 and it's a year later after the landslide and the work that has been carried out by the Mayo County Council and the budgets by the OPW and the great work that they have done on drainage, and open drains that were neglected over the 20-30 years, they have done a fantastic job, all the way from Barr na Trá right around Inver past Pullathomas, Glengad and all that area and the Mayo County Council has all new bridges put in to that area and they have all the roads tarred, by-roads tarred and I must say that they have fantastic work done after the landslide. The graveyard is all done up, a lot of the local people worked very hard in it, there was money put in by Eamon Ó Cuiv towards the doing up of the graveyard, there was also private money put in to do up the graveyard and the people, to see them there, months after the landslide, doing up the graveyard and it's a fantastic job. It's nature that has grown back on the landslide mountain where it was taken away and to look at it now it looks like nothing ever happened to it, so the change is amazing, the change that has taken place and the work that has taken place and the spirit of the Mayo County Council and the OPW, the work that they have done – it's fantastic, it's a year later and to look at it today, it's just that you would never think that that landslide came there, you could see the tracks on the hills alright, along the hills, where it is still there – plain to be seen – and now they are doing a structure – a fencing structure – to stop any other landslide from taking place because I believe, in my opinion, that that landslide will happen again but the only thing – the difference with it if it does happen again that there is better drainage done now, they have better bridges put in – that would make a big difference to the landslide and to where we were caught out on that night because it will take most of the water away from the roads. On that night the bridges they had in and the pipes that were in weren't good enough to take away that impact of water coming down and stone and rock and everything like that so there is a change and I have got an invitation from the local people, the local committee, to attend the anniversary and recognise the work and the help I gave the people in the area and the same letter is going out to Eamon Ó Cuiv and the politicians so it will be an honour for me to be there, myself & Teresa, on the anniversary of the landslide, a year later. Also, the farmers whose land was damaged on, and that's including the land that I have in Glengad as well, it's all put back again and it's all producing grass again and it's growing and the OPW went in there as well and they drained up most of the lands, the drainage in all the lands that were damaged and I had a machine in there for about a week, just cleaning the middle of the land and it's all fenced back again. I put, on my land, all the fencing and the wiring again and also the neighbours at that area too, the same thing has taken place, that it's all fenced and wired and a lot of the farmers appreciated it and then there's some more of the farmers there that were shouting about how their land was damaged and that they got no money for it and they'd be talking about 4 or 5 acres

Interview 3
Marian Finucane's Radio Show

Marian
We are now going to Pullathomas - a beautiful, beautiful part of North Mayo but it wasn't the scenery that brought us. I know that you would have heard other people talking this morning about what happened and the devastation that happened there as the awful landslide frightened the living daylights out of the people, or nightlights as it was, in truth. In our Castlebar studio this morning I am joined by Patrick Flannery from the area who was on our programme that day, at the outside broadcast from Pullathomas. He told a story that truly had me and an awful lot of other people in the country riveted, and given the news this morning, particularly this morning, coming from Cork, has a sad poignancy.

Patrick
We left the house that night, about for about two hours and I did think that we wouldn't make it but I didn't say so at the time. Teresa and the daughter were hanging on, her daughter was very bad at that stage and we were hanging on to each other. I told them to keep their legs moving to get the blood going and not to panic and that we were going to make it. But at the back of my mind was that we weren't going to make it.

Marian
Did you think that you weren't going to make it?

Patrick
But lucky enough Teresa took a lamp somewhere out of the car when I was gone, a small little lamp, and she said that she had a lamp and the prayers were said. I said that I would look around to see if there was any way out and Teresa was afraid of me going. I told them to stay there until I would come back and I went up the hill. Each side of me was gone at this stage, we hadn't much movement, trapped, the cliffs were gone each side of me and the water was coming down and I looked up and I said to them before I left "The moon is coming up" because I seen over the hill, like a light flashed, but then it went dark. So I went up anyway as far as I could and I watched the nearest cut on the mountain and the narrowest was about five foot and I jumped that and jumped it back, even if you fell, you were going down fifteen foot and I knew that the only hope I had was to try to get them back out

there. So I brought them up to that and I told them that I would jump across and I would reach out and they could reach for my hand and I would pull them across and that's what we did. When we got over there then, I said that we would hold hands and we were going through the muck and the slubber and trees, it was awful. We went through that right up to Paddy McGrath's pub and when we got to the pub the people that were in the car that I had told to follow me were still there, there were five of them and they were very frightened. If they had followed me they were gone, definitely gone. And I told them that I was going onto the next house, to Tony Mc Grath's, to see how things were there. At that stage we got to Tony's and we sent for the other five to come over. I must thank Breda McGrath, she was there with two young kids, her husband couldn't come in because at this stage all the bridges were gone, and nobody could get in and then the Fire Brigade came, and Breda took down all the clothes from her wardrobes, gave us dry towels, gave us cups of tea.

Marian
That's what neighbours are all about.

Patrick
I have to thank her for all the hard work that she done for us. At five o clock the fire brigade and the rescue services took us across to safety.

Marian
What a night, you will never forget it.

Patrick
I will never forget it Marian and I am not easily frightened. I was a fisherman all my life, I was in tight corners but I found my way out, but I was frightened for the three people that were with me. That night when we got to Mc Grath's that we were safe then, that we were on dry footing or at least half dry footing. I thought that there would be lots of lives lost that night. The four neighbours that were in their houses and were flooded and the walls cracked in them, my heart goes out to them but we all have to thank God that there was no life taken.

Marian
Absolutely and indeed somebody said the word miraculous I think yesterday. Listen thank you for that. Just to give our listeners an idea of the rain and of what happened, when we came down yesterday, Peter Hynes of Mayo County Council took me around to show me the various areas of the devastation.

Peter Hynes
It just stopped here short of the traffic control point, if you look up to the left between the two peaks on top of the hill, you can see a major depression onto the right of that, two smaller depressions which are actually the origins of the slide, which ended up in the graveyard lower down.

Marian
Right, so you can't really see that from down below, so it kind of came down at an angle really?

Peter
The land failed or the peat failed further up and it was intercepted by a ditch which you can't actually see very clearly from here at the moment, but a lot of the material ended up in that ditch and then the water flowed over the ditch and came down the hill, picked up trees and shrubs as it accelerated down the hill and deposited those in the graveyard.

Marian
But only one was really affected, isn't that right?

Peter
There was the older graveyard which escaped by and large, it was affected by the river which you can see just a little further down, and then there's the newer graveyard which had two cut threw it, ten maybe twenty metres in spots wide.
Marian
Just to describe it for people, it's on the side of the hill.

Peter
Yes and quite a slope.

Marian
Quite a slope. Just over the road, above the road and then immediately below the road is the sea.

Peter
Yes quite a steep drop into the sea at that point as well. As we move down the hill, we can see the river which actually catches all the water from the back of the hill, and follows it in almost a palm shape and it all comes down to this point and it did an enormous amount of damage to the bridge. It actually two channels both sides of the bridge, cracked the actual bridge structure, and it is an area along the graveyard, which

it picked up the retaining wall, basically broke it into pieces and away some of the graveyard itself, you can see that just along here.

Marian
Right, and there's a sign there 'Danger, threat of landslides in this area'. Presumably that's in people's consciousness at the moment. Now you can see here on the right hand side, just on the sea side, where the rubble came down, or the muck, I suppose.

Peter
This is debris that was deposited by the water as it swept around the corner. You can see the damage that it had done to the graves and the graveyard over here on our left. Then it flowed, both sides of the bridge, the channel both sides of the bridge and flowed out to sea and left all of this memento behind it.

Marian
Were there coffins swept out to sea?

Peter
We understand that a number of graves were disturbed, yes.

Marian
That's very upsetting for people.

Peter
Yes, very.

Marian
This hill has a lot of scrub and bushes and shrubbery on it.

Peter
Looking up here what you see as the crest of the hill isn't actually the top, it's just a change in the slope and there's a lot of hill behind the line that you see as being the crest. You can see the two channels that were out, the local community have done enormous work here in the couple of days that they have worked cleaning up and clearing up and restoring order. This was a complete mess on the Saturday morning and all of this road along here was probably two to three feet deep in muck and completely impassable.

Marian
That was Peter Hynes bringing me around yesterday afternoon.

Now Michael Carolan said that when he and his daughter heard and clicked what was happening that they rang the services, for want of a better word. Ian McNulty, you arrived at the scene at what point? Where did you get the call and what did you see?

Ian
We received the call just shortly after ten o clock saying that there was a landslide down in Pullathomas.

Marian
Were you surprised? I mean landslides? And places, I don't think of North Mayo?

Ian
Here, there has been a number down through the years but on that particular night, I was very surprised because it was dry in Belmullet. There was no rain at all. So like to hear that the land was being washed away down in Pullathomas was quite a big surprise.

Marian
Because the distance isn't that great?

Ian
Well you are talking about twelve miles. When we received the call, we responded, and headed down to Pullathomas. We were coming in at Knocknalower, up until that point it was all dry, that's where the rain started. It was ferocious, torrential, it was that bad that when we actually went in there that we had switch off our warning beacons.

Marian
Why?

Ian
Because the blue lights were reflecting back and blinding the driver.

Marian
Good lord, from the water?

Ian
From the rain, yes. So we continued on down to Pullathomas, down past the post office and we met a car that was there, stopped on the road. So basically he told us that there was no way that we would pass down. So seen as thought we had to go to Barrnacellew - where we

received our initial call from - we headed on down towards the bridge and then we seen parts of the bridge in the middle of the road. At this point, the actual road looked more like a river than it did a road, there was three to four inches of water actually flowing down along the road. We continued on in and we got as far as that and we couldn't go any further. So the crew got out and we went down to investigate what was happening down at the bridge. By then the water was just flowing over it. Some of the crew went back up to the appliance, put cones across the road to stop it. So we headed on down and we made our way across the bridge and just as we crossed the bridge, we received communications from our own appliance that the ESB lines were down. On route we had called the other members of the council services like the road section because we had been warned that the bridge was blocked. So they arrived as well on the scene.

Marian
Were the lines actually physically down?

Ian
Yes they were.

Marian
Which is a very dangerous situation.

Ian
Yes it is, that's what I was just going to say to you. At that point the ESB advised us not to go up the hill until they got the power switched off. We could see lights on the hill and we were discussing whether it was actually power lines or torches, I think that's what Patrick was talking about earlier, it was actually power lines.

Marian
This is where you thought you saw the moon Patrick?

Patrick
Well I thought that the whole top of the hill lit up, it was like the moon, right across the hill.

Marian
Was there lightning?

Patrick
We were told since that there was lightning earlier on, that there were

lights seen and that there was a ball of light on top of the hill going towards the radar tower. It could have been the power lines lighting up but it lit the whole sky up because I told Teresa, my partner, that the moon was coming up, that there was a bit of light but we only saw the light for about five minutes maybe.

Marian
So Ian, what would your purpose be? To get to people's houses to see that they were ok?

Ian
Our mission was to go up to Barrnacellew. Because we had received the call from there that there was a woman who was to go into hospital. We were going up there to see what the story was up there.

Marian
And did you get up there?

Ian
We did, yeah, but what happened was when we crossed the thing??? And the ESB advised us, we decided that we would make our way across to the nearest house that we knew was Tony Mc Grath's. That took quite a while to make a path through there because the road was actually impassable. We had to use chimney rods which are a metre long, and join them together to prod along to make sure that we didn't cross any holes that we couldn't see. We couldn't get by on the road at all - there was about four or five foot of stuff in it - we couldn't actually walk through it, physically, so we decided that we would find another route up through the cemetery. That's the way we eventually found a route there, a fairly straight route to pass in and out of.

Marian
This is the cemetery that was, well one part of the cemetery looks as if it wasn't damaged and then the other side looks very badly damaged.

Ian
Yes but as you go from the bridge over towards Pullathomas, we'll say Mc Grath's pub, the near side of the cemetery which would be the first bit that you would meet, was the worst of it, towards the middle of the cemetery. We plodded along over there and we made ourselves a path over and when we got to the other side of the cemetery by the Barrett's house, we met Patrick Flannery and Anthony McGuire.

Marian

What a night, I don't suppose that any of you will ever forget about it. I should tell the listeners again that we are in Pullathomas and Glengad was very badly affected too, where the landslides occurred last Friday week, and people are still recovering and figuring the cost and indeed a lot of people are out of their own homes. I am now joined by Superintendent Tony McNamara. You were at a wedding on the night I gather.

Tony

I was indeed Marian, I was in Athlone at a wedding and shortly after ten o clock I got a number of telephone calls from the Gardaí on the ground and I soon decided that the situation here was developing fast and decided there and then to call the major emergency plan. I left the wedding and travelled down immediately and got here about three o clock in the morning. The scene, Marian, was one of utter devastation. As you said yourself, this is a beautiful area, and these are beautiful villages but the scene that I met that morning was unbelievable, unreal.

Marian

Well presumably it was pitch black?

Tony

It was quite dark and the enormity of the situation really didn't reveal itself until the following morning, as day broke at about eight o clock. Then we saw the through extent of it. But at that time of the night, all the services were at hand, they were doing an excellent job as part of the major emergency plan that we called out, we called out the services of the Irish Coastguard from Ballyglass and they did great work. As you can appreciate, it's a very big area.

Marian

And what did they do?

Tony

They assisted the Gardaí the Fire Brigade and the Ambulance services.

Marian

What, to get from house to house?

Tony

Yes, because that was our main concern, to be sure that nobody was hurt, nobody was injured, that nobody was trapped in their houses and as it is being described to you here this morning, it's a huge area, and really in the darkness of the night, it was very difficult to get about. The power lines were down, landslides in several areas, rivers bursting their banks, bridges taken away so our immediate concern was the safety of the people.

Marian
Right, and then it is extraordinary that nobody was last?

Tony
It is miraculous, there is no question about it, to see in the cold light of day, as I was saying, as dawn broke, to look from the top of the mountains as we drove up to the radar station, and to look down and see the extent of the landslides and see how closely it missed some of the houses, it was miraculous, there is no question about it.

Marian
Were you not nervous travelling up there?

Tony
Well at times like that, people never think of their own safety and you are just concerned about the well being of the people.

Marian
Because going up there yesterday, I was kind of looking at it, and saying 'stay grand and quiet there now until we're down again!'

Tony
On reflection now when you drive around and see the damage that the water done and the landslides done that night to the area and to see the caverns that have been cut, you realise that it was an extremely dangerous situation and the rescue services did tremendous work that night.

Marian
When you say the rescue services, who are we talking about?

Tony
We have the Fire Brigade, the Gardaí the Ambulance Service and the Ballyglass Coastguard Unit. They did tremendous work, they have a number of personnel who come out and help out on various events and they did great work that night. They helped to carry the elderly to safety.

There was quite an amount of water in the water course and you could see that something terrible had happened.

Marian
I presume that people are nervous in case something terrible is going to happen again.

Tony
Of course they are.

Marian
Bridget, you are out of your own home. Tell me now what happened in your place, everybody is mentioning McGrath's pub. You are the proud person of McGrath's pub! Where are you now and where are you staying?

Bridget
We stayed with a friend. We were on our way home and we had to reverse all the way up to the friends house so we met our son-in-law coming down to my daughter-in-laws house where she was at home with three kids and he got stuck in the water. So he tried to walk but the graveyard came out in front of him, so he ran home and he phoned the Gardaí

Marian
What are the conditions like? Why are you not in your own home?

Bridget
Because it's a pub, it's closed. We were told by the Gardaí to close and for everybody to leave their homes.

Marian
And was there any damage done to it?

Bridget
It was all flooded, there was about four to six inches of water in the house / in the pub. In the kitchen and the whole lot was flooded.

Marian
Have you been back in it?

Bridget
We got it cleaned out. All the neighbours came and cleaned it out with us.

Marian
And there was one house that I saw where the gable end was into the mountain and that was knocked down, but other than that there were no houses actually, to the naked eye anyway, badly damaged.

Bridget
Not really I believe but I don't know.

Patrick
Yeah, there is yeah, one house there in Glengad was taken completely away, half of the house, down under where the tower is, when you look down there.

Marian
Explain to people about the tower. What is the tower?

Patrick
The tower is, well what we are told, we're not too sure!

Marian
Maybe it's better to talk to Michael Carolan about that, I don't know if he is still here.

Michael
It's the radar tower for the planes flying out.

Marian
Yeah, Michael is here actually. Will you explain about the tower? Aren't you involved with the tower?

Michael
It's the property of the Irish Aviation Authority, it's a radar tower, it monitors the transatlantic flights.

Marian
Oh right. And it's quite substantial and it's actually quite a nice building.

Patrick
Well it's an eye soar Marian, because most of the people, about 95% of the people that I have been talking to all along Glengad there are looking up at this and asking questions. I asked a question at a meeting about how much drilling they do? How much blasting they do when they were putting that up on top of the mountain? That mountain in Glengad goes on into Graughill and it goes onto Pullathomas, so all them mountains are connected up and all the landslides are adding up towards that tower. I'm told that there's a storey and a half that they drilled down through the ground to put down a foundation and I did ask that question about how much drilling that they did. But nobody seems to be answering that and the people that are out of their homes all along there, for five miles, are scared of that tower and I would like somebody to answer this question - did lightning hit that tower that night? Because they put earths away from the tower, if the lightning came that it wouldn't hit the tower but it would hit these earths on the hill and that would cause a split in the hill. So there are a lot of questions that have to be answered on that tower as well, for the people. The people asked me to speak for them this morning. They are staying in my holiday homes, Marian, there are four, I've almost five families staying in Flannery Holiday Homes in the village. That's the question that they keep coming up with and somebody will have to answer it to them.

Marian
Can I just come back to you Bridget, because you are one of the people that is out of your own homes, I mean can you go back and forwards and get clothes and all that kind of thing?

Bridget
Well the pub has been closed ever since.

Marian
And the house is attached to the pub?

Bridget
Yes it is, it's a family run pub.

Marian
So when are you going to go back to your own home?

Bridget
Whenever we get permission after this Friday.

Marian
Will you be nervous?

Bridget
Not really, no because it's our home and you are never nervous going back into your own home.

Marian
But you wouldn't be afraid that the mountain would slip again?

Bridget
No I wouldn't!

Marian
You wouldn't! Well fair play to you, that you are happy enough about that. Now Father Declan Mac an Comhghaile, were you here on the night?

Father Declan
Not on Friday night, I picked up the story on Saturday morning and it just fits in with all that has been said before. The first news of seeing a countryside devastated, or getting one view coming westwards from my own house, I am two miles away, and at the time that all the trouble started from nine o clock on Friday night, I was putting stuff into my van at the back of my house, walking in and out in my short sleeves because it was bone dry, while this torrential rain was falling just back the road from us. Anyway Saturday morning the countryside seemed like it was wiped out, it would remind me of the pictures that I seen Hiroshima on the morning after the bomb, it just seemed devastated. And of course there is a parallel there because there was so much energy released here within this concentrated area. As the first news was that the graveyard was totally awash with muck and dirt and the road blocked and the bridge being repaired. All the services and the voluntary people were there doing an excellent job.

Marian
Can I just ask you about the graveyard? Was there any attempt to recover bodies or coffins or that kind of thing or was that relevant?

Father Declan
At the first light that morning it wasn't relevant, it took time to recognise what had happened, that in the modern graveyard that it was very much covered with a lot of debris, stuff have come down the mountain and

gravestones could be seen broken and upended all over the place. But in the old graveyard it took a while before people realised that one little corner had been taken away and five graves were actually swept out to see but there was nothing that could be done about that, at that given time. Then I went around the hill on the far side and this brought home the extent of the devastation that was caused here because it wasn't a landslide as you rightly recognised earlier on - there were twenty landslides in the area - each one would have been an eye opening wonder of it's own right, but there were twenty in an area six miles long and three miles wide. The first impact was the visual of all the material that had been moved and then the second was to recognise the human impact of people just shell shocked just looking at their homes and wondering about in shock, the third thing then was the great army that was in action already, right on Saturday morning, the voluntary workers that were in there, around every house, trying to pick up bits and pieces, trying to shovel away muck and dirt. The services deserve great praise but also the voluntary people deserve fantastic praise for the way they just go in and got on with a job. That followed on for the next few days until Wednesday, especially the work on the graveyard. The meitheal that was down there would just open your eyes and in spite of the tragedy and the damage that is done, it is so heartening to see the spirit of people and react. The work that was done on the graveyard up until the evacuation order on Wednesday morning - the amount that was done was just unbelievable. Then when people were asked to leave, they walked out in an orderly fashion and I think that there was a change of mood on Friday when the council had their next meeting with us in the local chapel - that was the only place that we had left to meet. No fault of theirs but they weren't able to give a definite forward plan as to what was going to happen next and I think that a weariness descended on people - I could feel that at the weekend. At the weekend mass there was a kind of a weariness as to what was happening next. Like they were away from home and were wondering when they would get the word for them to go back into their homes and start living our lives again. All we can do is live and hope that that day isn't too far away. I would just like to say, I am a person outside the evacuation area, and I cannot talk for the trauma and the fears and the upset that all these people have experienced and went through on that Friday night.

Marian
I presume there was a special atmosphere at mass on Sunday, was there?

Father Declan

Yes, there was, extraordinary. Just one tiny little example of it, when we say the prayers of the faithful, we say Lord hear us and the response being Lord graciously hear us, and when I came to pray for the people who are out of their homes and for a quick return to normality, the response went up by about twenty decibels.

Marian

Their commitment to prayer had been obvious

Father Declan

That's true.

Marian

And I believe Patrick that you were praying as well.

Patrick

Oh God, we prayed hard.

Marian

I am going to have to take another break now. I'm in Pullathomas in North Mayo talking to people about their experiences last week.

Patrick

Every morning I look out my window I am looking up at it and it has been there for hundreds of years and the old people say that there was never a landslide like that because this is a massive national disaster of an area, for about six miles.

Marian

But it had been very dry

Patrick

People's houses have been cracked, I have them in my own house, one night I hardly had a bed for ourselves and I'm talking to these people every night and the fear they have. They want answers - did the lightning hit that tower that night? Did it scatter the mountain?

Marian

One of the other things that is being said is that it was an extraordinary dry summer and that then there was this downpour.

Gerry

Just to put this into context and I know that a lot of people are very concerned and traumatised and you can feel it here today and we have been feeling it for the last week and indeed some of our own people are quite traumatised by what they went through as well and what they have being working at over the past week but to put it into context, we have one of the largest landslides that we know of in the country - perhaps even internationally. It's a total of twenty individual landslides - perhaps more if you were careful counting them.

Interview by Marian with other residents shortly after the landsides

Marian
We are coming to you from one of the most beautiful areas, sitting in a kitchen, the kitchen of the McGuire household which looks out across at two graveyards, which sadly, are perhaps the most famous graveyards in Ireland now. We are in Pullathomas and Glengad in North Mayo where twenty landslides occurred on the 19th September. John Joe [Barrett] where were you on the night?

John Joe
Good morning Marian. I was having dinner with my family in Belmullet town. We left the house at quarter past eight that evening and after dinner we left Belmullet at twenty to ten. When we left home, the lights were on and the fire was on and everything was rosy and we said that we'd only be an hour and on the way, about a mile and a half from home, it had been sort of misty rain till we got to a mile and a half to Michael Carolan's house here was the first instance that we seen where we thought that the tide had come up over the road that we were driving along coming towards us about thirty feet high, it was like the tide.

Marian
Like a wave coming over the road?

John Joe
Like a wave coming across the road, it was so frightening. We're still shaken and frightened after it. The car spun around and we took off and as I said I thought the tide was over. So we came back and down here by Paddy McGuire's pub, down to the graveyard. At the graveyard we met the same thing coming up on this side of the village.

Marian
Another wave?

John Joe
Another wave, a huge wave, probably thirty feet high of water coming. We reversed up to the top of the road and from there we could see the house light up but we couldn't get anywhere near it. It was so frightening. Prior to that, a mile or two miles down the road it had been dry, the wipers were just coming on now and again until we got to these two exact spots.

Marian
Right. And what was the rain like at that point?

John Joe
It was more than heavy, every drop was like a forty gallon barrel of water, it was unreal.

Marian
And how did you get out of there?

John Joe
When we got to the top we couldn't get back until six o clock the following morning, in the daylight, when we seen our homes and the villages surrounding us. Looking back the road that particular morning it was like the place had been bombed.

Marian
How did it happen as it were in your life Michael?

Michael
The first thing that I noticed was at about five to ten and the commercials had come on from the Late Late Show, our electricity went. It was at that point that my daughter who was with me at the time in my own household set about getting candles and when she had done that she had said to me that there was a strange noise outside and wondered where it was raining from. I told her that it was from the North East and she said that she had never heard that noise before when it had been raining. At that point both of us went to the front door of the house and what we encountered there was that my daughter got a hold of me and said that the sea had come to the road.

Marian
Mary, you thought, rather than the mountain coming down on top of you that the sea was coming up at you?

Mary
Yes, it was just the sound of the water. It was unbelievable, we thought that the whole world was going to end at that very moment. With the sound of the water and you couldn't see anything. It was just listening to all the water going over the bridge, I actually thought now that the water was actually up to our house, because you just couldn't see anything - that was the worst thing about it.

Marian
Because of no electricity?

Mary
Yeah, you couldn't see a thing. If there was light or some sort of way of seeing over there, you would be able to see that the bridge was gone but you couldn't see anything.

Marian
And was that what you had heard, the bridge been swept away?

Mary
All I heard was the mud and the water coming down from the mountain and the ferocity maybe of the waters going through.

Marian
What did you do then Michael?

Michael
My first reaction was, as I turned to my daughter was, that it was the river and I knew then what had happened and I knew that no traffic would be in a position to travel through it. It was at that point that I saw a car coming from the Inver/Barnatra direction and I ran with the hand light to stop them from going by but they just stopped a number of feet before going near where the water was, and at that point I went to see where the water was and it was a wall of water travelling at twenty feet high, as the eye of the bridge had got blocked and the whole lot was just caving over the ???. I took the two girls up to the house and following that I left the hand light with my daughter to watch the road. I called up the services and I must pay tribute to the services that night.

Marian
They were on the spot, they were brilliant

Micheal
They were on the spot

Marian
Patrick, where were you?

Patrick
Marian, first just to welcome you to Pullathomas.

Marian

Thank you very much indeed. It is very beautiful, I know it's not for the reasons of the beauty this morning but anyway.

Patrick

We left the house that night at about ten past nine to come over to Paddy McGuire's to a fundraising quiz. When we left the house, myself and my partner Teresa, her daughter Siobhan and Anthony McGuire, her boyfriend, it was starting to rain that time but it was nothing unusual. We are only about five or six miles from where we were going anyway. So when we got over a couple of miles over the road, the rain was starting to get heavy, very heavy and we came down as far as the graveyard here in Pullathomas. Anthony's car was just ahead of me and the next thing that I seen was the wall was collapsed from the graveyard right across the road and into the sea. The sad thing was that there were wreaths floating all over the place at that stage in the morning.

Marian

From the graves?

Patrick

From the graves, yeah. I knew there was something wrong so I flashed at Anthony, even the water that time would be two or three foot high. I reversed back and I flashed at Anthony again and I let down the window and I shouted at him to get up over the hill to get home. Now this hill would be about a mile and a half maybe two miles to get up, it is a very steep hill. We got up but there was a car at the pub that time, at McGrath's, and I let down the window and I shouted at them to follow us because the mountain was coming down.

Marian

You knew the mountain

Patrick

Oh yeah, but I didn't say it to the ones in the car. I had more fear for their lives, their three lives than for my own life. We got up to the top of the hill. The next thing I saw was Anthony's car, at this stage my car was stalling because the water was too strong and there was dead sheep coming across the road. It was like the mountain exploded and it was like as Michael described it, it was like the ocean. I never seen the likes of it and I have been in many a tight corner, but I never seen anything like this. I saw Siobhan and Anthony's car and it was like a cork, it was just floating. It was floating over the cliff, we are very close to the sea there. At this stage, Teresa was fearful for her daughter and she was roaring and I was trying to calm her and I told her that I was reversing down the hill, but I wasn't, I was being taken away, it was like the ocean. We were taken down to the bottom of the hill and Teresa said that we would take off. I told her to put on her seat belt and then we decided that we would take them off because..

Marian
You thought that you were going into the sea?

Patrick
That's it and we let down the window, at least we would be found somewhere. My car then came to a stop and the water was flooding down and it was difficult to see anything. I could see Anthony's lights dimming, dying away with the water and his car hanging over the cliff. I turned to Teresa and told her that we would be sound where we were and not to panic and I forced the door open in my car. I had to go over to Anthony's car and take them out of the car because I knew the next thing that would happen was that another part of the mountain or trees would come down and take them over the cliffs. I went up against the heavy water and at that stage I knew if I fell that I was gone. I had the fear of Teresa in the car as well.

Marian
How high up on you was the water?

Patrick
It would be up to waist, three foot or three and a half foot.

Marian
So you got out of the car and she was still in the car?

Patrick
Yeah, so I got back up to where Anthony and Siobhan were and I forced the door open and I told them not to panic. The water was in their car at that time and they were holding on to each other. They had said goodbye to each other, they told me after that. I shouted at them to try to control them and I did a bit of f-ing to control them and I told them to hold on to each other's hands and I was taking their hand. I told them not to look up because the water was coming down and that we would go with the flood and to follow me. So we went with the flood to my car and at that stage, Teresa came out and I told her to hold our hands and

we went in a line down three yards. At this stage we didn't know that only three yards from my car there was a twenty five foot drop into the sea and that it had cut the road right up to the top of the hill, fifteen to twenty foot. You could hear the water roaring as the young lady said there and it was frightened to hear the water and the trees. So we pulled into a side, just the width of ourselves on a little height, hanging onto a little gate, for about two hours and I did think that we wouldn't make it, but I didn't say that at the time. Teresa and her daughter were hanging on - her daughter was very bad at that stage - we were hanging on to each other. I told them to keep their legs moving, to keep the blood going and not to panic and that we would make it but at the back of my mind was that we weren't going to make it.

Marian
You did think that you weren't going to make it?

Interview with Marian one year after the landslides in September 2004

Marian
Patrick Flannery, good morning to you.

Patrick
Good morning Marian.

Marian
I'd say it brings it all back to you, does it?

Patrick
God, it does. By listening to it there now, it does bring it all back to me.

Marian
It was a very, very frightening night for you all

Patrick
Well it was terrible Marian and thanks for asking me to come on the show.

Marian
Oh a pleasure and I mean just thinking of what happened to that poor woman in Cork yesterday and how you thought that your number was up this time last year.

Patrick
Well it's funny Marian. I watched that on television last night and I prayed for that woman, God love her, and her kid, and to see what happened to her, it made me lucky and the people all around the area, how lucky we were to have survived that landslide

Marian
Yes, that's right. Have you put it behind you or is it something that dogs the back of your mind?

Patrick
Sometimes it does, but you kind of move on. The other people I got involved in the area that time and listening to other people and of course when you see something on the television like that poor lady and her kid, it does remind you, and to see out abroad, hurricanes, it's only

the other day that I was saying how terrible it is out there to a neighbour, the hurricanes and all that. And he said to me, that it wasn't that long that yourself was in that, and so was I.

Marian
Yes, indeed. When we were down there a lot of people had moved out of their homes and were living outside of the area. Is everybody back in now?

Patrick
Marian, the most of them are back in now. I think that Tom Sheeran and Peggy are going back in on Sunday and then Anne Taylor hasn't gone back into her house but all the other people are back in their houses again now. The ones that cannot go back are being re-housed, I know there are one or two that the Council have helped to re-house.

Marian
There was all sorts of speculation and figuring out why it had happened and eventually the report said "very heavy rain after a very dry summer"

Patrick
Well that's right but sometimes people have their own opinion on it. They are putting up barriers now, I think that there is over a million granted for barriers to go up now. That was a dry summer

Marian
It was a very, very, very dry summer

Patrick
I would agree with that Marian, but there are a lot of tall hills around the neighbouring villages but it didn't happen. My own opinion on it is..

Marian
Is this the Radar Station?

Patrick
Well I remember being on your show, Marian and thanks to you that done it in Paddy McGuire's pub in Pullathomas at the time and it highlighted the whole thing and I did say that time, that my own opinion on it was the station and I still have this opinion. That's what they say but why are they to put barriers up now? Are they frightened that the hill is still not safe? Why don't they tell the people - they are telling them that it is safe. But my opinion is why do they have to put barriers up? If

it was the dry summer and the landslide did happen as a result of this, why are they putting up barriers then?

Marian
To ensure, I presume that it wouldn't happen again.

Patrick
That's true, it's true. But the hill on the top is still opened, parts of it. To me, I feel, I asked the question that time and it was never answered and I did say and I have to give credit where it is due now, I did say that the drainage that time and the bridges that was along that road were neglected for thirty years, but Marian, I cannot say that now because the OPW made a fantastic job after that, in drainage for ten or maybe fifteen miles, all around the whole area and the Mayo County Council put all new bridges in, in every area.

Marian
Well that's fantastic

Patrick
They also made a fantastic job of the roads that we hadn't before that so I have to give them credit for that

Marian
Full credit for that?

Patrick
I have to, I cannot take that away from the OPW or the Mayo County Council

Marian
Are there sheep on the hill?

Patrick
There's not much sheep on the hill now, they'd be a bit. That issue was raised, that it was over grazing but Marian it wasn't over grazing. Because that's not deep bog, you wouldn't have half a bog in that, it's gravel and rock.

Marian
So are you doing anything in the locality as a commemoration or as a celebration?

Patrick
Well I was always the outside speaker Marian and the committee there, they have organised at the graveyard on Sunday at four o'clock, a lot of people are invited to come and they are having a mass there and afterwards they are having a do in Paddy McGuire's pub, so I have been told, with food and everything and an awful lot of people are invited to it.

Marian
That will be great

Patrick
And also the graveyard, the local people put in fantastic work at the graveyard, I seen them after the landslide there, in the muck and the slobber so the local people did an awful lot of work on the graveyard and including Eamon O'Cuív, he put a lot of work into the area and money and that. When you drive along there now Marian, it is a totally different place now. You'd have to look up and you could then see the track of the landslide all along the hill but the landscape in itself, and I had land there in Glengad too, and I thought that it would never be the same again, and the OPW went in there and they drained up the land and the locals, like myself, we put in machines and we cleaned up the middle of it and we fenced it and it looks now like nothing ever happened in that area.

Marian
Great! I gather you won an award yourself

Patrick
Yeah I did Marian. I was entered for an award by Teresa McGrath and Siobhan and Anthony and there were fourteen people got bravery awards through the island and I was one of them. There were two hundred entrants and I got one. They said that I did save their lives on the night and the part that I played.

Marian
Well that's fantastic!

Patrick
Well it was an honour for me but at the time I felt sadness that everybody wanted an award.

Marian
Right, ok. It is nice to talk to you and I hope you enjoy next Sunday and I hope you enjoy the following Sunday too by the way.

Patrick
Well thanks Marian to you and to your show and as I said it is an honour and a pleasure to be asked to come on your show after you being in Pullathomas at the time, that highlighted the whole lot and thank you for that. I would like to wish my cousin who is in Castlebar hospital, in intensive care, Christy Flannery, that he will be alright and how the nurses are looking after him so well. I go in every day to see him but the nurses told me to ask you for Mayo tickets because we are going to win the match. We are going to bring Sam home and good luck to the lads!

Marian
More reasons for celebrations! Listen Patrick Flannery, nice to talk to you again and thanks for coming into the studio.

Patrick
Thanks Marian for having me on and God bless you.

Chapter 7

My Experiences as a Fisherman

23rd February 2005 - Lost at sea - German diver
Lamb at the side of the cave - chances at sea again
Mother's worries with us all at sea
Gerry Ginty telling story of us fishing in the rough seas
Funny neighbours in Graughill
Story of the donkeys - ran into the sea to get away from us
'The Dancing Mermaid' boat - bad night - landing at Belderrig
Other fishermen turning the radios off and us in trouble in the rough seas
Jealousy amongst the fishermen
Fishing on the 65 Foot trawler, Killybegs
Differences between working in America and England
Fishing in Kilalla - chances at sea again
Always worked, always made money on the fishing
Life at home - big fire, turf, own food etc, Electricity coming to the house, Visiting Houses - Boxing on the television - Missions
Teresa - my first girlfriend!

Every year the sea takes someone, people are always getting lost at sea. Today is the 23rd February 2005 and there's a cold north west wind blowing, hard, cold weather. Last night I saw the bay all lit up with lights and search lights and the rescue helicopter out searching. They were searching for a father and son that were out cruising on whatever type of cruising boat that they had, off Erris Head, about two miles off. The father fell out of the boat and was lost. Today the search is still going on out in the bay there. I'm looking right out on the bay and I can see the Lifeboat out there and they are still looking for this man. Every year the sea takes its own and a lot of people fall over board and get lost at sea. At times, people have taken big risks out at sea. The sea that they don't know, and the risk they take, sometimes have to pay the price. And that man paid the price last night. I just hope that they find him or the body. I said a prayer this morning that he would be found, to give some comfort to the family. I just heard on the news that it was an Englishman and his eighteen year old son that were on the boat. A lot of these cases at sea like this, especially this time of the year, you'll hear about a lot of people around the coast getting lost at sea. It's very sad and always when the sea takes someone, and the day after or the few days after, it seems to get up and get rougher. It did last night. It was blowing a gale last night after that. My father used to tell me that after a drowning, the sea would always get up, a storm would come. And it's true. The sea goes mad when someone's life is taken. It's a tough life, you always have to be aware that the sea is more powerful than man. You always have to be careful out there. I remember a few years back, six years ago, a German diver used to come diving around the coast and the caves. He used to come here and he turned out to be a good friend of mine. He used to come with his wife. He used to tell me about the caves that he was going into and he was taking pictures all along the coast here and these caves go right into the cliffs and the sea. All you can see is just the cave and the water goes in and you get in so far in the cave. There's like another land and a beach there, but there are some of them that we would not go in to. I used to be out with my father hunting for seals and they used to be in all them caves. There was one cave that this German used to go into that my father wouldn't go near because he said it was very, very dangerous. But I used to tell the German about that dangerous cave. He was saying that he was well used of doing these things. But one time, he took out this couple and their child from the Belderrig area. They went out on a small boat and the sea was very calm. As he was going into the cave, it was a big long cave, the sea got mad and rough. Even if it was very calm outside in the bay and the ocean, that cave would always get a big flush of wind and the sea would get up in the cave. It got up that day and the boat was smashed and they were washed right into the cave and up on the shore and he was killed, drowned. They were there for a couple of days and nights and the rescue boat was out and they stayed over there in Belderrig looking out. There was loads of people and boats going out and the fishermen were all out there, trying to rescue or to see were they dead or alive. Two divers went in to the cave but one of them was killed. The next morning they were able to get into the cave because the tide was very low. They got the couple out and the child - they were saved. It was an extraordinary experience for them, an experience that they will never forget. That German man lost his life. He was telling me that he knew the sea and the caves but it proves that you don't. Even I used to challenge the sea but I would never defy it. I respected it. But some people don't realise that. And them people lose their lives.

I remember another time at that cave off Belderrig, we used to be fishing all along there down as far as Downpatrick Head, lobster fishing, myself and two of the crew. We used to have lobster pots all along that cave as well. But we would always keep them out further than along the rest of the coast line because there was such a strong current in the water going into that cave. One time, down at the side of the cave, there were sheep and a lamb, and they were there for ten days. The next thing the sheep were swept away off the rocks and the lamb had climbed up to the side. He could never get up the cliff. When he went down the cliff he would never get up. We were watching them for about ten days as we were along there fishing. One evening on our way home, the sea was calm and I said to the crew that I was going to swim in and get that lamb. I put on my small light life jacket. I took my clothes off and I jumped off the boat and I swam in towards that cave. When I got in, I thought that it was calm. The lamb wasn't in the cave but down at the side of it, on the stone flats that are down there. When I got in near the cliffs, I nearly lost my life in that strong current of the sea. It was lucky enough that when I went up the side to catch the lamb that the lamb went away up the cliff and I just jumped back out again to the sea and came out. I knew that it was a risk that I took that time too. I could have paid the price for it. But I swam back out again to the boat, which was so far away from the cliffs and the crew on it lifted me in from the side of the boat. One of them said to "Jesus, you are crazy to have done that". So I realised that I was. I was younger then and foolish.

When we used to leave home to go fishing my mother used to take down a bottle of holy water and always throw the holy water on us and tell us to bless ourselves. To bring us luck and to bring us home safe. I suppose it was the strength of her and our prayers that always brought us back safely from the sea. My brothers were all fishermen and my father was also. So she had a lot of worries, having four or five sons and a husband out fishing and I'm sure she said a lot of prayers to bring us back safely and thank God we always were. Even in all the rough seas that we were fishing in and all the chances that we took at sea. Today I visited her grave, brought her a bunch of roses for her grave. She is dead a year and a half now and I still miss her. But I go to the grave and say a few prayers. She was a good mother to us and I pray for my father as well. I hope that they are happy in Heaven. They gave us a lot of education, they both educated us very well in life and the way to survive in life and to respect and to be respected. They gave us that legacy.

This is Gerry Ginty telling of his experience as he watched me and the crew fishing with the trawler out in a storm force ten. It was almost a hurricane and we were trying to make it back into Ballyglass Pier. He is telling the story of how himself and his father watched us, God be good to him on them times.

Yeah it was 1989 when this happened. He was coming up from the Stags(rocks). They were fishing cod. It was the cod season that time and there was an awful bad forecast for that day. The wind was getting up and it had gone back to a North West wind and it was very, very strong and it was rising the sea up terribly. There was a big swell in along the rocks, and further out in the sea then there was a big swell as well. And I remember my father asking me 'Did Patrick Flannery go up yet, all the other boats are gone in'. I said that I hadn't seen him going up yet. We were told that he was on his way and we stood out looking for him. The 'Little Mary' was the name of the sixty five foot trawler, and we could see her steaming up by Brandy Point and he kept her well out. The wind was blowing Storm Force ten, it was nearly a hurricane level at this time. We were saying that we might pick him up near the lighthouse and an almighty swell struck him at the lighthouse. The trawler went out of sight. My father blessed himself and he said "he's gone". She came up again in the swell and he faced her out and he went out for about a mile or a mile and half. He turned her again and he gave her full throttle in. The next thing he had sailed up past the lighthouse. But she was gone out of sight for two and a half minutes anyway and we couldn't see anything with fog and mist, till she landed up at the pier in Ballyglass. My father, the lord have mercy on him, was a very experienced fisherman as well. He knew that day that it wasn't fit to be out. They should have come in long before that. My father, God rest him, Paddy Ginty was his name, died in March 1995.

This is my experience of what it was like growing up in the village of Graughill. The neighbours were funny neighbours really and I was very confused growing up as a young lad. The neighbours never got on with each other. Every second household were fighting with each other, fighting over land and disagreeing over things. I could never figure it out. But I knew Patrick and I'd be only young at the time when he moved into the village and I always got on well with him. He was a good neighbour. A good hearted man. He is very good hearted, he'd give you the shirt off his back. My father and himself were very good friends as well.

I remember one day there was two donkeys on the road and they were between my people's house and the next door neighbours. And the next door neighbour chased them up the road and was firing stones at them. My father returned the dose and started throwing stones at the donkeys to chase them back down the road. This went on for about half an hour and it left me wondering and confused. At the end the two donkeys jumped the fence and they ran towards the sea - it was the only way that they could get out of it. Even the donkeys were confused!

END OF GERRY'S INTERVIEW

There was another time when we were out fishing cod, it was about the 1st of February and we had a bad winter with heavy seas and rough seas. It was the first time that one or two of the crew went out fishing, including my brother Andrew. We were fishing off Belderrig. It was a Sunday when they were hauling the fishing gear. We got a lot of cod and the seas were getting rougher all the time. I could hear on the radio that the boats were heading for shore because the forecast was bad. So we kept hauling the gear, and taking the cod away back and boxing it. It was starting to get dark in the evening time, and we headed for home and the wind was north west. So we were going to land in Porturlin. The 'Dancing Mermaid' was the boat that I had at the time for fishing and we were going back against the heavy sea. Finally, the engine started to lose revs, to go back again in the heavy seas. We knew that we wouldn't be able to get back towards Porturlin - we were fishing about four miles away north east of Belderrig that evening. I called the fishing boats that were about three miles away west from me. I told them that I was in trouble, that the boat wasn't give enough revs and that there wasn't enough power in the engine to go back against the heavy seas. I didn't know what was happening at the time, it was dirt that was coming up through the diesel pump. I told them that I wouldn't be able to make it, that it was too bad. I kept going back for about another half a mile and I figured out then that I wouldn't be able to do it. I radioed the fishing boats that I was talking to and they turned their radios off. They were people that I had grew up with, fishermen, there was at least two of them that knew that I was in trouble. They went ashore and I knew that I was on my own, that these so called friends of mine were not going to turn back to help me. So the only way that I could do it was to steam the boat around again and went with the sea. The boat was giving me enough revs then to go with the sea and then the only place I could land that night was in Belderrig. Belderrig had a pier that nobody would land, or think of landing, such a night. Someone put out the word that I was going to land in Belderrig and they called the people in Belderrig. They were all out on the shores, up along the cliffs, all the village people. They were watching us land because they thought that we wouldn't make it. I thought that this was it. But I would prefer to be downed in along the shore than out in the deep ocean. I told the crew to put their life jackets on, there was only three lifejackets on the boat and there was four people. So I was the one who wouldn't have a life jacket. There was one fella that I told to tie a rope around himself as soon as the boat hit the rocks. He started panicking, and you could see that he was scared. I shouted at him and shook him. And I said "as soon as that boat hit's the rocks, you better jump for safety". We hit the side of the pier and the rocks and you could hear the planks cracking and breaking and hit the shore and that young fella did jump. He tied the rope around the rocks and we got off the boat. Coming ashore we were all thanking God and then we left the boat there that night and the people in Belderrig were very helpful. They were down tying the ropes on the boat to try to hold her on the shore. We went up to Belderrig pub and there was soup and sandwiches and everything made for us that night. Everyone was delighted that we had made it because they thought that we wouldn't that night. We left the fish on the boat, the water was coming in and out of her. The tide was going out then so she was beached that night late. We stayed up in the pub until about two o'clock in the morning and then we went home. I thank God that we did make it and that was an experience that my crew said that they would never forget. Indeed I said the same thing in my own mind but there was no choice. When you are battling with the sea, you have to make choices and you have to make them fast. The sea doesn't give you the second chance to make the choices. That's the choice I made that night. I had to bring her into Belderrig and take my chances in the rocks and the heavy seas. The Belderrig people were very helpful to us that night.

The next morning when I got up I called the boat builder. The seas were very calm the next day when we went over to the boat so we were able to work on her. We were working there on the boat for eight or nine days and we re floated the boat again and we planked her and headed back out to sea again fishing the cod. It was a tough life but it was a good one. When I look back on it now, God was with us all the time.

The cod season finished around the middle of April and we had a good season. We made good money that year. Two of that crew that were with me that night that we landed in Belderrig never fished again. They finished the cod season and they said that they would never fish again.

So them two lads gave up fishing completely. My brother still fishes to this day, Andrew. He has his own boat now. We were brought up with the sea. But them two lads that were fishing with us that time weren't brought up by the sea, but they knew that there was good money in the fishing and they wanted to make some of it. They didn't realise how tough it was as a way of life. A lot of lads that fished with me over the years only stuck it for a couple of years and then packed it in. But until this day, there are an awful lot of lads that I grew up with that are still fishing. But that night coming in as well, people had the big lights up along the shore and I think they were trying to show us our way into the channel, coming in from the sea. But we couldn't see the pier at all with the heavy seas that was there that night. We had the boat well lit up that night. I was talking to my brother the other day and he said that it was an experience that he would never forget. It was terrible but we made it.

That night when I was radioing the other two boats that were still out at sea, they could have turned back and put a tow rope on us, and towed us to safety. That's all we needed was some back up but they never did. I never fell out with them either but it proved to me that the people that I thought were my friends weren't, by switching the radio off and us in trouble. They weren't too worried about us getting drown that night. I often thought of it afterwards. I wouldn't be that type of person. If someone was in trouble at sea, I was there. No matter how bad the seas were, I would turn back and I would tow them ashore.

There was a lot of jealousy in the fishing too. If somebody got a bigger haul than the other person there was jealousy. When the fishing seasons were over, the salmon, lobster, crab and mackerel, the fishermen all towed the line again and never fell out. But during the season there was a lot of greed. Greed set into people's lives. But the fish was plentiful then.

There was another time that I fished down in Killybegs, on a hundred and sixty foot trawler, and we used to fish for white fish, like haddock and cod. We had to go to Rockall and that's where the boat was to take the fish off. I remember one trip we were forty five miles away north of the stags and it blew an awful storm. We were trawling at the time and we shot the gear. They used to trawl in very bad weather. The boats were good enough to do so. But this time the boat was giving enough revs with the heavy seas and the nets were out and we couldn't haul them in for two days. We dragged and trawled for two days and on the third day we were able to lift the net and we were able to go back into shore because we had some engine trouble. That's what that boat was supposed to do, we were supposed to be going to Rockall and fishing off Rockall, and that was our trip. There was about two double crews on and two skippers on the boat. So I spent a while in Killybegs doing that and I finished up on that boat and I went on another boat and she was called 'The Girl Pat'. It was a different type of fishing again, we were out in the deep and we'd do trips for five days fishing. But it was a good experience and I enjoyed it. In Killybegs there were a lot of fishing boats. All types would be landing early and late in the evenings. But the pubs were always opened and there was a lot of drinking going on. A lot of the pubs had twenty four hour licences for the fishermen coming ashore, all hours of the night. I used to drink that time as well and I got fed up of that and I gave it up. I remember buying a van with a cold room in it at the time and that's twenty years ago. I'd be something like twenty eight or twenty nine at the time and I started filleting fish and selling it around to the villages. All around the Erris area and I went into Killala a couple of times and it went very well for me. I made a lot of money at that, buying fish and wholesaling them to the people and the customers at home. I done that for a whole winter as well. Then the next winter after the fishing I decided to go to America.

I went to America and I worked over there for about four months at the time.

There was a huge difference between working in England and working in America. The English always looked down on the Irish - we were still a 'Paddy' to the English. You would always be looking over your shoulder while you were working and living in England. In America there was more freedom. They respected you. You had the rights to work as an Irish person. If you were Irish in America you were wanted whereas if you were Irish in England you weren't wanted. A lot of the Irish thought that they were great to have the work in England but most of them, ninety per cent of them, were used as slave labour. One out of a hundred thousand would do well in England but most of the Irish people that built England was with slave labour. But in America, if you worked you got paid. You got equal rights in America as an Irish person. To be Irish in America was very good, you'd be proud of it and you'd be proud of yourself and you'd be proud of your country. A lot of the Americans that I got to know when I was out there used to ask me about Ireland and what it was like. An awful lot of them had never been on a plane, had never been outside America. There was only five per cent of Americans that own passports. So they would never leave the country. So I was telling them what Ireland was like and the beautiful country that we have and they were very interested. I always noticed, and this is going back nineteen or twenty years ago, they always advertised well - no matter what business they were in there was always big signs all lit up. I learned a lot from that as well. When I came back and started the Knitwear business, I put up signs that would catch your eyes when you'd be passing, that you would take notice of and I learned that from the Americans. Good sales people. When we were working on a job over there the boss used to tell us not to be looking side ways at some of them because they would sue you. People were putting in big insurance claims that time in America, we wouldn't have them in Ireland that time. There was no such thing as people claiming off each other that time in Ireland. But it was a big thing in America if anyone got hurt at a job or if anyone looked the wrong way at a girl.

I loved America and I meant to move back. I wanted to move back but my wife, at the time, didn't want to leave Ireland with the kids. She didn't want to leave while her father and mother were alive either, because she was very close to them. She spent a lot of time with her father and mother . But we didn't move back and I hated leaving America. If we had gone back that time I could have started my own business and I had the intention to go back again but I didn't. I came home to Ireland and the kids were young and I missed them and it was hard to leave them so I went back out fishing again. That was my experience in life and no matter where I went I always made friends along the way. I always spoke to people and talked to people and that was a gift that my mother gave me. She said to me one time 'while you have a tongue in your head you'll never go astray' and it is true. I have used it all my life so it was a marvellous experience to work in America and I made money as well. That time I was on seven hundred and fifty dollars a week and that was good money into the hand at the time. But yet the fishing was good as well. There was always fishing in our blood. So that was winter time that we wouldn't be fishing, so come Christmas and then after Christmas we'd be going back out fishing again and that's the reason that I came back and my kids were here and my family were here at the time.

I fished out of Killala as well and there was big cod and hake fishing going on at the time. I remember the boats being tied up to the pier in Killala because the weather was too bad to go out. When you got half way out the channel in Killala there's a big sandy bank where the waves were always breaking. They'd be massive breakers there and if you got through that and got outside it you would be alright. But the Killala people wouldn't go out if it was too bad. They'd see the massive waves at the sandy bank and the sea raging outside. I used to say to the lads "we'll head out, we'll try and haul the fishing gear out". My brother TJ was with me and two more lads, Martin Ginty and there was another fella. Anyways the lads were saying that it was bad and that it wasn't a good idea. I said "we're heading out". I was very forward. So we headed out of the harbour and the fishermen were there at the pier watching us. I'd say that they thought that we were mad! When we were heading out it was calm. When we got outside the bank, there was these massive waves that was coming in and the sea was blowing a north west wind. It was a very bad morning, a terrible morning. But I had to swing the boat around again and face her back up for the pier. When I faced up for the pier, I told the lads to get up on the bow because I thought we would sink or swim on this bank. The waves started breaking the stern of the boat and I gave her full steam ahead. With the power of the engine and the speed of the sea behind the boat, we got through it. It was breaking right up all the way ahead of us, so it was a very bad experience and I remember landing in to the pier again. We tied up the boat and there was lads there and they were saying "Jesus, you had a near one". We didn't say anything. We went up to the pub and the bar man said "ye better have this one on the house, ye are very pale looking". They were very pale so we started telling the story of what happened out at sea earlier. It turned into a drinking session for half of the day. Two days later the sea was calm and we headed back out fishing again for cod. That was a bad experience but challenging. I never would defy the sea but I was challenging it. I wanted to get out because it was our cod season to make money but the majority of my experiences at sea were beautiful. We fished in some lovely, calm weather and we got massive hauls of fish. We caught lobsters, cod, salmon, haddock, all types of fish that we used to catch in different seasons. We fished the seven days of the week. Sometimes you would only get two hours sleep and it was time to be back out to sea again. We would off load the fish, get some food, get a couple of hours sleep and back out to sea again. This went on for seven weeks and it seemed like a whole year because you never saw much daylight and if you did it was out at sea. You never got much sleep, it was work all the time. But we were fit men and strong men. You would eat well to keep your strength up. But they were great moments though, when you'd see the boats in the morning hauling in the salmon gear and then the boat loaded up with salmon. To see the dawn breaking, it was beautiful, and the rocks and the cliffs and that type of beauty was marvellous even though we seen that for years. Out at sea in the morning had it's own beauty. It was a nice experience, good fishing in them days, we always made a living out of it.

Since I was about twelve years old I was a skipper on boats. That time there would be smaller boats. I'd be out fishing in Porturlin. Your father would teach you how to be a skipper on a boat at a very young age. So I skippered boats all the years that I fished. I was my own skipper. The fishermen, years ago, when they had the twenty six foot fishing boats, the smaller boats, used to take out the nets before they would ashore. The nets were cotton, and they'd hang them over beams along the coast for drying. In the evenings then they would put them in the boats again. When I was eleven years old my job used to be coiling the nets for the skippers and have them ready for the evening when they would come to go fishing at night. And I would, I'd have them coiled and for doing that, they would give me a night out fishing. Whatever catch that they would get that night, they would give me a share of the catch. Many a night I went down to the shore coiling the nets and I would have a pair of sandals on me. These white sandals and very light clothes on me and the fishermen would be in a hurry to get out to sea and I couldn't get home to change clothes. They'd give me that night out with them and my mother wouldn't see me again until the morning. At the early stages, when I was young, I used to suffer from sea sickness but there wouldn't be much heed taken of you. The crew that time, the fishermen wouldn't have much sympathy for you. They would be laughing and they'd tell you that it would harden you up. But the fishermen in them years were very good to me. They'd always give me a night out fishing, this was before I went out fishing with my father. I remember that I used to get a lot of nights out on different boats and I had a lot of money to get at the end of the season. I remember my youngest sister being born and my mother went to the hospital. The last two that were born in the family, she had them in the hospital but all the rest of us were born in the house. We had a two bedroom house, we didn't have electricity at that time. There wouldn't be water from a tap, we'd have buckets of water. There wasn't any cookers, it was the open fire that we used for the cooking. My mother reared us all like that. But this particular time that she was in the hospital giving birth to my younger sister, Celia, and when she came out I had one of these big prams with four wheels bought for my younger sister. I had all the bed clothes that goes with it. At that time I was only twelve and a half years old and that was from my fishing money. So we always had money and made money on the fishing. It was a happy home that we had even though there was no electricity, no television. I remember when the electricity came into our house. There was no bathroom, we had a heavy steel bath that my mother would boil pots of water and that's how she used to bath us. She always kept us clean. Back then it was very hard times for my father and mother, the way that we were brought up.

But we were brought up with love. That's the way it was that time.

I remember we always had a big fire. The turf was very important in them years. They had all their own turf, and of course the fish from the sea, and that's what we were mostly raised on, the fish. The only time we would get meat was when my father would kill some sheep. I remember him killing pigs as well many a time. So we would have fresh pork and I remember him killing the cows on different occasions. So everything that we had to eat was our own, it's not like going into the shop and buying it. Of course we had the potatoes as well. It was all healthy food. When I look back on it now, growing up them days was tough. When I look at the homes that we have today, the bathrooms that we have today and the complaining of young couples today. It's a different life today. The food was the most important thing that time. If you had enough food to get by then you were rich. Now it's all a challenge with money. It's all around money now a days. But I remember that time we used to get snow in winter. We'd have the mackerel cut and salted. They'd be barrels of mackerel salted for the winter months and that was our supply of food. Sometimes my father would salt other fish, like pollack and all that type of stuff. In them years there was no freezer, there was no fridge, you couldn't go freezing fish. I remember in the winter time you'd be around a big fire and the snow would be coming under the doors. I seen on some occasions the snow coming up as far as the fire from under the doors. My mother or my father would have to put a bag at the bottom of the door. There was all flag floors in our house growing up, big open fire place and there was no bathrooms, no electricity. I left home when I was fourteen and a half. As we were getting older we were moving on and the majority of my family were brought up like that, except the youngest ones. Then there was a new house built when I was ready to leave home. At least the newer ones had bathrooms and electricity and a TV. It made things a lot easier for my mother.

I remember the electricity going into the old house then, the first time that the electricity came to Porturlin. The poles were put up all along the road and later on in the year the electricity was put into the house then. There was no television in the house then, but we did have a radio, and we'd listen to the radio a lot. Then we had visiting houses that we used to go to in the village, we used to go to John Hackins and Pat and Maggie O'Donnell, they lived in the village and they had no family of their own. They were the two houses that we used to go visiting to and there would be a gang of lads there. Sometimes up to about twenty lads in the house and we'd sit down and talk and we used to look so forward in the evenings to go visiting. Then we'd walk up the roads and chat and talk and everything was discussed in the visiting houses. All the dances that we went to were discussed and everyone at them. We went dancing when we were very young, and the night after the dance we'd be back at the visiting houses and we'd be discussing everything. If somebody had a girlfriend, we'd all discuss it there and talked about her there. We'd talk about the farming and the animals, sheep and cows, the fishing. There was a lot of control in the visiting houses - they'd be joking and blackguarding but there was no badness in it. When I look back on it now these visiting houses was an education in itself. They'd be very respectable people that lived in these visiting houses. And then there was another house that we used to go to - Terry McAndrew and Peter - they were bachelors. And that was the story house. We'd all go in there and they'd tell us the old stories and you wouldn't hear a pin drop. They'd be telling us ghost stories and when we'd be going home we'd be kind of nervous thinking of the ghost stories. Then of course came the cards. The cards would be played until about ten o'clock - twenty five, in for a penny and maybe the last game would be two pence. It was good, there was great chatting. I remember one time, Mohammad Ali was fighting and we heard it on the radio. It was to be shown on the television. We walked three and a half miles to go to Cornboy, in to O'Malley's to see the boxing on the television. They were friends of my father's. My father and their family were very close and we grew up together. There were girls there the same age as myself. There was a girl there called Teresa and she was my first girlfriend that I went out with. She would be in the corner watching and I'd be looking sideways as I was very shy. But she was more grown up than I was even though she was younger than me. We used to meet up at the Missions in the church. There was times that we sat together in the church and that's the sort of a relationship and courting that we used to have. Then we went out dancing and we used to go out with each other. She used to cycle to Porturlin. She told me years after that, that the reason that she used to cycle to Porturlin was an excuse to see me. She used to steal her father's bike. I used to be very shy and she was very open. She used to be telling people that she was going out with Patrick Flannery. When I'd be around the table eating the dinner, my oldest brother, TJ, would be always teasing me about Teresa O'Malley. I used to have to leave my dinner after me and walk out because they'd be laughing at me. I used to be mad about it and when I'd see Teresa I'd tell her not to be telling people about us. She'd tell me that she wouldn't but she'd still do it! She used to come over the hill on her way to visit her friends, the Gallagher girls. I used to call her "the girl from over the hill." We had to cross the lake, so she told me that the reason that she had to come down to Porturlin was to be looking across the lake where I was in my parent's house. It was young teenage love and they were good times, when I look back on my childhood, they were very good times. But I remember then I was about sixteen or seventeen and Teresa was talking about going away to America and she was only sixteen at that time. I remember meeting her at the church, two nights before she left for America, and she said I should go to go to America too. But my heart was in Ireland, I would rather to live in Ireland. So she went away to America. But it was like, the day that we were only twelve and thirteen, my father and her father were match making for us. The two fathers wanted us to be together and they'd discuss it in the pub and the two of them got drunk over it. It was them that was bringing us together all the time, it was like a planned relationship. Teresa was a very nice girl but she was more open than I was, she was very open and she would talk about us and I wanted to keep things quiet. I was very, very quiet growing up and anyhow she went away to America and made a life for herself. But we always remained friends and we always will be. Her father, God rest him, is dead now and my father and mother are dead now, God rest them. Both fathers were very close and we were brought up together. We would walk to the church. She lived beside the church there so we'd always see each other, from time to time, as youngsters. It was teenage love. When she came back from America, I was engaged. I was about nineteen, very young, and she couldn't believe that I was engaged so fast. After that she went back to America and she met a fella called Patrick and that was the man that she married. She also has a son called Patrick and I have a son called Patrick. I don't know, it was just the way it happened I think. She made a life for herself in America and that's where she still is. When she used to come home after that, I was married and I mightn't see her, and if I did see her it would be the day before she was leaving and it would be in a shop. I always remember I'd be in a shop and she'd be walking or looking in a window and we'd meet in a shop to talk and she'd always ask my mother about me. And how I was doing and she always wished me well in life. At Christmas 2004 herself and her sister were over and we just talked about when we were growing up and really how sensible we were. We were very sensible as kids and as teenagers. And how well we've done in life. All of mine and Teresa's age group all did well in life. When we look back at the way that we were brought up, it was hard, compared to the way that kids are brought up today. We hadn't it easy, there was nothing easy about it. But we were more content, had more peace of mind and we were happier people. We had the time to have a good laugh and a good chat. That time it was all clean fun and there was no love making or sex in our relationship. It was just clean fun. There was no such a thing that time as girls or boys going out having sex and if you had sex with someone, ninety nine per cent of them ended up marrying them. That's the way it was, and I have happy memories of those happy times of my teenage years growing up. I used to always call her the 'girl over the hill' because I lived in Porturlin and she lived in Cornboy at the church and it was over the hill. We had great connections indeed the two families had. But as I said I was more shy and she was more outgoing and very forward. She was way ahead of her time and she'd be always on about me to people and I used to get mad about it. I used to go pure red in the face when the boys would be blackguarding me. One of them would say that they were talking to Teresa and that she was asking for me. She was the first girl that I ever went with.

Chapter 8

<u>My Work Experience at Sea as a Skipper</u>

Drinking
Fighting with T – me and my father's fights with him
Talk of the Town in Bangor
Travellers
Leaving the Talk of the Town
Fishing / Drinking / Bad Weather conditions
Large Families / Sons – Fishermen!

After that night with the row in the pub I came home and the next morning was Sunday morning. I remember a fella from the next village coming to the house and he said that the guards were on their way. There was a lot of damage done to the pub down the road. He was on my side but he said that the guards were coming out and the next thing the Squad car landed up the street with three guards. They asked me what happened on that night and I could barely remember half of what happened and what I did and I just said to them "whatever happened I'm guilty of it"

With that the guards went away and I was taken into court. I think it was two weeks later and in the court the case was heard on what happened on the night in question. I pleaded guilty to it. I didn't fight the case even though there was a strong case against me by the landlord of the pub. He had better memory than I had and the case was heard anyway. Tony, the Sergeant in Belmullet at the time, stood up for me and I didn't ask anyone to stand up for me. But he spoke on my behalf. He told them how I was dragged into it and anyway I was found guilty. I was fined £1,700 at that time for damages to the pub and bound to the peace for a year. My case was finished on that day.

But as time went on, I didn't go back into that pub for years after that. It was only after me getting sober, that I used to walk five miles a day keeping fit. I always kept fit. It was years after that and I was passing the same pub, walking up the road, and the landlord was outside. He called me and he said "Patrick, come here. I want to talk to you". So I went in and he put out his hand and he shook hands with me. He said

"I hope there's no hard feelings on what happened with me and you". I said "no, that it was the best thing that ever happened to me today that you shook my hands". He said "we knew you had a problem, that's why we didn't press too much charges on you". But at the time it was enough. But by him putting out his hand and shaking hands with me, it was the best thing that ever happened to me in that present day. He forgave me and that I was guilty of it. After that we turned out to be good friends. I always liked him after that. I never hated him at any time. But strangely enough, as the years passed, when I was in America, I heard that Mr McGrath had died, this landlord has died. I was very saddened that he had died. I called the local undertaker and I told him to put the best wreath that he had on him and that I would pay him when I'd come home. He done that and the family sent a memorial card to me after him dying as well. So he wasn't a bad man, God rest him. But these are stories that happened to me through my drinking or through what I call the "wilderness in my life". I always kept things away from my wife at the time and my family. I protected them very much. I was not a violent man when I came home. I always worked, no matter what; to make sure the kids and the family were looked after and I made money. My youngest daughter never seen me drinking, my son never seen me drinking – the only one that ever seen me drinking, and it wouldn't have been too many times, was my oldest daughter. But I was lucky in that line, that my kids never seen me drinking. Anyone that I was around that I had time for or respected, like my mother, God rest her, never seen me drinking. Many a time I'd go out at a weekend and I wouldn't drink at all. I'd go out with the wife at the time, and then maybe something would hit me on Monday or Tuesday and I'd go on the drink. I was a binge drinker. I often gave it up for 6 weeks but it always brought me back, I could never stay off it.

But when I was very young, I think I was about 12 years old maybe – I wouldn't be much more, we used to be outside the pub – our local pub, "Doherty's". All the men would be in the pub drinking on a Sunday night and we used to meet up there, boys and girls. We'd have a chat, innocent talk, sitting outside on the wall. We might get 'Tayto's' sometimes, if you went in, your father would buy you a drink and 'Tayto's' and you would go back out again. I remember one time outside the pub with my oldest brother. We were sitting in the car outside and there was a gang of us. We heard awful shouting and roaring inside. A man came out and he told Jack to get off him and they were going fighting. He didn't know who he was going fighting with; he was just off his head. I remember my father walking out the door and him hitting my father. My father's head hit the wall and nearly killed him.

He was covered in blood and we were there watching this. I was just stunned. There was nothing we could do about it - well there was nothing I could do, I was too young. I remember my father had to go to the doctor and I think he got stitches. He was all black; his eyes were black and everything. My father would never fight. He'd never lift a hand to anyone to fight. That always stuck to me. Later, down in the house, beside the fire with my father and mother, there was a load on my heart to see such a thing happen to my father. I remember the man that done it, this T. He came down to the house and his father was apologising to my father. He brought a bottle of whiskey for my father and sweets for the kids. He came in and I think he was frightened that my father would press charges on him. But my father would never press charges on anyone. He was that type of a man. He wasn't a violent man. I was standing at the fire and he left his hand on me. He said, "How are you?" and I replied, "Fuck off". I told him to fuck off. It never left me. As I was growing up, this man used to speak to me all the time, so it went away a bit. But it was still always at the back of my head.

All these things used to come to my head. That was one of the things that used to come to my head. I remember one day I was down in Glenamoy, the crew and myself. We were fishing but the weather was too bad so we went to Glenamoy pub. We were there all day drinking and there was a good few in the bar. There was a cousin of mine. That same man that hit my father came into the pub. We were minding our own business. He was very contrary and he started to pick on me for no reason. I just told him to back off. And for no reason he caught me by the hair and he tried to pull me to the ground. I broke the grip and I put him flying at the counter. He went out the door and he wanted me out to fight him on the street. The publican at the time, Mr. Healy, said not to go out. They didn't want me to go out – nor did my cousin – but I went laughing. It was a pleasure. The minute he said that, I just thought of my father so I said to the boys "I have a score to settle here". So we went out on the street where he was and he was supposed to be very foul at fighting. So I said to him "I have something to settle with you. Do you remember the time that you hit my father, you fucker you"? With that I hit him. I would have killed him. He wouldn't be good enough to fight me anyway but he thought he was. I hit him again and the boys knew that I would have killed him. They stopped me, they were trying to stop me and I hit my cousin – he had a black eye the next day over it and it was just that he came in the way. The boys pulled your man away. They lifted him up off the ground, or wherever he was and they pulled him away. They had him up at the house across the road – and I jumped in the car and I went for them in the car. I just missed them by inches. They pulled him across the wall and I just lost it. I have a very bad temper when I start and I couldn't control it. I just saw red that day. I would have killed him but for the lads were there. I left there then and started to make my way home. The next thing I just thought of it again and skidded on the road. I was going back again to get him again. I thought I'd get him coming home. I thought that the boys would have let him go. But they didn't. They kept him there at the house. My car went into the side of the road. The next thing the Squad car came and the Garda said "Get out of the car". I got out and into the Squad car and he said "I'll bring you to where you were all day, the pub!" And they did bring me to the pub. I went in there drinking for the day again and I came home that night and forgot about it. That was bothering me for a long time. He was very lucky that he had lads there to stop me from killing him that day for what he done to my father. And this was a lot of years after that happening to my father, a lot of years. But that's the way it was. I never went into a pub looking for trouble but I never backed away from it either. I guess I was never a doormat for anyone when I look back on it. As time went on, it was forgotten about and he forgot about it. We ended up talking and became best friends again but he knew I wasn't one to fool around with. He had a name for fighting too but I think his fighting days are over!!

These are things that used to happen to me when I was drinking and the next day or 2 days later, I would be back out fishing again, working at sea. I would forget about it and work hard again. That's the way it was – when we were drinking, we drank hard and when we were fishing, we worked hard. I used to feel very guilty after drink. I promised myself so many times that I would stop drinking. I used to say to myself, "I'll never do that again, that's it, I'll never drink again". There were times I'd be coming home and I'd say "God please help me, please help me" that's when I would be on my own in the car, that's when I would ask God for help.

When I went to manage the pub in Bangor – 'The Talk of The Town' - I had to learn how to pull the pints, how to run the pub, tap the barrels, and clean the pipes. I had to learn how to do all that at the time in the bar. When the bar changed then, when I was in it for a while, the crowd started coming. There used to be a big crowd in the pub every weekend. And at that time no weekend went by without a fight in there. There would be a big mixture of people. You'd always get a row in the pub. This was all new to me; I was only young, 22 at the time. I remember many a time I'd have to go out and stop the rows because I was the Manager of the Pub. I had to stop the fights as well outside. At that time there were no bouncers - you wouldn't be hiring bouncers in the pub - you'd have to do your own bouncing. And I remember it was weird for me for a while that I would have to do this. But one time a fella came into the pub and he was nicely on it. He had a good few drinks taken and he had the name for being a tough fella a fighter. I remember the staff telling me to keep away from him because he was dangerous and he'd clear the pub. There were young lads in the pub on a Sunday evening, in after a match. He started picking a fight out of the whole lot of the people in the pub - fucking and blinding and using abusive language. I told him to be quiet, I said to him "please leave the lads alone and be quiet". He said "I know about you too you 'Porturlin Tinker. I know where you came from and there's no fucking good in ya". I don't think that he knew anything about me, as I was new to Bangor. I was new to the place and the area. I didn't know whom I was dealing with because of the whole mixture of people that was coming in. I didn't say anything but he called me an f-en bastard and abusing me for about half an hour. Then he left and banged the door going out and it was in my head all the time. That night we had music in the pub as usual. We used to have music and had 7-8 staff working at the time. Anyhow that night, maybe an hour before closing, he came back into the pub again. I remember him coming in the hallway where there was a young lad standing up with his girlfriend. I remember him drawing out and hitting him. The lad had blood all over his face and he fell down on top of the table of glasses. Your man was there and when I looked up at the other door I saw the local Sergeant coming in. He knew that there would be trouble with this man around. He just nodded to me to go for him - just gave me the nod - and I ran for him. I gave him full wallop on the head and put him down the hallway. I lost my temper again and I put him straight out the hallway and out the door. I was about to close the door when he gave a kick to it and just missed me by an inch - between myself and the door - it would have jammed me against the wall, but it just missed me. He took his jacket off and he asked me out to fight him. At that time people gathered around when they'd see a fight. I remember on the other side of the street there was another pub and people came outside to see it. I just said to myself 'well it'll either be me or him'. I thought that if I was going to run this pub that I would have to show them who the master was. Otherwise I would be finished because there would be rows going on all the time then. With that, I went out and I hit him. There was a car behind him and he went straight across the bonnet and down on the road. He got up and I hit again and I jumped on top of him and I gave him a good hiding, a hiding he'd remember. There was another fella with him. When I was on top of him beating him, he gave me a kick in the side and he ran for it - he ran away but he didn't hurt me because when I lose my temper I feel no pain. He got a good beating that night. He'd be older than me. But that was the start of me controlling the pub and showing them who the boss was. I remember looking around me and saying 'the next fucker that will ever rear up on me or call me a bastard, I'll kill him'. I went back into the pub and the rows began to start to get smaller. If a row would start, I was able to control it before it would get out of hand and I'd put them out the door. I used to have three rings on my fingers for this and I done all my own bouncing. There was a lad there in Bangor, Jimmy, a good friend of mine, and he was always behind me when the rows would start. He was the only lad that did back me up on putting people out. But I was able to manage the pub after that. Nobody came into the pub and started a row that I wasn't able to handle. The pub then started to clean up - even the local sergeant said that there was one thing about me – that I was able to stop the fights myself. But he did say that if I wasn't able to handle it at any time, to give him a call. I said that I would. He was supposed to be, according to the neighbours, a bad man. They were saying, "He's a bad sergeant". But at the time I thought he was very good, we turned out to be very good friends. When I was doing over-time in the pub one time he was outside the door at half one in the night, trying to get into the pub to catch everybody that was in it. I pretended that the door was locked. I didn't open it for him. I did things like that in the pub. One time there was a fella down in Porturlin area and he sold 'poteen'. He made gallons and gallons of 'poteen' and sold it to everybody that would buy it from him. And I remember that there were Ballycroy boys looking for poteen and they asked me if I could get it. I used to get ten gallons of it at a time from this fella and I'd put it into whiskey bottles, and I would sell it to them or give it to them when the bar was closed. I'd sell it over the counter to them or 'under the counter'. They used to pay me and I used to make so much a bottle and I thought that that was good. They respected me because I was giving them the poteen. The sergeant said to me that there would be a few fights on the street - that they'd be a good few fights on the streets - and he used to say to me 'how come that every time that they come out from your pub that they are fighting out on the street, are you giving them some drink that you shouldn't be'. I said to the sergeant 'would I do that, would I now be so stupid as to do that'. And he used to laugh about me and tell me that he could never figure me out and he went away but I sold a lot of poteen like that. It was crazy - I know now that what I was doing was crazy - but that's the way it was that time. The pub was never my scene. I had to make a lot of different choices to be in the pub and it was a rough game to be in at the time. People would come in and share their problems with you. They would start talking about their problems and you would have to be a good listener when you were running a pub. Both men and women, sometimes a man maybe giving out about his wife or talking about his wife and you'd have to listen to him or I also remember a lot of young women would be coming talking to me and telling me about their boyfriends and the problems that they had in life. At the end of the night I used to go outside the bar and be shouting to get the customers out. There was one famous saying that I had - THIS IS A PUBLIC HOUSE, NOT A LODGING HOUSE! The people used to get a thrill out of that! Sometimes young women would be catching you by the arse so you had all these things to be dealing with, mostly in fun. There were some lovely customers coming into the bar, some nice people. I often gave money to people too. You know they might not have enough for something - I used to lend money to them and some of them - most of them gave it back. Some of them didn't give it back but that's the way it was. I never held it in for them - If you don't get it back you don't get it back. But the majority of them spent an awful lot of money in the pub and the pub was taking in a hell of a lot of money at the time and the business was good. I look back now and it was the worst move - the worst business that I went into - it really took my life over with drink. Even though I tried not to drink much in my own pub - I always drank outside my own pub. I never remember being drunk going behind the counter. I was always able to work in the bar and run the bar. My wife and I had good staff on as well; we had very good staff working for us. They were all young people that worked for us - young girls and they were good fun too. There were nights there, maybe Saturday nights that we'd have the Jukebox going after the pub being closed. Most of the people would be out and there might be seven or eight lads staying over and their wives or their girlfriends for a drink afterwards. They would ask if they could stay over for a drink and I used to do a lot of that overtime. The Jukebox would be going - country and western music - and the girls were so fond of the crack in the pub after time that they wouldn't even bother going dancing. They'd stay there and there was many a time that I would be out jiving with them and having the crack like that, so there was good fun in it too. That's the way it was in them days.

There was one time that travellers came and parked outside Bangor. There were a whole lot of them. About ten or twelve caravans and most pubs wouldn't serve them back in them times. They wouldn't let them into the pub at all. Two of them came in and they asked could they be served. I told them that they could. They really wanted day drinking - it was wintertime. So I had a bar down away from the lounge and they used to come in and drink there. During the winter, the day trade would be quiet but somehow that winter was very quiet. They left a lot of money, they used to buy that time around one hundred and fifty pounds of a carry out most evenings and they'd leave. All Guinness long neck bottles that they would buy and they'd go out. They were there for a couple of weeks - about three weeks - coming and going and I had them limited too. I told them that when I'd see them getting drunk that they'd have to leave. So there were two of them that were the bosses over the rest of them and when they would say to move, they would move. I had no problem with them but then the Publican next door saw how good the business was doing. The traveller's would be drinking in the pub and they'd be gone at the weekend. They wouldn't come at the weekends and he decided that he would let them in. Anyhow they were only there two days when the rows started and they nearly broke up his pub and the Guards were involved at that time getting them out of the pub next door. The next day they came back again to me and I had no problem with them but I limited them. I told them that they had to be out of the pub at seven o'clock in the evening. This particular day they were in the pub and I was away and they were getting very rowdy. They were very drunk and the two that I had in charge to keep an eye on them were fairly drunk themselves. They were getting really cheeky and I came back and I knew that they were out of control. I went upstairs - I used to always have my automatic rifle under the stairs and I went and I got that and I came around the back so as they wouldn't see me. I came inside the counter and I pointed the gun on his head. I said that if he didn't go and take the whole lot of them out of the pub within seconds that I would blow his fucking head away. He told everybody to get out quick. I never saw people get out as fast. And they moved on and I met them after that. The day after that the travelling community moved on and I always found them ok and they were moving on anyway. He never held it in for me; he said "would you have shot me if I didn't move" and I said "Well you didn't stay long enough for me to let you know."

They moved on and I remember a year later meeting that particular fella in Ballina. The two of us had a good drink and he was heading off to Sligo - they were always moving. But even in them days, I found that it was wrong. I thought it was wrong that they wouldn't be served in the pubs - they should have the same rights as other people served in the pub. I remember them years that they'd be no weekend without two rows or maybe three rows. I remember three rows one Saturday night in my pub and that wasn't from the travelling community. They were locals, and you'd have to handle them as well - but that was all you had to put up with running a pub in them days. It wasn't easy; it was another tough stage of my life that I had to put up with. If there was a row you couldn't go looking at the staff or you couldn't go looking at your wife to stop the rows. They'd all look at you - and I'd have to be the one to do it. But I think that I used to handle it fairly well. There was only one fella that I barred while I was in the pub. A fella that I had the row with over the night he cleared the people out of the pub and he insulted everybody. He called me a 'bastard' and he called me a 'tinker' and he said that where I came from that they were nothing but tinkers - that was Porturlin, where I was brought up in. That was the fella that I brought outside, that he'd thought he'd beat me but I beat him. I gave him a hiding so the word went around after that that I was able to handle myself. Somebody said that the way he fought he must be a boxer but I was a bit of training that I got with these people - these Northern people - I got to know. They self-trained me a little bit to handle myself and that happened in Lincoln when I was out in Hornecastle in Lincoln and it happened in the North of Scotland. I never wanted to fight, it's not a good game to get into but I was always able to handle myself when it came to fighting. I wouldn't definitely be a doormat and I think that in them days that you had to be that way, I think that I had to be that way to survive. If I walked away, turned my cheek away from these things I would never have been able to run my pub. It was the way it was. I think I had to stand up for myself - all my life I had to fight for my rights, fight for what I believed in, all my life I had to do that anyway. But I remember there used to be great crowds coming to the pub - they used to look forward to coming to the pub and it was the Number One pub in Bangor. They came from all over. From Porturlin, Belmullet, Inver, Pollathomas, Sraith, Mountjubilee and Ballycroy. They came from all over in them years when I was in the pub - they even came up from Killala. People deep down had good respect for me. So had I for them but the pub was definitely another experience of life. I think sometimes in life that you have go through these things to realise what life is all about. I suppose I had to go through this to find out what it was like. But it wasn't an easy road either.

I remember my oldest daughter was in the pub with us when we moved there. My wife had to go into the hospital when she was due to have our son while we were in the pub. My son was born in Castlebar and that night there was a big night in the pub. I came home because I had to run the pub but I kept in contact with the hospital to see when the baby would be born. I remember the staff all waited back for me to make the phone call after the pub being closed. There was about 6 people in the bar as well that had stayed in for the over time. I made the phone call anyway and the nurse was able to tell me that there was a son born to me. I came off the phone and they said, "Is the baby born". I said that it was and that I had a young son and everyone started celebrating in the pub that night. We bought a drink for the whole lot in the pub. I was told not to go up until the next morning that they were both fine, my wife and the baby were fine and that they were sleeping. So I thought that I would be up the next morning and that night we celebrated the baby boy. I remember leaving the pub at maybe 1 o'clock and heading down to my father and mother to tell them the good news. I couldn't sleep but dying to go up the next morning to see the young baby that was born - my son. That was a happy moment that happened when I was in the pub. The next day I went up to see the little fella and they were both ok, thank God. That night in the pub they were all coming in congratulating me. As I had a fishing background, I remember saying to them that I would have to order another fishing boat now as I had a young son and he'd be going to sea. They were very proud moments in the pub, and the baby coming home and the christening and all that goes with it. That little ladeen was born when we were in the pub and I used to call him Jason. There was a Western and Cowboy films and I always loved them films and that type of life and there was one fella who was called Jason. I said that if I would ever have a son that I would call him Jason. And that name was picked out for that baby. But I remember my oldest brother and his wife was expecting a baby at the same time and he was born two or three days before my little son was born. They called him Jason so they robbed my name away and then my son was called after myself - Patrick. Patrick grew up to be a very tough little baby. I remember we put him into bed in the cot and when he started walking. He used to shake the cot upstairs in the pub and he'd come out the bottom and he'd roll down the stairs and he'd come into the pub with just his nappy on him. So he was a very giddy little fella in them times. I remember Caitrina, she had a toy car, she was only a couple of years old as well, maybe three or four, probably four and she would pedal the car down outside the petrol station across the road. She would stop until the man would fill her up with petrol. They were happy little kids; my kids were brought up very happy away from it all. One day, as we used to get tired, we used to take a break from the pub. I remember going upstairs changing to come down for the night. I was at the bottom of the stairs and I heard the roaring and shouting. I went up again and I looked out one of the windows in the rooms. I saw the man outside shouting, telling him not to jump. I ran into the other room where the window was opened and my son was out on the step, outside the window. He would have fallen down on top of barrels and concrete. Two storey or more and he was only just walking at the time. The man was shouting not to jump and I just grabbed him. That was a very frightening moment for me and I thought the child would have been killed stone dead. It was after that really that we decided to get out of the pub, that it was no place for kids. They hadn't much freedom; there was no such thing as a back garden with the pub. We had our own home built. The house was built a couple of years before that and it was standing there, all ready to move into. It was furnished and everything, a good home for them. So that was one of the times that we decided that we would move out of the pub for the sake of the kids.

I remember the night that we left the pub. There was a big party and the pub was packed out, a busload came up from Killala. There was so much drinking done in the pub and it went on until all hours of the morning. Part of me was very sorry to be leaving the pub. I had a lot of friends made at the time there and we decided anyway that we were going to get out. The night of the party, a massive party, and a lot of people went up making speeches. The local sergeant went up and made a speech and was saying how I'd be missed, that they would miss us around Bangor and praised both of us highly. The local guards as well as the Sergeant were there. Afterwards, there was about ten of us around the bar drinking when everyone else was gone. We drank until seven o'clock in the morning and the girls went upstairs and put on rashers and sausages and brought down food. We sat around the counter drinking. The guards and the Sergeant were steamed as well and that was the final move out - the next day I moved out of Bangor. I moved down into my new home with the family and I started back out fishing again. But I could never get back proper the way I was when I was fishing. There was something in me all the time and I started drinking more heavy then. I was a binge drinker. I was so well known, if I went into a pub during the day, I might only be going in for one drink and of course they'd be someone in the bar that would always buy a drink for me. They had a great time for me since I was in the pub when I was good to them. The next thing they'd buy a drink and I could never say no to the second drink and I'd be there maybe for the day drinking. Then I'd try and go off it again but it was too late - the drink had me beaten at that time. There's a very thin line between a heavy drinker and an alcoholic and I think that I had passed that line as I look back on it now. My life was taken over; I could never get my life back proper again. I went back out fishing again and it wasn't the same. It was like my life was taken away from me. The thing I loved - the fishing - it was like I lost everything - there was something lost that I couldn't gain back when I went back out fishing. The fishing was all right well it was good enough. But it was like that I had lost that will to fish and work hard again on the sea. I could never gain that back. Then I started neglecting my fishing boat and everything started going down hill for me. For somebody that had everything before I went into the pub, had everything I wanted. All I wanted in life was my fishing boat, my family and my own home. I worked for that and I had that, I had that even before I went into the pub. I had started that and I was able to do that and then all of a sudden when I left the pub it had changed me completely. I don't know what it was but I was like a lost soul when I look back on it. One time before I went to America I remember the engine went in my boat. I got a mechanic down to fix the boat and he was a heavy drinker too. He took the engine apart and I just looked down and seen all the parts all over the boat. I thought to myself that it would never go back and I said to him come on leave the fucking thing. We left the boat there, tied up to the pier and we went out to Ballina and we started drinking. Then after that I went away to America. And do you know something, that engine never went back. It was taken out of that boat and I got a JCB to dig a big hole in the strand and I buried it - good parts and everything - I just buried it. A fisherman said to me that there was a good starter in that boat and the alternator and the gearbox was good in the boat. But to me it was bad memories, so I buried the engine and I went away up to Malin Head and I bought a brand new engine for my fishing boat. It was a stronger engine, more horsepower and a better engine. I re-engined the boat and I had already taken over the 65 Ft. trawler and I was back out fishing with her.

I remember leaving Killala on a bad night with the 65 Ft. trawler and we started the cod fishing. It was a very bad winter that year and we had a lot of brand new fishing gear for the cod. There was big money in the cod then, up to 50 pound a box. We were fishing away North East of the stags and we used to go West of the Stags so we were following the shoal for cod, every couple of days the cod would be moving, so we'd know the cod was moving. But that year we stuck the whole Winter fishing all bad weather, we stuck it out there cod fishing. All the boats were tied up in Belmullet – the 40 footers, they weren't able to fish because the weather was too bad. There was another trawler fishing but he wouldn't fish as many days. He wouldn't take the chances that I was taking, fishing out at Ballyglass as well. We'd be heading out over the lighthouse at Ballyglass and you'd be listening the forecast. They'd be giving up to Storm Force 9 and 10 in the mornings and we were heading out to sea, facing the North West wind and the North wind. The boat that I had was a fine sea boat – it had big horse power - 320 horse power and the crew sometimes were scared because of the bad weather that we stuck out. We were landing good loads of cod. I remember one time North of the Stags and it was blowing up to Gale Force 9 and we were hauling in gear in the worst of weather and we had ninety boxes of cod, that is ninety hundred weight, they'd be one hundred weight in the boxes. I think the prices went to 55 or 60 pound a box that time because they were scarce. Malin Head used to call me sometimes and they were saying that the weather was so bad and that there wasn't any other fishing boat out, not only even in Donegal would fish at that time. The nights and the days were too bad but we still fished it. I was off the drink at this stage and I was definitely challenging the sea and trying to make up for lost time but definitely I took big chances. There were a few times out there that we were thinking that we wouldn't make it back like one night we were fishing off Downpatrick Head and the Ceide Fields with the straight North wind. That night all the Porturlin boats and all them would be tied up, they wouldn't be good enough to fish in that weather. We were coming back on that Wintery night about maybe 11 o'clock and the crew wouldn't be on the deck because the sea would be coming across the deck when I'd be steaming home. I was coming out over the Stag rocks, over Porturlin, and I was going to go North of the Stags. But then I thought that I wouldn't that I'd go between the Stags and the Mainland, it's about two and a half miles from the Mainland to the Stags. But in rough weather it doesn't look like it's two and a half miles. It looks a lot less when you have a big North West swell coming through the Mainland and the Stag rocks. The trawler used to go down in the swell of the sea and the swell would come right out over it and you wouldn't be able to see anything for five or ten minutes. I was going by my equipment – the radar and sonar at the time that we were using. On the radar I saw a beeping and that means that there is a boat away about four miles ahead. It was steaming East and I was heading West at the time. The sea was so bad that I thought he was going away north of the Stags. But it was coming closer, closer and closer all the time on the radar system. It was blinking and I just opened the front window of the wheelhouse of the boat. I saw that we were gone away up on the swell of the sea and I seen the trawler right down under us. It was like we'd be nearly coming down on top of him and he just slid back by the side of my fishing boat and out. I called him on the radio and I fucked him out of it saying, "What kind of navigation are you using". He apologised as he had fallen asleep. He set his boat on course and he didn't take it off course and he fell asleep. It was a Killybegs fishing trawler and he was heading in because the weather was so bad. Afterwards he told the fishermen in Killybegs that it was the closest one he had ever had from the two trawlers running into each other and the whole crew would be lost. I'll never forget that. All I could see was that we were going up in the sea like a mountain. It was a massive high swell that we were up on it and when I looked down all I could see was him going back by the side of my boat. That's how close we were to being lost and we'd all have been drowned. I was steaming hard and he was steaming harder because he was going with the sea, I was going against the sea. That was an experience. Even the crew who were in the wheelhouse were looking out. I remember one of the lads blessing himself and all I said was "our day is not up lads, our day is not up". There were close times in fishing and my experiences at sea. So that winter was getting worse after that. One night we were out North East of the Stags, about sixteen miles offshore. We were hauling the net. A very bad heavy sea but I thought that we would get all the gear hauled, before the evening time. It was coming up late. There was another trawler from Ballyglass heading home because it was getting so bad. He was telling me that we should turn back as well. The weather forecast was bad. I didn't turn back. We kept fishing and hauling the gear in. The cod was good it was good fishing. I'll never forget that day. The crew were all on the deck. Sometimes they would be hanging onto something on the deck because the sea would nearly be washing them off the boat. That's how bad it was. Anyway, we got all the gear hauled in and at that time the storm was up around ten. It was the roughest day that I ever spent at sea. That trawler was very small in them massive waves, in the North, North West winds. The forecast was giving up to eleven for that day. I swung around and I headed out to the sea. Out North to go fishing again, to go shooting the gale. I remember Pat Walker at the time, he was gone in, telling me how bad it was and I was giving my position. I turned around to go shooting the gear. I didn't even tell him that I was shooting the gear and the next thing I saw was one of the long term crew lads , Michael Noone, being swung around with the net and the wave. All I could see was him going flying past the side of the wheelhouse of the boat and lucky enough the net broke. We just broke the net, we had bouey at the end of it that floats whenever we set out. I just said to Michael, my brother Tony and Tommy Riddy, "Let it go lads, get in off the deck, clear the deck". We put all the fish down below. As the fish was coming in we were putting them down below in the hatchet and we headed for home. It was so bad and the next thing Pat Walker was on the radio to me again asking where I was. I was making no headway home at all, the sea was so strong, even with the power of the engine, and the sea was stronger. We were dodging waves and trying to make it home and finally she was picking up speed. The sea was blowing, I would say, storm force eleven at this stage. It was the roughest day ever that was to be seen at sea. Pat Walker called me and said, "You'll never make it Packie". They used to call me Packie that time. I said to him, and the crew beside me listening in the wheelhouse, "she'll either sink or swim now" and that's the way it was. We were in God's hands; I used to always think of that, that we were in God's hands and at His mercy. We headed for home. I remember coming back in after hours of us battling with the sea. The sea was so bad, all along Glengad and all along the coast. You couldn't see the land, all you could see was the sea going across the land. You couldn't see Ballyglass Lighthouse; the sea was going right across it. So I came in then and I let her around. I went back as far as Erris Head nearly back between the Bay before I could chance to come around because the sea was so heavy. I got around then and I got the sea hitting the stern of the boat. Then the boat went with the swell of the sea so we were heading in towards the lighthouse. I came then, for about half a mile, before the Lighthouse. I couldn't see it so the whole cliffs were like the sea, with the sea going across it. We were told that there were people along the cliffs and people outside at the lighthouse looking out to see would we make it. When I came within that half a mile, I knew that if I kept going on that course that I would land probably up on the Lighthouse because I couldn't see it. So I had to swing it back out again. That was the worst because when I swung the boat around, you were hitting all the swell's coming in. I brought it around in a sharp turn and I gave her full steam ahead out against the sea again. I went out again for about a mile and a half before I could turn around to come back into Ballyglass. The crew at that stage, I remember one of them, was very pale, frightened. That mile and a half that I got us turned around again, gave her full steam ahead, and faced her for Ballyglass. We headed in and just as we were heading in we just seen the lighthouse on our port side. The sea broke at the lighthouse, right across, when we got into the lighthouse. Then the sea wasn't as bad but it was bad enough. So that was an experience that I will never forget at sea and we had about sixty boxes of cod when we landed in. Pat Walker and the lads there couldn't get over the sea that we stuck out because they were fishermen and experienced fishermen. They said to us that they didn't think that we would make it. But they were some of the experiences that I had at sea and I had a good lot of them but God was always with me.

There's another experience that I had at sea one time. I was skipping my father's boat. We were fishing for salmon at this stage out at Porturlin. We left Porturlin and it was a very strong North wind, bad at sea. When we were heading out there was a lot of boats heading in because there was a bad forecast. We had lost time on fishing so we were trying to make up for time. One of the crewmen was Brendan Garvin that was fishing with me at the time and we headed out East and way off Downpatrick Head. Then we headed North of Downpatrick Head. We were steaming out before we started shooting the fishing gear for salmon. The sea was so heavy that one time the boat came down off a swell of sea and the sea hit the boat off the side. Heavy seas hit the boat on the side and we cracked a planck. One of the crew said that there was water pumping in at the side of the boat. The only thing that I could do was to go with the sea and we headed for Killala. The pumps were going flat out keeping the water out of the boat. We were going with the sea, so the boat wasn't taking as much water as it should be. But when we were going into Killala Harbour, the water was nearly half way up on the engine at that stage. We landed fine into the pier but when we had just got off the boat and within two minutes the boat sunk at the pier. The side of it was all damaged; she had sprung more leaks underneath with the roughness of the sea. The next day we floated the boat and the boat builders were brought down and they re-planked the boat again and we headed out back again to sea, fishing for salmon.

That was some of the experiences that I had at sea and my crew that was fishing with me and at that stage my father was with me too. But we had some great times fishing. We landed some great hauls of fish; we always made a living at the sea. It brought it's own beauty the sea; the nature of the sea always brought us back. We were always brought up never to defy the sea but I used to always challenge it because we were hunters. Hunting for fish in the sea, to raise our families and to make money. Money that would keep us going for the rest of the year so we fished while we could. When the weather was too bad then the boats would be tied because these were only 36 ft. boats. It was a good lifestyle as well; parts of it were tough, hard work at sea. While we were fishing we had to fish, we had to take a certain amount of chances out there. I suppose from a young age the sea air had lived in me. I was fishing at eleven years of age. Yeah sometimes I used to be frightened but as we went on in years the fear had left us. We had no fear. The sea made us men before it was time for us and made us brave. If you said that you were frightened out there at sea too, the crew would laugh about you. You wouldn't be saying that you were frightened because then you weren't a man. You'd have to be strong and I suppose that was the way that we survived in them years. There was another time I was fishing with my father off Ballycastle Bay. It was nighttime and we were hauling the fishing gear. The net got caught underneath the boat and it stalled the engine. It was another bad, cold Winter's night, very wintry for the month of August, fishing again for salmon.   Because I was the youngest and the lightest I was the volunteer that would go out on the rope. They tied a rope around me and they put me into the cold, ice water with a knife in my mouth. They would let down so far and I'd feel my way around to try to find where the net was caught underneath. The sea was hitting me against the side of the boat, but they were holding onto me with the rope. Now if anything happened to the rope, if it snapped or anything like that, I was gone. I eventually found where the net was caught and cut it off the propeller and freed it. That was another experience that I had at sea, you had to be prepared to do all things. You had to be prepared to take chances and if something like that went wrong, it was the youngest fella that would be put out in the water. After freeing the rope, they pulled me back in and we went down to the bunks with the light on. I was shivering with the cold and I took my clothes off and squeezed them dry and they were put back on again. It wasn't a dry sweater that they gave me and my father told me to take a good drink of whiskey to warm me up. That night we stayed all night fishing and we went back in the morning. That's the way it was with fishing at the time, they were experiences of a lifetime at sea. It was beautiful in the dawn heading in for Porturlin Pier. It was the nicest sight that you would ever see; you were heading into shore, after your night's fishing. It was lovely to see all the boats coming in with lots of salmon. Salmon was very plentiful in them years. You'd land at the pier in Porturlin and they'd be lorries at the pier buying the fish. The fish would be weighted and the owner of the boat would get the docket. You were paid after fishing for six or seven weeks all together. That's the way it was that time. But the lorries that were selling the fish were also selling drink – whiskey and beer. You'd see a lot of the men that drank that time. I didn't like drinking that time because I hated it. They'd be there in the morning and they'd drink two or three glasses of whiskey and Guinness. They'd be talking and discussing the night's fishing, the catching that fellas caught and then they'd all go home. At home my mother and the other mothers in the village would have the breakfast ready for them at that hour of the morning. A lot of times we'd have salmon. My mother would boil it from the night before. She would have it cooked for us and we would have it the next morning and the homemade bread. After that we'd go to sleep for a while and when we'd get up we'd be heading out to sea again. It is a healthy lifestyle although a tough one.

In them years every house had big families. My mother reared thirteen kids in our house. Most of the village people had big families as well; they'd be ten, eleven or twelve kids in most of the houses. When one of the wives would have a son they'd congratulate them that it was another fisherman; the fishermen always wanted sons for the sea in them times.

At a beach in Rin Roe talking into a tape & writing my book.

Touring Porturlin with Martin McGuinness; the flag was flying everywhere we went. August 2001

My tractor for working the farm. Bought for £1,400 in 1990.

Laying a wreath in memory of Michael Gaughan and Frank Stagg, hunger strikers who died for the freedom of Ireland. April 2003.

Opening of the Wildlife Centre at Flannery Village 1998.

My brother Tony helping out with the fund raising dance for Sinn Fein. Jan 2003.

With Derek Warfield of the Wolfe Tones and Theresa at a fund raising dance in January 2003.

Contratulating Willie Corduff, winner of the Goldman Environmental Award in Belmullet, May 2007

With Theresa at Sinn Fein fundraiser, August 2003.

The Fighter!

Brother TJ Flannery with rare Leatherback turtle caught in his net off of Ballycastle in June 2006.

In 1995 my brother TJ after fishing all night and caught nothing. Next morning he went back out and caught a big haul of salmon.

My brother TJ, his 2 sons Tommy and Johnny & nephew Michael Gallagher with staff of Kilalla Co-op.

Meeting first-ever girlfriend Teresa at SF fund raiser in January 2003.

The view from my home looking out at my stock.

At the Talk of the Town Pub, Bangor Erris getting ready for a wedding in 1976. Wife Marion and staff Ann Lindsay, Breege Carey, Mack, Maureen Cuffe & Maureen Deane.

Martin McGuinness congratulating me on my nomination to run for Sinn Fein in Erris at meeting in Paddy McGuire's pub in August 2003.

On a 5-day yacht trip in Stillwater, Minnesota on a mission to tour America in 1993. Taken with skipper Johnson.

Discussing politics with Sinn Fein TD Martin Ferris. Castlebar February 2003.

The standoff in Bellanaboy against Shell in 2005. Protestors gathered at 6:00am all day through. Day after day they kept the campaign going.

Arial view of Flannerys Village taken in 1998.

Leaving Iniskea Island with John McGuinness and his son, Emmet August 2003

Taken in McGuire's Pub with Paddy O'Donnell who left Graughill for New York at age 16.

Summer 1997 with Gerry Adams at Flannery Village Memorial Plaque Commerating the people that died in the Battle of the Boreen in Graughill.

Fundraising do run by myself and Paddy McGuire in August 2003 for Sons of Erris Sinn Fein Cumman. Music by the Wolfe Tones.

Martin McGuinness (5th from right), Patrick Flannery (2nd from right) with Staff at Udaras na Gaeltachta, Beln

I took Martin McGuinness to Teach Iorras, Geesala to see Brendan Grace 14 Aug 2001

Leading the picket against the gas in Geesala summer 2001. Being interviewed by RTE1

Meeting Frank Fahy, TD & Minister for the Marine & Natural Resources when I was PRO for the Northwest Salmon Fishermen in Jan 2002.

Looking out on Porturlin Harbour on a summer evening.

Picketting against gas
in Geesala, summer 2001.

Presenting an Taoiseach Bertie Ahern
with Flannery Knitwear in Geesala, Sept 2001.
TD Beverly Flynn on right.

Myself & Paddy McGuire ran a fundraising do
for Sinn Fein in Geesala in January 2003.

With my good Mother Eileen at her
70th Birthday Party in Sept 2001.

With Joe Leonard (centre) and friend
in January 2003 I had the Wolfe Tones
in Geesala in memory of the Hunger Strikers.

Showing Taoisich Bertie Ahern damage from the Pullathomas Landslide in October 2003.

Welcoming Derek Warfield of the Wolfe Tones to Geesala for a fundraising do I ran for Sinn Fein in January 2003.

Playing for tourists outside McGrath's Pub, Pullathomas 1998.

The free beaches in Erris - my island!

My son Patrick with Gerry Adams in the Flannery Knitwear shop, 1997.

Patrick at age 26.

Taken in Scotland with my beautiful baby daughter Katrina 1977. One week old.

Two cousins: granddaughter Nicole Flannery and grandson Nathan Flannery. May 2004

My daughters Maria and Katrina modelling Flannery Knitwear 1991

With Martin McGuinness at Blacksod Lighthouse 1996

With Martin McGuinness celebrating his daughter's wedding in Derry, June 2002.

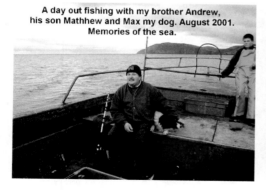

A day out fishing with my brother Andrew, his son Mathhew and Max my dog. August 2001. Memories of the sea.

Martin & Bernie McGuinnes with my son Patrick, his partner Lisa and granddaughter Nicole. Aug 2001.

McGuires Pub, with Paddy McGuire, Derek Warfield of the Wolfe Tones, son Patrick and grandson Mark on his baptism day in August 2003.

With Martin McGuinness leaving Iniskea Island. August 2003.

With Martin McGuinnes and Paddy McGuire in McGuire's Pub, Pullathomas. August 2001

Martin McGuinnes with son Emmet and John Healy (centre). August 2003.

With Martin Ferris at his office in Kerry August 2005.

My sister Kathleen's wedding day to Padraic Barrett Sept 1976.

Martin McGuinness and his wife taken with Tim Quinn (far right) and JT Gaughan on our visit to Belmullet 1997.

L to R: Alex Banahan (SPAR), Patrick Flannery, Mary Davis CEO Special Olympics at Mansion House for SPAR Local Hero Awards 2003.

My daughter Maria with Gerry Adams in our family home 1997.

Guest singer with a country & western band at the Broadhaven Bay Hotel, Belmullet Sept 2006. The dancefloor was full of jivers.

Deputy Lord Mayor of Dublin congratulating me on Local Hero Award in Mansion House.

Outside Paddy & Mae McGuire's home, before interview on Marian Finucane's radio show. Sept 2003.

Taken in Killybegs Harbour.

Flannery Knitwear wins local race in Geesala, ridden by Nina Carberry (famous jockey). Aug 1999.

My Grandchildren, from left: Mark, Nicole, Shane, Nathan & Cian taken in 2005.

The Pig Island off Porturlin, owned by Christy Flannery.

Noel Coyle presenting the Shaw Cup that my horse won in Geesala August 2000.

Winning the Geesala Races August 2000.
(L to R) Theresa, my brother, daughter Maria.

I led the protest against Shell when the Rossport 5 were jailed on 29 June 2005.

Taken with Gerry Adams in Bellanaboy 2005.
Presenting him with Flannery Knitwear.

Gutting freshly caught mackerel at sea.

As PRO for NorthWest Salmon Fishermen
signing salmon quota agreement
in Dublin Government Building, March 2002.

Fishing off Porturlin.

The Little Mary tied at the pier in Killybegs.

My 65-foot trawler, the Little Mary (le Petite Mimi in French) tied up at the harbour.

American Indians from the Sioux Tribe stayed 3 weeks at Flannery Village in 1993.

1972 Myself (2nd from L) with brother TJ (far right), Aunt Margaret and Sean & Seamus Farrell coming home from a hard day's fishing. * Years later Sean Farrell lost his life at sea.

Lambs let out of the shed into grass on the farm.

Flannery Farm Triplets

Birth of baby foal

A White Christmas 2000 in Flannery's Village
Katrina, Nathan and Theresa

My daughter Maria
was chosen
Miss Punchestown Races
in April 2004.

14:57

Gerry Adams in 1996 in the kitchen of my family home.

Home Sweet Home!

The Flannery Brothers 1999

Flannery brothers on Andrew's wedding day in July 1986. From left Patrick, TJ, Richie, Andrew and Tony, outside mother & father's house.

Celebrating my 50th birthday with my family & friends at a surprise party at McGuire's Pub. April 2006

My 50th Birthday in Paddy McGuire's Pub. Daughter Mark, Son Patrick, Grandson Mark and Grandaughter Nicole.

Bertie Ahern giving me a clap on the back for being a good Irish Republican.

Fair Day in Belmullet Aug 2001.
With Martin McGuinness & Gary Bohan.

Opening Day of Flannery Knitwear Factory Shop
summer 1996. (L to R) Martin Coyne (Udaras),
Seamus Caulfield, local Inver priest,
Kathleen Campbell (mother-in-law)
and mother Eileen Flannery.

Flannery Knitwear Brochure designed by Patrick in 1997

Liam and Roisin Tighe from Shraigh.
Liam won the All Ireland for Irish Dancing.
Picture with Tim Quinn and Gerry Coyle.

My Mother with her sisters and brothers at her
surprise 70th birthday party September 2001

My nephew Mairtin Flannery.
Don't mess with The Cowboy!

My good, long-time friend Eddie Crozier from Derry, April 2003

Brother Andrew with his son Matthew hauling in net full of mackerel off Porturlin.

27 Jan 2007. Welcoming Eamon O'Cuiv, grandson of Eamon DeValera, to Erris. With Councillor Tim Quinn.

Eamon DeValera came to Belmullet in the 1960's and people came from all over Erris to shake his hand.

Meeting an Taoiseach Bertie Ahern in October 2003 to discuss the needs of Erris.

Meeting President of Ireland Mary McAleese in July 2004

Theresa threw a surprise birthday party for me in April 2000. With my kids Katrina, Maria and Patrick.

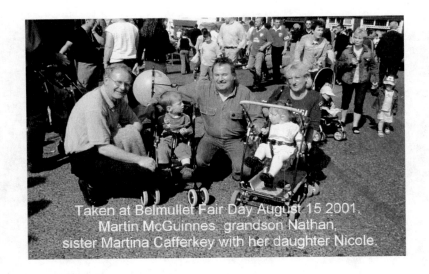

Taken at Belmullet Fair Day August 15 2001.
Martin McGuinnes, grandson Nathan,
sister Martina Cafferkey with her daughter Nicole.

On holidays with two of my kids
Patrick & Maria in Bundoran 1992.

Vising the Famine Walk from Louisburgh
to Leenane. Many died of hunger
due to the neglect by English landlords.

Taken with my sisters and brothers
at Alan & Karan's wedding.

14 October 2006

With my mother and sister-in-law Breege at the Flannery Village Annual Christmas Party 2000

Relaxing at home, babysitting my grandson Mark. August 2003.

A Special Child with a Gift

I always said to her mother that if Christina could bottle the nature and kindness she shows to people she would become a millionaire overnight. But money couldn't buy the gift that she has from God.

Wherever Christina goes people are always drawn to her. She's a child that will always do well in life.

Interview 4

<u>Paddy and Anthony O' Donnell Interview (2002)</u>

Interview with Pat O'Donnell, who is from Graughill but left there many years ago, and Anthony O'Donnell his brother. The interview is telling the story about what it was like to grow up in Graughill in them days.

Patrick Flannery
What was it like for you growing up in Graughill as a kid?

Pat O'Donnell
Exciting in a primitive type of a way. We got together a lot

Patrick Flannery
When you compare them times with today, do you think that they were hard times?

Pat O'Donnell
They were hard times, a lot of hardship. But we were never hungry. We always had a bit of fish, bread, potatoes and a pig for a bit of meat!

Patrick Flannery
So you had all your own food?

Pat O'Donnell
We had all our own food, and it was all provided from a little piece of land

Patrick Flannery
And what would you be talking about? About nine acres of land?

Pat O'Donnell
Yes about eight or nine acres of land

Patrick Flannery
How many kids were in your family?

Pat O'Donnell
There were seven children in the family and everybody got on well together. We were all a very happy family and I have great memories of it. Christmas dinner was the big day, once a year. But my father used to go to England in them days for the Summer and my mother did the work

Patrick Flannery
And the women worked very hard in them days?

Pat O'Donnell
Very hard. They cooked all the bread, made all the meals, spun all the wool and made sweaters and socks. Washed the clothes by hand, milked the cows, fed the cows, fed the hens

Patrick Flannery
They were marvellous people

Pat O'Donnell
Very hard, harsh work. Carried the potatoes from the field on their backs on a creel

Patrick Flannery
Did everyone in the village do the same thing, as a family?

Pat O'Donnell
Every family in the village practically lived in the same manner and did the same thing

Patrick Flannery
And were ye all born in the house? Do you remember your mother telling you?

Pat O'Donnell
Three of the children were born at home here but there were four born in America

Patrick Flannery
Your father went to America?

Pat O'Donnell
My father and mother went to America on the 23rd November 1923

Patrick Flannery
And what was America like then for families that moved out there?

Pat O'Donnell
It was harsh, very harsh

Patrick Flannery
Was it a bit better than staying here?

Pat O'Donnell
I don't think that it was any better, in fact I think that it may have been harsher over there. For a few years things were very good but then they had the Wall Street Crash in America and the depression. It was very, very hard, especially for migrants

Patrick Flannery
So things weren't great over there?

Pat O'Donnell
Things were not great over there for migrants at that time. There was very little for them

Patrick Flannery
Do you remember, here in Graughill, the cargo ships coming in with food? I've been told about the currachs rowing out to get wine and drink and food off them?

Pat O'Donnell
Oh sure, I remember when the Spanish trawlers came in, we'd get a couple of hens or ducks then we'd go on and get some brandy or whiskey or whatever. We'd trade with them

Patrick Flannery
And would they give ye fish at the time?

Pat O'Donnell
Fish wasn't what the villagers wanted. They wanted a little bit of spirits!

Patrick Flannery
To do a bit of partying and drinking?

Pat O'Donnell
A little bit of spirits for the party!

Patrick Flannery
And how did the neighbours in Graughill get on? Did they all agree with each other or were they jealous of each other at that time?

Pat O'Donnell
My recollection of it was that there would be very little agreement amongst them. There was always animosity among the neighbours and feuding over petty stuff, unfortunately

Patrick Flannery
Like over lands?

Pat O'Donnell
Over a little bit of land or a little bit of bog, who had one cow more than the other one, and all this type of stuff. There was always that in the village. There was feuding over the cattle going into another person's land, or sheep or the dog chasing the wrong cow or whatever it may be. It was very petty type of stuff

Patrick Flannery
Would the neighbours all fall out with you over that? Would they stop talking to each other over that?

Pat O'Donnell
Well my recollection would be that some of the neighbours were not friendly with each other. But most of the children got on well together

Patrick Flannery
The kids got on alright?

Pat O'Donnell
Most of the time

INTERVIEW WITH ANTHONY O'DONNELL

Patrick Flannery
What was the experience like for you Anthony growing up here in Graughill?

Anthony O'Donnell
Well there's not too much that I can add to what my brother Patrick already said. Except about the women. They would also be down on the shores with the creels on their backs, bringing up the seaweed, to

put on the meadows

Patrick Flannery
That was the manure that they used to put on the land. How old were you when you left, Anthony?

Anthony O'Donnell
I was sixteen when I left here

Patrick Flannery
But you kept coming back every year?

Anthony O'Donnell
For the first couple of years and then I got sort of lost in the wilderness! (early 1950's)

Patrick Flannery
Made your own life over there?

Anthony O'Donnell
Made my own life, yes

Patrick Flannery
What was the fishing like? They used to fish with the currachs, I believe, at that time?

Anthony O'Donnell
They used to fish with the currachs

Patrick Flannery
So they kept themselves going on the fish as well there

Anthony O'Donnell
They were out in the currachs regularly. They used to catch the fish and put them in a wooden barrel and salt them and you always had a bit of fish

Patrick Flannery
For the whole year round?

Anthony O'Donnell
For the whole year round. They would also kill a cow or a pig and do the same things, salt it and soak it

Patrick Flannery
So the money was scarce but at least they had their own food?

Anthony O'Donnell
They lived off the land. They lived off the chickens mostly. They'd sell the eggs and buy the groceries with the money, they'd buy a ten stone bag of flour at the time

Patrick Flannery
What year would that be now, Anthony?

Anthony O'Donnell
Well I left in 1947, so that would be in the 1930's and 1940's

Patrick Flannery
So the women worked very hard? The mothers worked very hard?

Anthony O'Donnell
They did. They were doing the house work and the field work and a combination of the two

Patrick Flannery
When ye were young what leisure activities had ye? Used ye be at dances or were the dances in the houses?

Anthony O'Donnell
There used to be dances in the houses, we used to have them here in the house in Graughill, one a year

Patrick Flannery
One every year?

Anthony O'Donnell
Yes once a year. It would be chock o block and the money they made out of it would go along way towards buying clothes and different things, shoes for the kids. When we wore them! We didn't wear shoes very often

Patrick Flannery
You were in your feet?

Anthony O'Donnell
Yes we were in our bare feet. You would bring a couple of sods of turf

with you under your arm down to the school to keep the school fire burning!

Patrick Flannery
And the 'school dances' they were called?

Anthony O'Donnell
The school dances, yes, they were traditional. They used to run for two weeks for two shillings. There would be a piece of bread and jam and a cup of tea thrown in for that as well

Patrick Flannery
And did you walk?

Anthony O'Donnell
Well you walked everywhere! There wasn't even a bicycle about then

Patrick Flannery
Do you remember ever walking into Belmullet from here?

Anthony O'Donnell
Oh God, dozens and dozens of times

Patrick Flannery
And that's eight miles?

Anthony O'Donnell
There used to be one man in the village, I forget who it was now, and he had a bicycle and they'd be five or six of us running behind the bike into Belmullet, and you would do the same coming back at night, run back again behind the bike

Patrick Flannery
So the cows, fish and chickens would be sold in Belmullet, at the fairs?

Anthony O'Donnell
The cows yes, they would always take in a cow or a young calf and sell them. It used to be the 15th, the 15th of August was the big fair, the Lá an Logha

Patrick Flannery
Your father too would have worked hard at the time?

Anthony O'Donnell
Oh definitely, if you are bringing up seven children, you've got to work pretty hard

Patrick Flannery
And there was always big families at the time?

Anthony O'Donnell
Always big families, always six or seven children

Patrick Flannery
And what about girlfriends in them days? Were they like now, the dances, were they all virgins then?

Anthony O'Donnell
The girlfriends side of it - we were probably too young to mess about with girls at fifteen or sixteen!

Patrick Flannery
But there was no such a thing as going out, girls going out

Anthony O'Donnell
The parents were very strict on them. They wouldn't come in late. If you were visiting they would shout 'Home and go to bed'. And you didn't answer back

Patrick Flannery
You obeyed your parents?

Anthony O'Donnell
Oh you did yeah

Patrick Flannery
Do you remember if the girls got pregnant at the time?

Anthony O'Donnell
I can't remember of any girl here in Graughill or around the area that I know of that got pregnant

Patrick Flannery
What would your reflection of the Graughill people, as neighbours be? Were they friendly people or were some of them falling out with each other?

Anthony O'Donnell
They'd have little arguments and forget about it because when you'd be reeking your hay, all the neighbours would come and help out and visa versa, when it was their turn. And cutting the turf was the same, most of the neighbours would go around and cut one man's turf one day and then carry on to somebody else the next day

Patrick Flannery
Do you remember your parents talking about the 'Battle of the Bothrin'? Where the people were killed, Mary Deane?

Anthony O'Donnell
No, not really

Patrick Flannery
That was kept kind of quiet, wasn't it?

Anthony O'Donnell
Well yes, I never heard them going back into history much

Patrick Flannery
Back to Pat O'Donnell again now. Do you remember any ladies getting pregnant here at the time?

Pat O'Donnell
Not in my memory, but it was brought to my memory. I had an aunt that got pregnant and immigrated to America that had a baby in Graughill and she never did return probably because of that reason

Patrick Flannery
It was a big shame?

Pat O'Donnell
It was horrible. I don't know if that was the reason that she never returned but she never did come back. But I do know that she had a baby, it was a kind of a tragic thing when that happened in them days

Patrick Flannery
Would you think people were odd that time? Why were the people ashamed of these things?

Pat O'Donnell
They were ashamed about having a baby without being married because I think a lot of it had to do with religion or church or up bringing. They were odd in that way. They were also very odd about having autistic children or children with special needs. They kept them in theirhomes and were never exposed to the public. That was very odd and strange. So yes they had primitive ways a lot of them

Patrick Flannery
Would you think today, looking back on these times, was it a lack of education? If you look at today we are not ashamed of these things today, it's a gift really today from God

Pat O'Donnell
It was a lack of education and dictatorship from the church. I think that the church dictated to the people how to live their lives in them days

Patrick Flannery
Tell me what it was like going to school for you. Were the teachers hard?

Pat O'Donnell
They could be quite pleasant at times but they could also be very harsh and abusive towards the children. I never experienced it much myself because I didn't have a problem with whatever learning I had but there are children out there who cannot learn very well so the teachers were abusive to them

Patrick Flannery
At the time when I was going to school, I left school at ten and a half and I could never read or write. There was a big dunce cap put on me and I'd be behind the blackboard. Was that the type of attitude in your time as well? That if you couldn't read you were considered thick?

Pat O'Donnell
I don't have any recollection of it because as I said I could read and write. I have a recollection of children who were not able to read or write or learn very well, were not treated properly, they were treated harshly at times

Patrick Flannery
I'll go back to Anthony again. So Graughill for you growing up was hard time?

Anthony O'Donnell
It was hard times but happy times. I couldn't really remember of anyone being unhappy. People worked to survive and they were very, very friendly - most people anyway, of course you would get the odd one. The ignorant person putting a cow over the fence eating the neighbours grass

Patrick Flannery
Your brother, God rest him, Johnny, how old was he when he came back from America to take over the farm?

Anthony O'Donnell
I'd say it was about 1931

Patrick Flannery
I remember Johnny, when I came here to Graughill, and that's twenty-eight years ago, and himself and his wife Kathleen were very good neighbours to me. They were one of the families in Graughill that welcomed me to Graughill. I remember being in Graughill when I was nine years old too and I used to stay in Tom Cafferkey's house, the neighbours used to go down with the carts in the very early morning, bringing up the seaweed. But even as a kid, I remember some of them even if they filled more or if they had a bigger cart they were kind of jealous of each other, I thought at the time. And some of them didn't speak to each other at the time?

Anthony O'Donnell
Well they didn't, I guess that they didn't like strangers coming into the village I'll be honest with you and you had to go through that I suppose

Patrick Flannery
Oh I did, I did

Anthony O'Donnell
It always has been like that in Graughill. They didn't like that and my father had big problems too because he came from Aughoose

Patrick Flannery
And they didn't accept him?

Anthony O'Donnell
No they didn't, no not at first. But eventually they became friendly with him and at the end of the day, they had to accept him

Patrick Flannery
But they find it hard to accept any outsider at all and I think that that is still here today too. So we'll move on, did you fish Anthony?

Anthony O'Donnell
Oh yes, I used to be out in the currachs fishing mackerel, then take them on the back of the donkey and sell them then around the local villages from the back of the cart. It was another way of earning a little extra money. It was part of living in them days. We accepted things the way they were and got on with our lives

Patrick Flannery
I'll go back to Pat again about your brother, Johnny, how many kids did he have?

Pat O'Donnell
Seven

Patrick Flannery
Seven kids, God bless them. And your brother died when he was young?

Pat O'Donnell
Fifty one when he died

Patrick Flannery
And his wife Kathleen, died shortly after that?

Pat O'Donnell
She died at forty five

Patrick Flannery
I'm sure that you remember all that sadness

Pat O'Donnell
Oh sure, I was in America at the time of course but I do remember it very well

Patrick Flannery
The kids are all grown up now, thank God

Pat O'Donnell
The children are all doing fine, there are four of them in the London

area, one married in Brighton with three children, the oldest boy John is with the Irish Army, he's a sergeant in the Irish Army for over twenty years. One of the girls has just come back from England and bought a home around Ballaghadereen. They are all grown up and doing very well

Patrick Flannery
When Johnny died and Kathleen, I remember that they were a very close couple, they were the closest couple that I ever remember, and even to this day because when I came to Graughill they were the ones that welcomed me and we had only one kid and they'd baby-sit to let us out on a Saturday night because we were young, twenty at that time, and Sunday night was their night, and they gave us milk at the time and stuff like that. But how many years were between Johnny and his wife dying because I remember that was very close, was it six months or five months at the time, can you remember, or was it a year?

Pat O'Donnell
Three, Four or five months

Patrick Flannery
Yeah I remember that there wasn't much in it. And the kids, how old was the youngest and the oldest?

Pat O'Donnell
The youngest was three and the oldest was sixteen

Patrick Flannery
She died of heart break really?

Pat O'Donnell
Well she had a cancerous tumour in her head probably brought on by the loss and stress. Sometimes cancer is brought on that is there but may lay dormant for many years, but stress brings it on and I think that the loss of her husband brought that cancer on

Patrick Flannery
Your old house is still standing there. What's it like when you go up to that house now and look at it does it bring back memories all the time to you?

Pat O'Donnell
It brings back the good memories, I don't think of the sad memories, I think of the joyful memories. We had a lot of happy times there. I never look for the sadness. I look on the positive side of it and the happiness and the joys that we had in that old house, and the surroundings

Patrick Flannery
Would you like to come back here to live in Graughill?

Pat O'Donnell
No I'm too long in America now. And my children are there so I wouldn't move back. I love Ireland but I don't think that I could come back to live in this area

Patrick Flannery
Did we change any bit? Or did we get worse?

Pat O'Donnell
Oh yes! The changes are great! Some people don't think that they are but I think that they are great.

Patrick Flannery
Do you remember the pub down the road, Joe McGrath's?

Pat O'Donnell
Oh yes I do

Patrick Flannery
And what did you think of Joe as a character?

Pat O'Donnell
Joe McGrath was quite a personality - he had none! And I don't think he had much character either! But he never did me any wrong

Patrick Flannery
He was a tough business man, yeah? Would you think that he was a good business man?

Pat O'Donnell
I would give him zero for a business man!

Patrick Flannery
But yet the people went into him though?

Pat O'Donnell
Because they had no other place to go!

Patrick Flannery
Tell me how long are you working in the pubs in New York - you must be a long time in the pubs?

Pat O'Donnell
Forty five years working in the pubs in New York

Patrick Flannery
Doing bar work?

Pat O'Donnell
Yes

Patrick Flannery
And still today?

Pat O'Donnell
And still today!

Patrick Flannery
So you don't mind me asking you Pat, how old are you today?

Pat O'Donnell
Seventy two and I still work five days a week

Patrick Flannery
Well you don't look it! And your kids are reared and they are nearby and all that?

Pat O'Donnell
Well one is in Vegas but not too far away really.

Patrick Flannery
I'll turn back to Anthony now. Do you remember Joe McGrath? The publican down the road?

Anthony O'Donnell
I remember him well

Patrick Flannery
Do you remember the old pub? I was told about the old pub, I don't remember it though they were telling me about it

Anthony O'Donnell
Neither do I but I got drunk there and he had to take me home in the car

Patrick Flannery
Is that right?

Anthony O'Donnell
Yes that's true

Patrick Flannery
And what was the old pub like?

Anthony O'Donnell
It was like the usual pubs in them times. Sometimes you could drink there all day and other times they would just throw you out and they'd let you back in again

Patrick Flannery
Would they put you out if you got drunk?

Anthony O'Donnell
Well they'd clear the place if there looked like there was going to be a bit trouble. If the trouble makers weren't in you'd stay outside and you'd go back in there and you could stay there all night, it would depend on what mood they were in

Patrick Flannery
When people got drunk would there be a lot of fighting?

Anthony O'Donnell
Well if you didn't see a good fight every weekend, there would be something wrong!

Patrick Flannery
Is that right?

Anthony O'Donnell
Yes, mostly between families about some sort of an argument that they would have had at home. They'd be a few scraps and they'd go in and

shake hands and drink together again for the rest of the night

Patrick Flannery
So they would forget about it the next day?

Anthony O'Donnell
They would forget about it the same night

Patrick Flannery
And were they good fighters? Were they well able to fight? They wouldn't hurt each other too much?

Anthony O'Donnell
Most of it was one bloke taking his jacket off and two blokes holding him and if they let him out he wouldn't fight at all! It was mostly to do with the actions!

Patrick Flannery
What did you think of Joe McGrath as a character?

Anthony O'Donnell
He used to serve me and once he brought me home. I didn't have a lot to do with him to be honest with you

Patrick Flannery
The reason that I am asking about him a lot is because a lot of people mention his name. That he was fun to go into. I remember, myself, to me, he was a comedian with the things that he would come out with in the pub. He used to love see people arguing and he'd be telling them to shut up to frig and he'd throw them outside the door. He used to draw more arguments in the pub than stopping them!

Anthony O'Donnell
Well yes there was that about him.

Pat O'Donnell
He was abusive?

Anthony O'Donnell
I didn't get involved or encouraged him

Patrick Flannery
But there were a lot of people around here that time. The villages had a

lot more people than now

Anthony O'Donnell
There always seemed to be a lot of people in the pubs in them days anyway

Patrick Flannery
We're in 2004 now and hasn't the population gone down an awful lot in Erris since?

Anthony O'Donnell
Oh yes it has definitely. There is only four or five in each house now

Patrick Flannery
You must find it a big change. Do you remember the first dance hall then, the first one in Erris?

Anthony O'Donnell
Let me think, the first dance hall in Erris. The McAndrew's had a dance hall there in Gortbrack, you also had a hall in Foxpoint. There was a dance hall there as well. A lot of them used to go to Aughleam, the other side of Belmullet to go dancing. And then of course you had Glenamoy

Patrick Flannery
We're going back to Pat now again. Pat I want to ask you about the women in them days. You said that they worked very hard, which they did, I remember even in my time and I'm the next generation up to you, they weren't allowed into pubs? You would never see a woman in a pub?

Pat O'Donnell
Well, the women did not go to the pubs. It wasn't that they weren't allowed, they just didn't go to the pubs in them days

Patrick Flannery
Was that the women's own decision in them days?

Pat O'Donnell
It was I would think. I wouldn't think that they weren't allowed, I would think that it was their own choice not to go to the pub

Patrick Flannery
Going to mass in them days, tell me about the women. Could they not go into mass without something over their head?

Pat O'Donnell
Oh yeah, they had to have a scarf or something over their head

Patrick Flannery
Was that the church or was it their own choice?

Pat O'Donnell
I think that was the church. It was the teaching of the church.

Patrick Flannery
And we'll say a woman in them days, would they wear a low neck dress? Or would that be allowed at the time? Would it be a long dress? Would they be allowed to wear a short dress?

Pat O'Donnell
There wasn't that much low neck dresses at that time or short dresses

Patrick Flannery
You never seen any?

Pat O'Donnell
No, not in the forties or fifties

Patrick Flannery
There was kind of restrictions on how to dress for the women?

Pat O'Donnell
It was a modest wearing clothes at that time

Patrick Flannery
Because I remember when I went to school, and that's along time ago, forty years ago, in the little school in Porturlin, I remember a girl coming in with jeans on her and it was the first time that I ever saw a girl in jeans at that time and the teachers put her out of the school because she wore them. I remember the mother coming up and gave out to the teacher over it. So there was restrictions on how you dressed at that time. It would kind of remind you now of how things are in the Arab countries, how the women wear the scarves around their face, wouldn't it remind you of something like that when you look back at it?

Pat O'Donnell
It was a part of the old cultures of Ireland which were similar to some of the ancient cultures of the Arabs or the Indians in America

Patrick Flannery
So our culture was a bit like that?

Pat O'Donnell
Yes our culture at that time was a little bit like that. Some of our old cultures, like the straw boys and the wailing at funerals and some of those things are basically like some of the cultures that the Arabs and the Indians of America had and have

Patrick Flannery
The funerals back them days, do you remember them, the funerals in the houses?

Pat O'Donnell
Yes, very well

Patrick Flannery
And did ye wait up until morning?

Pat O'Donnell
Going to funerals as youngsters, especially if the person that died was old, a night of telling jokes and partying and wait up all night!

Patrick Flannery
Was there crying at these funerals?

Pat O'Donnell
I never noticed anyone! We were having a ball!

Patrick Flannery
Ye enjoyed them?

Pat O'Donnell
We were having a party! Free cigarettes, bread and jam, tea. It would be a couple of party nights out. I remember them very well

Patrick Flannery
Back to Anthony again. What did you think of the funerals at that time?

Anthony O'Donnell
They used to have to keep the body in the house for a couple of nights and called it a 'wake'. We all used to go to the wake and we'd all sit around and as Pat said have free cigarettes, free pipe tobacco, most of them then smoked pipes anyway. And then to the church, most of them wore shawls, black shawls. The men sat at one side of the church and the women sat at the other side. Men and women didn't mix in them days in the church

Anthony & Pat
And it was the same with dance halls, especially the dances that the priest was at

Anthony O'Donnell
You'd have the men sitting on one side of the hall and the women on the other side and you'd have to go over and ask them to dance with you

Patrick Flannery
Did you think that religion was a bit too strong on the people? Or did it keep the families together? Was it a good thing when you look at today?

Anthony O'Donnell
When I think back on it, it was probably a good thing. Maybe it was a little bit too strict, they could have relaxed the rules a little bit

Patrick Flannery
But did it keep families together?

Anthony O'Donnell
I honestly think so

Patrick Flannery
Marriages especially?

Anthony O'Donnell
Yes I think that it did probably keep them together

Patrick Flannery
Would you ever hear of a break up of a marriage in them days?

Anthony O'Donnell
No, it wasn't even talked about

Patrick Flannery
When you married, you married for life?

Anthony O'Donnell
Indeed you did, whether it was good or bad you stuck with it. There was no second wives in them days

Chapter 9

<u>The Break-up of my Marriage</u>

1999 - Brought into court - 300,000 settlement
Opening an account with the Credit Union / Banks giving me
hassle
Helping a man with a drink problem - Gerry from Drum - AA in
Glenamoy
15th August and Doolough Races
Teresa McGrath's daughter Siobhan leaving Ireland to go to
Canada
Horse racing again
Changes in Belmullet
Rosary said at home when I was young
Liam O'Donnell story again - already on another tape
The way our parents brought us up
Food / Americans / Fast Food / Overweight
IQ / Irish Cailín
Food again

In 1999 I was brought into court by my ex wife to bar me from my own home. She claimed that I used violent language. The Judge listened to both sides of the story and the case was dismissed. And it went on from there. I was brought back into court again by her solicitors and barristers for settlement. They wouldn't settle for anything less than three hundred thousand or two hundred thousand and everything that was going. Through it all I was falsely arrested by the police on three or four matters because I raised my voice to my ex wife, to try and talk some sense into her. With that my place was forced for sale. My business was forced for sale. I had a booming business, I had built up a million and a half, maybe a million and three quarters of property here, that's what it was worth at that time. My borrowings with the banks at that time in 1999 were very low. There wasn't much outstanding, maybe one hundred and thirty thousand pounds at the time. When my business was booming out here, the bank managers came out here pushing loans on me, wanting me to take out more loans because I was a good business man and everything was booming. But as time went on in the court case, around 2000, my ex wife's solicitors summons the bank managers into court to make it look bad for me. All they wanted to do was to force me out of business and get a good deal for my ex wife's, to get as much money out of me as they could. They never thought of holding property, that there was family here, that the kids were here or anything. I feel that I was paralysed for about five years but I never went bankrupt to this day, July 2004. But I'm penalised since the banks came into the courts because there was no more of bringing Patrick Flannery out for dinner or offering any loans or back ups and they really closed down on me in a nice way. I have kept the doors open on my knitwear since. I have kept the place. I have painted the place. I have made a settlement with my ex wife and honoured it all. I am making offers to the banks to polish off the loans that they gave me to take off the penalties and charges. About a year and a half ago, in 2003, I opened an account with the local branch of the credit union. I had up to five and six thousand sometimes in that account. I put it in and took money back out and I applied for a loan for five thousand for my business and they refused to give me a loan. I applied for some loans from the banks to try to get myself back on track again and they also refused me. The reason the credit union refused a loan to me is because they are all local people who work there. I know them all. They know me because they heard about Patrick Flannery's place going up for sale and it's a small community and the rumour went around that Patrick Flannery had no more money. My friends disappeared as well from me. I felt that the people I had there pushing me and looking up to me when they thought that I had money, just drifted away. This morning I went to get a loan for my car for eighteen thousand with a house that's paid up to date. And I was called on my mobile, the appointment was for half twelve, to tell me not to come in that I wouldn't be getting the loan in other words. And I asked them why. They told me that I should know why. I told them that I didn't because I had enough security to pay off that eighteen thousand. And it saddens me that this could be done to somebody like myself, and a lot more people, that the banks have done that too. So the banks, to me, are very slimy and rotten business people. The only thing is that the sun is shining for me today and I'm still in business and I'm going to get where I want to go. I said to a bank manager one time "all you'll ever see is that little room, you made your own prison when you went to school to become a bank manager". Today I have freedom, I have life and I have all my property yet. It's worth probably up to two million, between land and I have one site for twelve houses that I am going to build here. And I am not going to step down for anybody or give in. I am going forward. I definitely know who my friends are. When I needed help there were very, very few. It doesn't sadden me because that is human nature. I was always there to help people. I gave money away to people when they were stuck, they'd come to me. I'd often help them along their way. I had a few friends that did give me a few pounds here and there, that I will be paying back to them. But I have great will to go on. Like when I built Flannery's Holiday Village and I still have that there. I'm happy that God gave me the strength and the will to go forward because if I had to let myself down, with all the refusals from the bank managers.

It's Thursday night and it's the 8th July, again a beautiful Summer's evening. And I'm just after getting a phone call from a fella who needs my help with his drink problem. He said that it was the end of the road for him and he couldn't see any way out of it. He's very depressed and he needs to talk to me badly tonight. I had other plans made for tonight but I've changed them and I will just go with him. I always go out to help out people if they need my help with drinking problems and that's what I'm doing this evening. And I'm just hoping to God that he will see the light and go off the drink. All I can do is carry the message to him and talk to him and help him the best way that I can. He thinks that the only one that can help him is me, but the only one that can help him is himself. I can show him the way and help him to try to stay sober. I am taking him to a meeting in Glenamoy tonight. He was talking to someone in the town who recommended that he'd come to see me if he wanted help to give up drinking. I hope to God that I will be able to show him the right road to sobriety. It's a curse of a disease, once it takes over your life, and I always said that if there was ever a devil, he was in the bottle! This is another poor person who has suffered from alcohol abuse so we'll see how we get on tonight.

I took Gerry to the meeting in Glenamoy and I am after leaving him at home now back to Drum. He broke down at the meeting and he cried and he said that he wouldn't be there only for me. He had asked me for help. I told him that I would help him but the way that he is drinking he will have to help himself as well, just to leave down that bottle and stop drinking. I told him that if he doesn't that he will die. He will die if he doesn't stop drinking because it is a big killer disease. To see him at the meeting tonight, and there was a lot of lads there tonight that I brought in to their first meeting, and now they are doing well. Some of them are sober now for five, six even ten years. And it's good to see that and it's good encouragement for me to give Gerry. I was able to tell him "That lad there is sober for eight years and I brought him to his first meeting. He was just like you, he just couldn't stop drinking. Look at him today, sharing with us how his life is so good for him. There is hope out there." I gave him hope tonight and I hope to God that He will leave His hand on him and that he will stop drinking and get his life back. I told him to try to clear his head. You could see around his home that it was neglected. It's a sure sign of an alcoholic, the lawns not cut, the grass overgrown on the streets. It's sad and he's only forty eight years old. I remember him years and years ago back in 'Palm Court'. He always drank but he was never as bad as he is now. I told him that he has reached his quota, that he has gone over his limit. When you cross over that thin line there is no going back. Alcohol takes over your life then so you either stop or die. And that's his choice tonight. I gave him my three numbers and I told him that if he thinks of going to the pub to call me. And call me every day, every hour even, just to take one day at a time and he will get sober and he can have peace of mind back in himself. I pray to God tonight that he will get that. I feel good tonight too that I can carry this message and help people along the way.

Well today is the 15th August and everybody is getting ready for the big fair today at Doolough Strands and we are getting the horse ready to go in the race today in the local horse race. I have taken the cup three times there and today I look forward to taking the cup again. We don't know yet how it will go. I suppose that there will be good horses there today. I'm thinking that sometimes the races are sold out for the bookies to make money. All I want to do is to win the cup, I am not too bothered about the money prize on it. I just want to win the cup this time again. I am looking forward today to taking the cup again for the fourth time, if I take it, and if I lose I'm a good loser anyway. Today has a lot of hype and it's nice. Everybody's excited about the races and they are asking me if I think my horse will win. I tell them that he will win! So they'll be twenty two races altogether. People come from all over, people that left here years ago and went to America and they come for this big day of sport in Geesala. It's a week to eight days of sport. Everyplace is booked out, all over Erris. Anyone that is doing B & B, the hostels and Flannery's Holiday Village are booked out and there's even people camping out on the lawns because they have no place to stay in Erris. People rang me up yesterday looking for places to stay but I didn't have any vacancies. They tried everyone, the hotels and everything and they had to go out to the Downhill Hotel in Ballina, an hour's drive, to be here today for the races. So there's big excitement today and tomorrow then is another big day, the 16th August. It's changed from the 15th until the 16th because of the races. Tomorrow, Belmullet town will be closed off. There will be people all over, they'll be games and sports for the kids. It's a big day for the kids. Indeed it's a big day for all the people to meet up with the people that left here years ago. The people that are living here in Erris you will meet them all here that day. It's a day to be looking forward to. I certainly am looking forward to it today and tomorrow. I am not too bothered whether I win or lose. It's just a sport. I've had my thrill; I've taken the cup three years in a row and today might be time to be giving it away. That's my story for today. I went over to check on the horse and he looks good. He is over in Pullathomas, at Paddy McGuire's stable, that's where we're holding him. I never saw it before but the trainer was giving the horse some medicine to boost him up and some poteen. So I don't know, he knows better than I do, but I think that when I took poteen I got drunk and I wouldn't win many races! I'd be always a loser when I took drink! But the horse might be better than me! Everybody is hyped up, Oliver McGarry is here. Chris McGarry that left here years ago and went to Chicago is here. Martin McGarry that won the Golden Gloves is here, boxers with their own boxing club out in Chicago are here with their whole family - there's about forty of them. There's great excitement and it's a thrill. For the trainers - they are in it for the money - Michael Flannery who looks after the horse there, 'Flannery Knitwear' - he's in it to make money and we're in it for the sport and the thrill. I think I get more of a thrill out of it than winning money so it's a good day. I hope that everybody will enjoy themselves and we're always praying that the day will stay good and dry. That's the sports from Geesala on the 15th August and that will be our day so we hope that it will go well and I'll fill you in on the day tomorrow.

August 2003 - Last night we were at a going away party for Teresa McGrath's daughter, Siobhan, that was going away with Anthony McGuire that came from around here. They are moving to Canada. They are a young couple, twenty-two and twenty. Teresa put on a big party there and I was involved too in it. I didn't do much of the work, Teresa did most of the work. We had a great night and it was half two when we finished. There was good music, loads of food, the sing song, the sadness of people going away. Years ago I remember people leaving like that, like Siobhan and Anthony, and some of them never returned. It's a lot easier now than it was thirty, forty or fifty years ago, when the people left from around here. But thank God their kids kept coming back. They kept the Irishness going and the same thing will probably happen with this couple, they will probably keep coming back. But to see them going away is still sad for Teresa, I'm sure. But they have the health to go away as I said to her and the world is very small anymore. Seven hours will have you home from Canada on a plane.

Years ago they went on the boats which took weeks and weeks to get there. So it's not as bad as it was years ago going away now. It's good to see that the youngsters have the ambition and the go in them to go and make a better life for themselves. It's their own choice to go to Canada and make a better life for themselves, which they will. It was nice to see all the people there last night, wishing them well, farewell cards for them and wishing them the best of luck. It was an enjoyable night. And I, myself, wish them the best of luck and as I said it's a small world anymore.

The horse race went very well in Doolough, Geesala. There was about fourteen races altogether. My horse 'Flannery Knitwear' was entered in the local horse race and we won the cup again, the fourth time in a row. It was a very proud and exciting day. One of the biggest crowds that was ever there to watch the horse racing. There was a lot of people clapping for my horse to win, supporting me through the race. I was all excited and it was marvellous. Last night then after winning the cup Willie Coyle brought out a bottle of champagne to congratulate us for taking the cup, from the most important race on the day. I had a few pounds won as well but then afterwards we were celebrating around the ring with the people that sponsored the cup years ago. Then we went into Geesala to the party that was going on all night there. We left there then and we ended up down in Paddy McGuire's where the cup was filled with whiskey and brandy and everybody got a chance to take a sup of the cup. I was asked up, by the McGuire family, to come up to the stage and to say a few words on the night. It was good to go up there and to praise the people that were responsible for it. It was a dream come true for 'Flannery Knitwear' to take the cup again, like Michael Flannery, my friend that looks after the horses and trains them. Then I sang a few songs on the night and the night went into the early hours of the morning. We had food and celebrations there, clapping for the speech that I made and for winning the cup again. It was nice to take it back home again to Pullathomas and to leave it in Paddy McGuire's pub for another year. There's another year over but the races were good and I'm proud of 'Flannery Knitwear' for taking the cup for the fourth year. August holds great excitement for me. Today then was the 16th of August and we went into the big fair, where people come from all over the world and celebrate Belmullet Street Festival. It's a big day in Belmullet every year and all the people attend. There are a lot of people with stalls and people selling their goods on the streets. Everyone meets up around the streets and shake hands with each other. Back for years since I was a kid going out dancing I see them now and I'm forty seven years old and they're still around at the same fair that we used to go to then. Back then we would go out to 'Palm Court' and dance for the whole night and that's on there tonight as well. There's loads of dances on tonight for the young people. It's great to see that the tradition of the Belmullet fair carries on, it's an old tradition and it's still carrying on. People used to come home especially for that and today they are still doing the same thing. It's great to see that and see people happy, everyone around shaking hands with each other and enjoying it and that they are healthy. Today anyway, was another big day for us. August is always a good month for me, I love it, going out and meeting people. People that come from America, England, Europe - all over Europe - Germany, everywhere, and they all seem to be gathering around Erris. Erris people that left here years ago coming back still to see this fair.

A lot of these people are amazed at the changes in Belmullet and all around Erris. The fine houses that people have, how they are better homes now than anywhere in the world, and all the restaurants in Belmullet. I remember going into Belmullet when we were young, twelve, thirteen years of age. There would be no place to eat except one place where they done teas and ham and bread and the queue of people that would be there to have that. It was a big thrill in them times, to get the ham. The ham was so nice and the bread and the tea and we were thrilled with that. But being in Belmullet now there's a new Chinese restaurant set up. There are a good few other restaurants, one better than the other, and you can have any food that you want now in the town. In them days, when we were young, and all the food was cooked at home but the change around again was for the best. Belmullet has changed. I was talking to people that left here thirty five years ago and how they were in at the fair and how they were amazed at the town and how it has changed, and the fine homes in comparison to the ones in America or anywhere in Europe. And we have better homes here now, we have more solid homes. They aren't wooden, they are built with blocks and plastered outside. They are all oil heated and have open fires. I would believe that we have better homes here that in America or anywhere else. It's marvellous. In a lot of ways these changes are for the best. Younger people today are living in a totally different world compared to when we were kids. I think in some ways they have a lot more but in other ways then young people today are very mixed up. Back in our time you didn't have time to be mixed up because we were out fishing when we were young, from eleven years of age onwards. We were out on the boats fishing and we always had duties and jobs to do. But today I think that it's a lot easier - for the mind is debatable, maybe for the mind we were better off then - but in the line of progress and jobs, they are away better off now. They have choices of jobs now.

Back when we were kids too the Rosary was always said at home. I remember my mother would have to sit between us when we would all be down on our knees because we would be making funny faces at each other. She would laugh and then she would tell me to get serious. But the Rosary was said at home and prayers. It's an old saying 'who prays together, stay together' and that's true and I think in that way we were better off. People did pray together and did stayed together. And we were happy in our own way. But I love to see the change too and am glad that I lived to see both sides of it. I've seen the way things were when we were growing up and how it has changed for the people that are growing up in this world today and the differences. I'm proud to have lived long enough to see that.

I was very fortunate with the way that my mother brought me up that she wouldn't be telling us to go out and make as much as we could or to do better than the neighbours. She always said that as long as we had our health, food on the table and a roof over our heads we were very rich. We didn't have to prove ourselves to anyone. We were happy that way.

The only thing that I can see with the food side of things, there's a much bigger variety today. I see an awful lot of the young Irish people, like the Americans now, overweight, too much weight on and that's from 'Fast Food'. I see that it's just starting in Ireland now. Youngsters are putting on more weight now like the Americans. An awful lot of Americans are overweight, like twenty to twenty six stone. They wear these tight clothes and the fat hanging out of them and I can see some of the Irish starting to go that way. In the next ten years if the Irish don't cop on to themselves and stop going down the road to fast foods, they will end up like that. I think the day of healthy eating is going from a lot of the youngsters and that's the only thing that I can see - we ate healthy and we carried that with us. We did all the cooking at home, most of the time, than eating out. The youngsters are heading down the road of burgers and chips and it's a bad road for them. If they don't cop on I can see a big problem with weight in Ireland in the next six to ten years.

One time I spoke on people's IQ and it's very important. When I look at today, there is a high, middle and low IQ. I see today that a lot of young women are losing the 'Irish cailín' that we were all proud of. They're losing that respect for themselves and for their bodies. I'm not saying that they are all like that but there are a lot of them. That's a sad road to go down. I see people who have travelled to America and indeed Europe who are all on to this Fast Food road. It's like letting these fast food chains into Ireland was a big mistake for Ireland to do. To let in McDonalds was a disaster for health. I believe that all the cancer that is arising in Ireland today, and indeed all over the world, is coming from these fast food places. Fast food that is the fastest way and the easiest way that we can get the better for us today and it's not, it's a bad road to go down. People should go back to the way that we were brought up - natural foods that we were brought up and reared on and you'd have less sickness and less cancer and better foods. The good healthy food from the sea, growing your own potatoes. Indeed when my kids were small I always had the potatoes and fish. Fish that I fished myself and in the wintertime when I wasn't fishing, the fish from the summer season was put fresh into the freezer. I always grew vegetables, I used to milk the cow, take the cream off the milk and make the butter for the kids. And the kids were far healthier. Today they tell me 'Jesus, Dad we used to hate drinking the milk from the cow'. But they did. And that's the way that I was brought up. If we didn't milk the cow we had no milk in our tea and if we didn't fish we had no fresh fish. If we didn't set the potatoes then we had no potatoes. So the potatoes were set and the vegetables. That was the healthy food that we were eating. I never heard of anyone dying from cancer in them years.

Chapter 10

Fighting for Justice and my Property

Investing with First Active, Castlebar
Police again calling - Court again - Speeding on my way to court
Rose as witness for my ex wife
Splitting everything 50 : 50 - Flannery Village going up for sale
My sickness
Barristers / solicitors / engineers
Judge calling out to my place - settling things at last - Judge not wanting to see case up in front of him again
2 solicitors working against me - hers and mine
Sheriff calling to my house to put me out
Michael Ring calling me
English landlords / Me speaking out for my country / Jealousy after the landslide
Break up of marriages - men going through hell
Mr. B calling to my wild life centre - hypocrites in Erris
Beauty of the Erris area
1 of my daughters, her partner, & their 2 kids with him.
Another fella with relationship problems / His girlfriend

Today is the 30th September 2004. I got a call today from First Active in Castlebar. About five years ago I made an investment of ten thousand euros. Today it's due to be drawn out. They told me that I had less coming back to me, about nine thousand. For the five years this investment was in the bank I didn't even got my own money back on it. The time that I invested it the bank manager came down to the house. He encouraged me, if I had any money under the blankets, to invest it with them. They were doing a five year investment at that time and you were guaranteed to double your money. But that's what I have coming back to me after my five years investment - less than what I put in. I think that the banks have tricked so many people with these investments. They make out that they are going to double their money by investing with them and it's how you are losing out instead of gaining. Then the First Active in Dublin called me yesterday because they knew that this was due to come through and they wanted money towards the loan that I had there. My solicitor advised me to sign the investment over to them, so you are damned if you do and you're damned if you don't. It's just such a con with the banks and frauds and that's what I'm doing today now. I'll be calling my solicitor later on this matter. The first solicitor that I had was fighting the case for the break up of my marriage. When I was brought into court and it went on for at least five years, and I'm just after finding out today that he's the solicitor that acts for First Active. So it was very hard for me to win a case. I'm also being told today that he acted for my ex wife's brother, so it's no wonder that my case lasted for four and a half years, being conned. It looks like my ex wife had two solicitors, she had my solicitor and her own working for her.

After being brought into court by my ex wife in early 1999 I tried to settle the best that I could for the sake of my family and my business and everything that goes with it. Every Friday she had to get so much money for house keeping, so much money for keeping the house and she didn't work since 1998 in the business. I came back from selling knitwear one day and I decided to come in and talk to her and try to talk some sense. I thought that for the sake of the kids and the family that it was the right thing to do. I was giving her a certain amount of money, on a settlement, for her to go and never come back and to buy a house for herself some other place. And I told her that she was destroying the whole family. She was the cause of it. She was the cause of me taking over a pub - putting my hard worked fishing money into it. I never wanted to do that, it was her idea to go into the pub. But anyway I told her everything that I had wanted to tell her over these years. Things that she didn't want to hear. Things that I don't think that she realised that I knew about her. It hurt her. I told her I loved my family, including her. I told her that some day she would be sorry. I walked out the door and I felt that I had lifted a load off my chest. I went back into my holiday home where I was staying at that stage because I had moved out of the home by then. That was the Sunday night. By Thursday night I came home about ten o'clock and my youngest daughter came over to me to see if I was going out that night or was I staying in. My ex wife had sent her over to me to see if I was going out again that night. My daughter didn't know what her mother was putting her up to. I didn't know at that stage that the police had come three times to my place that evening. I told her that I might be going over to McGrath's pub for a game of cards. I usually went over there to get out of the house and for a bit of peace of mind. I told Maria, my daughter that I would see her the next day. But when she left, I could see out the window that my ex wife was going off in the car with my daughter which I thought was strange. I went to McGrath's pub, and at that stage, I didn't know that the police had come again and had missed me. I came home about twelve o'clock and I was in bed shortly after that. At half one in the night a knock came to the door. I answered it and there were four police men at the door. They asked me "Are you Patrick Flannery" and I said "Yeah". They read me my rights and they said "You are under arrest for the abuse to your ex wife, Marian Flannery, and the threats that you made to her". I didn't know that she had told them that I had threatened to get the IRA to kill her. I just went with the police and I told them that I had done nothing wrong. So I was arrested, I was brought in and I was locked up that night. The next morning I was asked did I want breakfast and I answered "I don't want your dirty breakfast". I was taken to Kiltimagh Court that morning. I called my solicitor and he was there to represent me. The case couldn't be heard that day because it was the day that the settlement on the property was coming up. The solicitor got the case put back then until the next court case in Belmullet. I was bound to the peace. The police left me home. I had to be in Castlebar that same day for the settlement on the property. I left there without any sleep, torn apart, being arrested for no reason whatsoever. Even the police hadn't the right to arrest me but I didn't know at the time, but my solicitor should have known that. I remember coming home, I told the girls in the factory that if anyone phoned for me that I was on the mobile. I left then because I had to go to Castlebar for half past three for the settlement of the property. When I was going up the Glenisland Road to Castlebar, I was doing over one hundred miles per hour. I saw my ex wife and someone else in the car with her, going up the road, on the way into Castlebar town. I overtook them at about one hundred and thirty miles per hour. The first time that I tried to over take them, she wouldn't let me pass her, then I built up speed to one hundred and thirty miles per hour and I flew past her. I'd be guilty on that, dangerous driving. When I got into the court, I asked my solicitor "What time will the case be heard?" And he said "soon". The next thing was that two police men came in, one of them read me my rights again. And he said "You are under arrest for the attempted murder of Marian Flannery, for trying to run her off the road". With that they arrested me again. My solicitor told me to go with them. And I was put in a cell. The advice that my solicitor gave me was that if I didn't agree with everything that she said that he would no longer be able to defend me. He wouldn't be able to fight the case, because she had a witness, Rose from Bangor Erris, her best friend. She signed a statement against me saying that I did try to run them off the road. He told me that I would get three months in jail because I had no witness to say that I didn't try to run her off the road. Then the settlement went on without me because I was in a cell at that time and she still wouldn't settle on anything. She wanted the whole place to be sold, every bit of land, all the houses to be sold and the money to be split fifty : fifty, and all the bank loans to be cleared. My solicitor and barrister advised me to agree on that. And I wouldn't agree on it. I remember being in the cell on my own and asking my father, God rest him, who had died years before that, to help me. I felt so tortured, it was like that I had no one. Not even a solicitor or barrister to advise me. I was totally on my own. It seemed that her word was fully taken by them and by the police and my word was worthless. There were a lot of phone calls coming in then, in support from Northern Ireland. Lads that I knew and they were calling the police station to see what were the grounds for arresting me. There were more people calling from Belmullet and the surrounding areas. I remember the Sergeant coming into me one time and he said "If we don't let you out of here tonight, we'll have to put on more secretaries here to look after all the calls that are coming in". But my solicitor and barrister came in and they advised me to let the place go, that I was a young man that could start a new life somewhere else, to let go of every single thing that I worked hard for. I finally gave in. It was about nine o'clock that evening and I signed for the place to be sold, which is what she wanted. With that my place went on the market. They let me out of the cell that night then at eleven o'clock. I came down the road and I never felt as bad in all my life. Everything that I had worked hard for was gone. I felt that it was gone overnight. It was the hardest thing that I ever had to do, was to put the biro to the paper, to sign away my land - the property that I had worked so hard for. I kept thinking what this would mean to my kids, there would be no property for them. I had three kids. None of the barristers or solicitors ever looked at the kids, where they were going to live, if all this property was to be sold. Because my ex wife didn't care as long as she got her fifty per cent of the money. She never once thought of the kids at that stage. But two days later, the auctioneer came down here, to sell my place. He put the 'For Sale' signs up all over the place. It was Flannery Knitwear he was advertising for tourism all over the world, for holiday homes and Flannery's Village. That's what I had to look at after two days signing that. Passing that every day and looking at them signs for my place and it went on and on to try to sell the place. Of course she was trying to sell the place but what she didn't know was the fella that she was going out with was a con man, she couldn't have picked a worse man in Ireland to go out with. He brought two of his friends from

Donegal to buy my place. They stayed in McGrath's pub over the road the night before and they came out to my place when I wasn't there. I didn't know that time that they were coming, it was afterwards when I found out. A lot of people came and looked at it and tried to buy it. Indeed there was neighbours as well, a fella that was smiling every day at me and that I thought was a good neighbour, and wanted to buy a couple of the fields as well. I have seen Flannery Knitwear and my business give a lot of money to local people but I saw when my place went for sale that I didn't have too many friends backing me. I remember one woman calling me, she had a hotel in Belmullet, and she said that if there was anything that they could do, maybe to raise money to help me, or to give me money to help me out. She was very good. I'll never forget her for it. More people said that the place would be lost if I moved out of here. A lot of people had genuine concerns for the place being sold. An awful lot of them didn't care, when you're going down they would like to push you down more. Anyway the place wasn't sold and I'm still here. The case was dragged on for about four and a half years and it was nearly five years before there was any settlement. About three and a half years after that started, nobody had bought the place, I tried to make a settlement, as good as I could, with my ex wife but she wouldn't settle on anything. She wanted everything or nothing. She wanted the place to be sold. But she brought it into court again, several times, over the years and then finally she settled for two houses and a certain amount of money to be paid over to her. I settled outside the court on the day and she accepted that. I was left with all the debt and sarcoidosis, I'd say that I had this lung sickness since 1997, I suffered with it in silence. It is getting worse and I've had two operations and they found out that this is what I had. I was on ten steroids a day for about a year and suffered pain and stress with the whole lot of it. But I came out of that even though it was going on when I was going in and out of court all the time. But a year later or a year and a half later, my ex wife decided that she didn't get enough and she wanted land with each house, a half acre or thereabouts, with the house and another three quarters of an acre with the other house. She brought this back into court again to fight for this land. That went on and dragged on again. I will never understand my solicitor and barrister, they kept telling me to give her what she wanted. It went into court and I was only out of the hospital five or six weeks. The second time that she brought me to court to fight for this land, the Judge took it on himself that there was no agreement. He asked how my health was and my solicitor told him that I was on steroids. He took it on himself to come out to the place to see what my ex wife wanted. What was she looking for? He came out, five or six months later, and looked at the place. Her barrister, solicitor and engineer were there. It was just my solicitor that was there. But the Judge, after seeing what she was arguing about, went to Westport at three o'clock that day to court. We were there in the courts again and my solicitor told me to give her the land and that I would be rid of her then. Of course he said that the time we settled previously and here we were back in the court again. I finally decided that I would give her so much of the land. I couldn't give her the right away going into my sheds because I needed that area for access. I marked out what I was going to give her. My solicitor went over to her and she wouldn't accept it. She said that the Judge would decide. So ten minutes later the Judge came out and he said that he was glad that he took the time to go out to see my place. He seen where it was and that I had built it up for the family, which I stated from the start. I built it up for the family and he saw how the houses were faced, looking out over the sea, a beautiful view of the bay. He said that I could have build the houses anywhere in Mayo away from there and they would have sold faster and he believed that the settlement that was done two years before that, the settlement that we had already agreed on and signed, still stood. Her barrister jumped up. But the Judge stated "I'm ruling on this case and it stands as it was agreed two years ago and I don't want to see this coming before me again. I'm sorry Mr. Flannery that it has taken so long to settle this case but now it is settled". Her barrister jumped up again and said "What about the right of way to the septic tanks". The Judge replied "I'm sure Mr. Flannery won't mind you looking at your septic tanks anytime you want, as long as you don't damage the property". The case was finally finished. I walked out of that court that day, saddened, that they had dragged me through the courts for all these years. Such hatred and badness. I'm glad that it's over. And I'm trying to pick up the pieces now and trying to get everything back on track again. I feel that my solicitor didn't make a good deal for me, he didn't really fight the case. All he kept telling me was to keep giving my ex wife whatever she was looking for. It was like having two solicitors fighting against me - hers and mine! But time moved on and thanks be to God that it's over and I can move on with my life. I enjoy every day of my life now. When I get up in the morning, I am happy. I'm not the kind of person who goes out of their way to take money from others. If I wanted to I wouldn't have built up the properties at all, I'd have left the money in the bank. But the property, to look at today, is far better. I can move on with my life. The few neighbours that wanted to buy the land, one of them behind my back, were disappointed because none of the land was sold. It's still there. The farm is still there today. I keep sheep, chickens, ducks, geese, turkeys, all free range animals. It's lovely to walk over there and see these animals around the place. People still come there today to my open farm, from all over the world. I'm proud of that. That was my dream from the start, that Flannery's Village would be built the way it is now so that people could enjoy the beauty of it. I just get enough money to keep it all going and that's all I want out of it.

I think that the solicitors, barristers and my ex wife wonder how I hung in there after all the hell that they put me through. But I have good faith and good will to go on and that's what keeps me going today.

Well today is the 5th October 2004. Yesterday at six o'clock there was a barring order issued for one of my houses that my ex wife lives in. First Active got a court order against me. Two weeks ago I paid them seven thousand euros to try to pay off some of the debt. I was trying to negotiate finishing paying them, to buy out the house. They called in the police and they arrived at my house at half ten this morning. We barricaded the road coming into Flannery's Village. They had to stay outside the walls with the police and we were inside. There was about thirty people gathered, mostly my relations, nieces, brothers, cousins, sisters and we defied them to come in. It was like the Battle of the Bothreen all over again. They wanted to evict us out of the house and this time we won the battle because I told them, that if they crossed the wall, that I would kill them. I was prepared to rot in jail for the life of one or two of them police. But they didn't cross the wall, they were cowards behind it all. We stood there. Declan Healy brought down sandwiches to us and chickens to the knitwear factory. We would have waited there for a full year but they weren't going to come into my property and take anything off me. My solicitor called me in the meantime. I told him that there was going to be a blood bath there unless that they were to accept twenty-five thousand for sixty-five - that they would write off forty thousand or they wouldn't see another cent. They had brought the sheriff to put us out of our houses. After the stand off, from eleven o'clock until three o'clock, they backed down and left. A phone call came through after ten minutes to say that they would back off for two months. It's a very sad day for me to see the banks trying to take my property. I have taken all that I am going to take. They tried to destroy my business and take my property.

DRAWING SICK MONEY, SOCIAL WELFARE AGAIN

Michael, who is involved with politics, called me today and told me how sorry he was to hear what happened to me. And if there was anything that he could help me with that he would. Except money, he didn't have the money to give me. But I never asked him for money, I never asked anyone for any money. But I'm going to come out of this, please God, and everything will be fine.

I had a call today from a protestant girl in Dublin. I told her what happened. I helped her out through her problems one time and she told me how sorry she was. She didn't think that these things go on these days. One time the landlords used to put people out of their homes now the banks are doing it. It's a sad day for Irish freedom. All my life I have been an Irish republican. I spoke out for the freedom of this country. I backed the freedom of this country since I was nineteen years old. Just to think the English did it to us then, our own people are doing it to me now. I always said that until the English leave this country there will never be peace. But before you would be able to beat the English you would have to shoot a lot of the Irish. A lot of the Irish in this country were spies, spying on their own people, jealous of their own people, the same as my neighbours are today. After the landslide here in the Pullathomas area, I was talking to a lady yesterday whose house was involved in, and she was talking about the bad feeling after the landslide. Such evil that set in it, the jealousy that was there. One of them afraid that the other one would get more money than them and all they were doing was talking about each other. That night we could have lost our lives. That was the attitude they had. It's sad. It's like the devil is amongst them. Money to some people is their God. I could never say that, that money was my God.

I've been down to my mother's grave and said my few prayers. I miss my father and mother. I went there to see Willie Doherty's pub where my father used to drink and I seen a relation of mine there that was supporting me today on the blockade. His marriage is breaking up and God love him he is just drinking himself to death, it's like he can't face it. The break up of a marriage and what men are put through is hell. Men are put through a lot more than the women and sometimes the women don't realize they're doing it. That they wouldn't try to come to some sort of an agreement and not let it into the court. Because when you go to court you are put through hell. The solicitors don't care about feelings or families, all they care about is money. Today has been a bad day for me but in one sense it has been a good day. We stood up for what I believe in and the rights of people. In this country in the next eight or nine years I believe that you will see every man, woman and child out on the street, fighting for their rights. Because the rights of this country are sold out. With all the laws that have been brought in, all the judgements against people, people put out of their houses. The banks are evil. What happened in my case, if it was in court, the Judge would probably throw it out because I didn't refuse them. I paid them up to seven thousand ten days ago and then they came and tried to take the house afterwards as the rest of the payment. There's corrupt law in this country. I always believe that you have to stand up and be counted. Today if they came in on my property and to try to break down that door to take the house, may God forgive me, but I would have killed one of them or two of them. And I still will do it if I have to. I believe that this is wrong.

The next day the sheriff called me up and told me that he thought it was wrong what was happening to me but that he would have to do his job. He had to come out to me because the bank sent him out. They wanted me into Belmullet barracks to sit down and negotiate with the bank. I had already made a one off settlement with the bank. There was only fifty thousand involved and I was giving them thirty two thousand. He said that he wasn't aware of that and that if he had known it he wouldn't have come out otherwise. But he was trying to cover his own arse. He has called me several times since to say that they got an awful shock when he came out to my place and saw all the men that were inside. All the cars out at the front of the drive coming into the holiday village, that they wouldn't get in anyway, the only way that they could have come in was across the wall. I've told him that if he or the police had crossed the wall that I would have killed one of them, that I meant it. I had good back up there with me as well. We were ready to fight if they came in. He said that in the twenty five years that he has been working there that he never came up against that. And he said "I'll hope that we'll be able to negotiate because I don't want anything to do with it". To me he is only a coward, just a fucking low life coward. He's no better than the English landlords that killed the people on the very land I own now, years ago when they couldn't pay their rent of the house and the Battle of the Bothreen. They were acting for the English landlords at the time. I said to him "There's no difference between you, ya bastard ya, and the English landlords. And it's the same way with the police in Belmullet. There's three of them in there to protect the Sheriff". They wouldn't be able to protect him anyway the way that I had organised myself on the day. If somebody crashed along the road, or if there was a fight in a pub, and you called these police in Belmullet, there would be no way that they would come out. But they came to protect their sheriff and their law, to put somebody out of their house. I did tell the sheriff that I thought they were scum bags with dirty low jobs (I know there are some police that wouldn't want to do that dirty job) that it wasn't a case that I wasn't going to pay them. I was negotiating with the solicitor and the bank at the time. But the solicitor that I had for them five years of in and out of court by my ex wife was also acting for the First Active bank, the bank that came out with the sheriff for my property. And he was behind it because he knew that this was happening. I didn't know anything about this until about five o'clock the evening before when I received a registered letter stating that they were going to evict my ex wife out of the house. I could have stood back and let them take the house. It wasn't my house, I was out of the house at the time. But I wasn't going to let them take her out of the house, or to take over the house either. The negotiations are still going on with the bank. They wrote to my solicitor two days later to refuse the settlement. So now it looks like it's going back into court again. I have changed solicitors since and I hope that he will do better by me than the last one. I'm prepared to go into court, I don't mind going to jail for something that I believe in. But I won't let anyone walk over me or my rights. When I say my country is sold out, a country that since I was nineteen years old, stood up as an Irish republican, and sympathised for the IRA, for the cause of the freedom of this country, and then when I look back on my situation, I just think that it was English working through the Irish again. A lot of this country was sold out by the Irish themselves.

The sheriff keeps calling me all the time. He says that he likes to keep in touch with me because he doesn't want to do this dirty job. The reason for that is that he is not man enough to do his job, the dirty job that he took as a sheriff, evicting people out of their homes. I told him "they should never send a child to do a man's job". That's the way that I see it. They are not able to do their job. I am not here to break the law but I'm not going to be used by the law either. The law in this country and indeed in a lot of countries, can never be trusted. They are frauds in amongst the law. A lot of people have been haunted all their lives by the law because the law picked on the easy target. I certainly wasn't one of them. God gave us all freedom in this world. The freedom to do what we choose and that's not to walk over people. In this case, I am not. I saw a lot of neighbours around as well, looking at what was going on and going around with the news then, that the police were there trying to evict us out of our houses. But I didn't see too many of them neighbours coming to help me when I needed them and that's the type of people that they are. They love to see people going down. But the only thing that I did say to a nosy postman that came "I always lived my life for what I believed in and worked hard and I have build up seven houses in this village so they cannot put me out of them all and I'm not asking to take anything for nothing, only what's mine and in this case the bank was wrong".

I must say that I don't owe the banks what they are accusing me of owing them. When the banks were summonsed into court by my solicitor and my ex wife's solicitor too, that day they tried to bankrupt me. They were no longer going to trade with me, they closed down all my accounts. My life savings, my insurance, my pensions - I had to sign them over to the banks at that time. I found out later that I shouldn't have had to sign over anything to them without coming to an agreement with them because I didn't need them again. So what they did in my case was put interest on interest and charges on charges and they shouldn't have. When they showed their evidence in court they should have ceased the accounts and interest should have been ceased also from that day to give me a chance to pay them back the borrowings that I had from them. But they didn't do that, they were so greedy. They wanted my business to be finished and also wanted me to pay back loans and interest on loans and borrowings that they had already closed down when they went into court against me with the ex wife's solicitor. So it's only a couple of years after that after getting advice from another solicitor that he advised me that I wasn't denying the loans but the interest and charges that they put on me when my business wasn't trading. That's the argument that myself and my new solicitor have with them. We are trying to come to an agreement, I have offers made to the banks to settle with me. The only bank that did come down on me to take my property was the bank that my old solicitor worked for because he was acting for the bank as well as me. When you go through things like this, you'll find that it's the ones you trust, like your solicitor and your barrister, the few friends that you would have in these cases and they would be very few, they'd all be pretending to be your friends and that they were for your good, but the most of them take pleasure in people's grief and people that's losing business and going down. When you're in a situation where you are dragged into court for five years and you are trying to hold onto the business, the property for your family, you are weak.

I feel saddened when I think about the old solicitor that I had. I did trust that solicitor. I feel saddened that he led me down the garden path. He talked down at me, very much. When I would go to him for advice or phone him up, he treated me like a child, that I had no brain at all. It was impossible to deal with him, even though I trusted him and believed him. I did what he told me to do, it was only afterwards that I found out that I shouldn't have done what he said. I should have left and got another solicitor. At least my new solicitor listens to me. He has a better understanding of the problems. He listens to me, to my side of the story and then he gives me advice on it. The old solicitor wouldn't listen. He said, and I had to listen. Any idea that I came up with wasn't important. I wonder sometimes was he looking down on me because I couldn't read or write. You will get educated bollocks that look down on someone like me who cannot read or write, and knowing inside in my own head that I would lose and find him. Maybe that's what happened in this case, he thought that I was stupid, that I wouldn't be able to come up with an idea. It would have to be his idea and that's what he done to me and he did me a lot of harm. But I'm going to come out of this ok, my kids will have homes out of it. I will have a home out of it. I'm proud of the work that I have done in that area. It saddens me sometimes that it had to come to this. That your place is broke up, your business is effected, but through it all, I never closed the door to my business. Flannery's Knitwear is still open. The sweaters are in there to be sold and that's what I intend to do.

I remember one fella coming down to my house one time when I was going through a bad time. He came down with a cousin of mine. He was from the Belmullet area, he was a local businessman from Belmullet. I wouldn't call him 'Mr'. He'd run across the street to shake my hand, he was such a nice man. He started talking to me and I thought that I could trust him. I explained to him how I built a stone building and I turned it into a wildlife centre and I got a thirty thousand grant for it, back in 1998. Just because I was under such pressure with solicitors and barristers and trying to hold onto my business and family, try to keep their homes. I explained to him that I took the wildlife stuff out of the stone building and I put it into the Knitwear factory, up on top where the tourists could see it. I turned the stone building into a holiday home - I had no choice. And he agreed with me. Six or seven weeks after that man being in my house drinking tea and eating my food, the Leader fund that funded me for the grant aid, came down on top of me, that I had changed the wildlife centre into a house. I would have to pay back the grant. And they sent me out several solicitor's letters and at the time there was nothing but solicitor's letters coming in. I could never figure out who did that to me. Then of course I thought that it was the ex wife or her solicitor but when I asked my solicitor about it, he told me not to worry about it. But these boys wanted their thirty thousand grant paid back to them. I had to put all the wildlife back again into the building and I had to take it out again later when they got off my back. Just to try to survive. Then later I went to the Freedom of Information, a friend of mine brought me there. I wanted to find out who reported me for the wildlife centre. It shocked me to find out that the man that sat in my kitchen, that I welcomed into my home, reported me for the wildlife centre. I thought that was sad. This is the type of some of the neighbours that we have in Erris, they are the nicest people to your face and behind your back they are hypocrites. They would go twenty miles just to gossip about other people and I would say that a lot of people in Erris are like that. They aren't bad but it became a way of life to some of them. But there are a lot of good people in Erris that more than make up for the bad ones. They would try to help people in need, good Catholics. Some people are the first to go to mass every Sunday, go up receiving and these are the type of people that go out the next day and talk about the neighbours. They live on people on the way down, the worse the news is the more they like it. They go up then and receive Holy Communion. To me, people that do that are hypocrites. It saddens me because we were not brought up that way, we were brought up well by my father and mother, thank God. They taught us how to go out and help people if we could, not to ever harm people. To do the best we could for people. I've done that. I help an awful lot of people, anyone that knocks on my door in need I help them. People that ring me up for help, I go to them, I would go any length to help them. I always speak out for the area with the media, for the Pullathomas area and the surrounding area, indeed all of Erris. The beauty of the whole thing is that I'm glad I did too because it is beautiful, it's one of the nicest parts of Ireland, the Erris area, Belmullet area, Blacksod area, Pullathomas area. All along from Céide Fields to Belderrig has lovely scenery. The reason I stayed around this area is because I love the landscape and scenery - it wasn't for of some of the people I came across. But today I pray for the them people. I pray for people that lives on the grief of other people. Not just mine, I'm only one person in Erris that has gone to hell and back. The only thing that I have to be grateful about is that I see the light at the end of the tunnel for me to go on. And that's what keeps me going. To see two neighbours watching, and loving seeing the police at my place and wanting to see what was happening. I wouldn't like to be depending on them neighbours. /

At the end of my years fishing I had one crewman that came from Rossport and he done a lot of damage to my family. My oldest daughter was only thirteen at the time and the damage he done to her went to the high courts in Dublin. It was dragged through the courts for two years. The case was put aside and never finished. And my daughter never got justice. And I believe today that it had a big part in breaking the family up. The man that done the damage to my daughter was represented by Barry White, the best barrister in Ireland. He was able to get him because his brother in law was in the police force. And his wife's first cousin was in the police force as well. He admitted in court and on a statement that he done the damage that he did to my daughter but, as I said, the case was put aside and never finished. And he was also protected by the law in fear that I would kill him. I was looking for him for the right moment everyday to pay him back for what he done to my daughter. The moment came, I was five yards away from him with a loaded automatic rifle, ready to kill him when my friend that was with me told me to think about it before I shoot him and think about his wife and kids - because he's only scum and he'll be looking over his shoulder for the rest of his life. He told me to leave him for another day. A lot of the local people supported him even brought him back out fishing for a living again. I sold my fishing boat after that and never went back out fishing even though I love the sea. A couple of years later he tried to do the same thing to another lady in the Rossport area. She reported it to the police and still nothing was done.

It's a beautiful Sunday, October 2004, I'm down at Rinroe at my father and mother's grave, saying a few prayers for my good parents that showed me nature, taught me not to be jealous, not to hate people and they taught me how to be strong as well. I won't be a door mat for anyone. I was never the one in my family to live off sadness or to hurt other people. We always reached out and tried to help people if we could. But it's changed now compared to what I was used to. It's like the nature is gone out of people. A lot of them hasn't the nature that the older people had, they seem to be losing that. There's more greed and evil in people now. They are jealous of each other, talking about each other. They are big changes compared to the past.

Today is a new day and we're ten weeks away from Christmas Day. I went up past Paddy and Bridgie McGrath's Pub, way up on the hill, looking at where the landslide was and out over the Atlantic Ocean, out towards Erris Head. Today is a dark, wintry looking day. The winter is here now. I'm looking out here on the nearest point to America, the tower here on Glengad Hill. We are right out at the ocean here, we see the winter but it still brings it's own beauty, even if it is winter time. The sky is so different, the sea is so different, cold looking waves but it's still beautiful. It's a busy day today, there's hardly a day that I don't get a call from somebody looking for help and advice. People that are in trouble with drink, looking for advice on business or relationships. Today I was talking to a fella who is in a ten year relationship with his girlfriend and they are breaking up. I am friends to both of them and they are both talking to me today and I'm giving them the best advice that I can. By listening to both of them, they just need space in their lives. I think that their relationship will be fine and I gave them the best advice that I can. I pray to God for both of them for guidance. I get a lot of that in my life, especially since I got sober, in the last seventeen years. People trust me to counsel them on different things like marriage and drink problems. There's a lot of drink problems in this area. But not these two today, neither of them drink. But it's good to be able to help people and give them the best advice that I can. They trust me because they know that I don't go around talking about them the next day or the next hour. What people tell me will go to the grave with me. It's good to be able to do it. I think I give them strength by talking to them. The fella is stronger now than he was yesterday evening when he broke down crying. To see a grown man of thirty years crying is sad. It's how the lady wanted space in her life. There was a third party involved. She had another fella that she met six weeks ago and she started telling this fella her problems and that she was unhappy. He's separated so he gave her the wrong advice. Her boyfriend found out about it, he heard a message on the phone where she told the other fella that she loved him. But I hope and pray that they will get it together.

Interview 5 Mid-West Radio

<u>The Break-up of My Marriage</u>

Interview on Radio and the price I paid for it afterwards
2 Children fighting with me over interview
Guards involved
Not letting me see grandkids
Maria standing by me
Good day for me - Tideway moving into my offices - forty
thousand euro
Flannery's Village & Holiday Homes - Guests staying / Nature /
Animals /
August in Erris / Fair Day & Races in Geesala

Mid West Radio Interview - The Prime Time Programme

Tommy
Patrick, Good morning and thanks for talking to us How are you?

Patrick
Fine

Tommy
You saw Prime Time last night?

Patrick
Yeah, I did Tommy, I watched it last night

Tommy
And were you surprised?

Patrick
No I wasn't but I think it's a shock and it's terrible what goes on in people's homes. The abuse that those ladies put up with and how the law did nothing about it

Tommy

Just to let listeners know that the Rotunda was the hospital that was the focus of the investigation by Prime Time. The doctors there were saying that about twelve per cent, in other words twelve of every one hundred, pregnant women who come in, have been abused. Either physically or sexually, battered, just sexually abused whilst carrying children and so on. I suppose it was a case of the doctors crying wolf this time and that it is time to expose this. Isn't that what Patrick the whole programme was about?

Patrick

It was yeah. It is high time because it goes on in an awful lot of houses. And it's not just women, it goes on with men as well. So like I suffered abuse at home and I had to leave my home over abuse. I was nearly stabbed with a knife a couple of times and getting the hot cup of tea thrown in your eyes. I'm a man and men do suffer abuse as well. But I think that this barring order is abused by some of these women that do such a thing. They use the barring order to cover themselves and then there are an awful lot of genuine women then that are really abused. The law is not doing anything about it because these people that rape these women, these husbands that batter these women, should be getting jail sentences, they should not be let go at that

Tommy

Of course they should be getting jail and this was a point being made by a judge last week, John Nealon, up in the Midlands. Where a woman retracted her statement about the abuse she suffered at the hands of her partner or husband. Then at the last minute when she was looking for a barring order and the judge said "Look you're not doing yourself or society any favours by letting him off"

Patrick

No, no I think it's terrible but I'm going back to my case, I suffered abuse as well. It's a thing that will affect you for the rest of your life

Tommy

I'm sure very few people actually believe that you suffered abuse

Patrick

No Tommy because I'm a man and you just don't because they will be saying that I'm talking rubbish. I had to leave my own home from abuse and then my ex wife went in and made a complaint against me and I was arrested. I was taken out of the home and brought in and arrested.

She was making out that I abused her, which I never did at the time. I never abused her

Tommy
And was the allegation sexual abuse of physical

Patrick
No, no it was just that I gave out to her and the police arrested me and kept me over night. I was arrested again when she made another complaint on the same thing. I think the law is terribly unfair. I got no justice no more than them poor women that suffered from abuse and I suffered from abuse as well. I was dragged through the courts for six years and I lost my business over it and I lost my health over it. It upset me last night just to think that we have no one in this country with the law so corrupt because they don't follow these things up. They should have, even in my case, looked into somebody that was stone mad and that's the words I would call it, totally unreasonable. And they should have checked this out and charged them and the same thing with these poor women that was on that programme last night. Their men should be locked up for doing things like this

Tommy
And when you were brought in for questioning, would you be put into a cell?

Patrick
Oh yeah, I was kept overnight, I'll never forget it. I was kept there overnight and let out in the morning with no charges. Even the police said "well we know that you didn't do it, she is the one with the problem". A couple of the police told me that. And yet they came again and took her word again and arrested me again

Tommy
But once a complaint would be made wouldn't there be a nonus on the Gardaí to investigate it?

Patrick
Of course there should be but they never do. They never ever do

Tommy
So when they questioned you, for example, when she said that you had verbally abused her, and you were questioned and you said that you hadn't done it, they let you off, nothing else happened?

Patrick
Not at all

Tommy
No apology from any party to say "look we upset your routine, we kept you overnight in the cell, sorry about that"

Patrick
No, no nothing and that was twice that that happened to me. I feel very bitter and when I was there last night, I'll tell you, the tears rolled down my eyes because I know what these women are suffering. I never hit my ex wife in my life or I never hit a woman in my life because we weren't brought up that way. We were brought up that to hit a woman was a cowardly way. But I know even when I go out to help people in different things and I see the abuse at home with alcohol in the home. And the wife scared and being bet and it's terrible. It's terrible that it goes on and the police or the law are not doing anything about it. There are a lot of these law people who are doing it themselves, abusing their wives at home. it's cowardly. The Judge is looking at letting these people go, because from listening to that programme and what happened to me and what happens to an awful lot of people that I have met since, it shouldn't be going on. These people should be locked up in jail. These people are insane to do such a thing

Tommy
Have you got your life back together again?

Patrick
I haven't, I'll be honest with you but I am trying to. But I haven't. And I was dragged through the courts then for six years and I lost my business over it. The only thing I have is my kids, thank God and they are going on with their lives. No I haven't and I never will get over what happened to me. There's a thing I'm doing on tape, I do it every day about my own life, since I was a child. And that is helping but when I play the tape and listen to it, I played it the other day, and I said I'll hate these people for the rest of my life. I'll hate them to hell

Tommy
Hate what people?

Patrick
Well the law and what my ex wife done to me. And these women that were on there last night, listening to them, they will never have a life

back. Even if they go into another relationship, it's always there, they cannot get their lives back proper. I think that society has failed these people

Tommy
So would you say that your confidence as a person is shattered?

Patrick
Yes of course

Tommy
And would you go into another relationship?

Patrick
Well I'm in a relationship at the minute, I'm working on it. But it's never easy because you are never the same again. I left my house, I'll never forget it, at half one in the night where my ex wife was gone lunatic, firing everything at me and threatening knives at me. I ended up at the doctor at one stage, I mean, like one time I wouldn't talk about this, but it's high time that people come out and do talk about it. And these people should be charged because they shouldn't be left in society, some of them. I feel very sorry for these - I was talking to a man yesterday whose marriage is over now because he has to leave his home because he was abused

Tommy
By his wife?

Patrick
By his wife, violently abused so you have both sides, there's men as well

Tommy
You are in the minority, you'd accept that?

Patrick
We are, yeah we are. I was talking to a close friend I know and I couldn't believe it that he put the knife to his wife's throat and I only heard that the other day, through a friend. And he pulled her down on the floor by the hair on her head because she hadn't fucking food on the table or something for him when he wanted it. So yes it's terrible. But I blame the law for a lot of this because they are closing their eyes to this

and when somebody gets killed then, well…

Tommy
..there's uproar

Patrick
There's an uproar, and they'll arrest him and he'll get away because he lost his temper or she lost her temper

Tommy
It's a huge issue

Patrick
Well it is but I thought in Ireland in society that we were more educated now besides this thing going on but I think that it's worse now

Tommy
By the way did you get any help, any professional help afterwards?

Patrick
No I didn't

Tommy
Or are you with AMEN or any of those groups?

Patrick
Sorry?

Tommy
Are with any of the groups like AMEN?

Patrick
I'm not, no

Tommy
So you're trying on your own?

Patrick
I am yeah, well I do counsel a lot of people. I go to AA and I help a lot of people through drinking problems and everything

Tommy
And did you have a drink problem?

Patrick
I did yeah. I gave up drink eighteen years ago

Tommy
Right

Patrick
I did but I didn't drink until I was twenty

Tommy
Anyway look, it sounds like you could nearly write a book?

Patrick
Well I am doing that and that's why I'm doing my tapes and I'm writing my book and I think it's sad. The thing is that I could have left my home a long, long time ago but my kids were young and they're grown up now. My youngest is nineteen, the eldest one is twenty-eight so my kids are reared now.

Tommy
Alright, listen the clock has beaten us but thank you Patrick

Patrick
Thanks Tommy

END OF INTERVIEW ***

After being on the radio, on Mid-West Radio, on the Tommy Maaron Show, and speaking out on about people that abuse at home. I was talking about men and women that suffer abuse at home and violence. I didn't go on the radio just to get one back on my ex wife. I was just speaking about what I went through myself.

Well today is the 31st May and I've been talking about my family and kids. It's the day after this happened. Today has been a good day for me. Tideway - a company that's working offshore for Shell - signed a contract with me today for five months for forty thousand euros. So God is working for me today and works every day for me. That will help me to pay up some bills and move forward. They are taking over the Flannery Knitwear premises. Well most of the factory there, except my shop will still be there to sell the knitwear. - I'm very happy with that. They are a nice bunch of lads that will be working there. They have all computers in my place, they'll be about twenty of them there with offices and computers. I will be there also with my knitwear and crafts. So when you are down one day there's something good the next day. I am moving on as usual. I don't let things get to me too much. A lot of times things do hurt me. But today I've seen my grand kid with the mother in Belmullet and they smiled at me. My other two grand kids that are across the road shouting across at me. Things move on and we all have to move on. Things get better. I always look at the bright side. Time is always a good healer. So today has been a good day for me, signing the contract for five months for forty thousand is a happy day again for Flannery's Village. I always have something going on in here. I have people also staying from Northern Ireland in one of the holiday homes, another one from Germany. I have Americans staying in another one of my holiday homes as well, from Florida. They are enjoying the walks on the hills here and walking along the shore, overlooking the beautiful ocean. All of my houses have a view to the sea. Yes there are happy moments. In my life there have been more happy moments I suppose than sad ones because I always say 'think positive' and no matter what I always smile. I look at the good side. Today I am also looking out at the animals in the field, the different breed of sheep I have - the Jacobs, the black sheep, the white faced sheep and also the donkey and the horses. And a baby foal that was born on the farm about a week ago. It's lovely to see them all and the chickens, the geese, the turkeys and the ducks walking freely on the farm. These people that rent my holiday homes see all that, it's all in Flannery's Village, all the animals and nature. After talking to the Americans yesterday, they were telling me that they felt so at home with nature, looking at the animals. And getting the eggs from the farm, I brought some eggs that my chickens had to them as well, free range eggs. Nature is a wonderful thing and speaking to the couple from Florida, they agreed. They loved to be among nature and the peace they have here. And they had heard of this Flannery's Holiday Village before they came here, from their son who was here visiting before. It's their first time in Ireland and they are out here with me in Flannery's Village. And I love to see people coming to enjoy the gift of the place. The freedom of the place, the beautiful walks and scenery that we have here to offer them. I love to see people enjoying the work that I did and the building of the properties. It isn't all about money for me. I never set out that I would ever take the last penny off any tourist that comes to me. I always try to give them all a deal, as good as I can. They say that my holiday homes are very cheap. I love to see people coming here and enjoying the place. It gives me a good feeling that I've done something in the place that people can enjoy. That makes it wonderful. It gives me a lift in my heart to see people looking and talking about the place and telling me that they had a great time here.

I walk over every evening, just before it gets dark. I walk around the place, the factory and up the road but I still miss the grand kids. Some nights when it's late and the lights are on I'll walk up there. I can see Mark and Collie and sometimes Nathan and the other grand kids in through the window. I look in at them and it's very hard because I do love the grand kids but I don't want to cause any problems for the kids. If they see me, they would want to be with me. My son and daughter are still mad with me because of the interview that I did on Mid West Radio about abuse. It's the price that had to be paid and it's me that's paying the price because they are keeping the grand kids away from me. It's not right. Sometimes I look at them kids across the way and I know that they want to be with me. I know it's not good for me to be going up and looking in the window at them because I can see them inside playing. I think that I don't know anymore what's in my kids heads for doing this to me. It's their way probably of punishing me but it's the wrong way. They will realise it when they are older that it was the wrong way, but I'll never blame them for it. I'll always love my kids and my grand kids and I just hope for the best. Time heals but for now I will have to keep away because they've told me not to go near them or the grand kids again. I've enough problems and I don't want to be making problems for my kids. If that's their choice then I will have to do with it. They are old enough now to make up their own minds. But it saddens me sometimes that this is the only way that I will see the grand kids, by looking in the window at night. But thanks be to God they are healthy. They are young kids yet but because I haven't seen them for a long time now I could see the changes in them last night. And their parents are looking after them well and that's good too.

I was talking to my other daughter Maria the other day and I was worried about her because she was going in for an operation in Naas. But when she called she said that they wouldn't be bringing her in for three months. She was delighted. I talk to Maria every day and that's great. She is very close to me. She has been like that since she was a little baby. We always got on, we discussed things and we could talk about everything. I always listen to Maria as well because she is a very level headed young girl. She's a great little girl. She used to follow me around when she was a little girl. She worked with me in the knitwear shop. She showed great interest in what I done. She looked up to me. She's a proud little girl but a very, very good girl. I miss her because she is in Naas a lot of the time but I'm always close to her. I know she has to do her own thing in life as well and I respect that. You have to be on the sideline for her and that's what I do and the other kids as well. If they ever need me. It's just good that I have her there and that she talks to me on the phone. She'll come home for August now and I'll be looking forward to that. I like August always here in Erris. The people that left here return in the month of August. You'll meet up with them out at the festivals in Belmullet and Geesala. I'm looking forward to the horse racing at the Geesala Festival. In the past four years I have taken the local cup in the Horse Racing Competition and I'm looking forward to taking it again in 2005. It's a big day out. Between eight and ten thousand people gather back there on Doolough Strand for the races. The horses come from all over Ireland for it. The horse I have will be racing in the local horse race and that's the big one. There's big celebrations for it - it's like the Galway Races! People place their bets there and I'm looking forward to it again this year. It's a big time in Erris, everyone seems to be happy, meeting up with each other. There are a lot of things happening in the Erris area during the month of August, it's a very busy time for people at home and tourists. This year we have a new hotel in Belmullet. A seventy two bedroom hotel - an absolutely beautiful hotel and I'm delighted to see that as well. It was built by a local man, Mr. Padden, and it is doing well. The hotel in Geesala, another local man, Tom Gaughan, is also doing well. I like to see progress, to see things going on in Erris. We have beautiful scenery in Erris. We have lovely beaches and now we have our hotel. There will be a swimming pool added later this year in 2005. So everything is happening out here. The weather has been nice. I've had tourists in the shop today and they've been telling me that they stayed in the hotel in Belmullet. They were telling me about the price that they paid and they were happy enough. The whole family stayed for one week for six hundred euros, including bed and breakfast. They were very happy that the prices were reasonable because I believe too in keeping the prices down for tourists. It's a part of good business management to keep the prices as low as you can afford to, with your own profit of course! I think what's been happening in Ireland over the last five or six years has killed the tourists coming into this country, with the prices that accommodation was. Some of the shops too were over priced. A bed and breakfast for thirty five or forty euros, sixty five, seventy or eighty euros for a hotel - it's too much. I was talking to a couple today who are paying six hundred and fifty in the Erris area for a holiday home which I think is too much.

Chapter 11

<u>My Friend Elke</u>

*Elke moving into my holiday village / Like a second mother
Elke going home and getting sick
24th April - my birthday party / Family around me / Farm
On my way to an AA meeting / Friend in trouble in Crossmolina
with travellers / the way the travellers were treated by the guards
Meeting in Castlebar with Eamon O'Cuív
Travellers wedding in Killala
2nd May - In court again - not honouring an agreement
Going into court again on the 24th*

In early 1998 a lady came from Germany and she wanted to rent a holiday from me, for her mother. Her mother wanted to move to Ireland and she wanted to buy a home in Ireland. I advised the young lady at the time to rent a house for a period of time, whether it was from me or anybody else, to see would her mother like Ireland and settle in here. And then if she did like it to arrange to buy a home for her. But this lady came over in 2001 with her daughter. The mother's name is Elke. I showed her around my holiday homes, she had a choice of three homes to rent. She choose a two bedroom flat with a sitting room, kitchen and bathroom - upstairs in a family house - to rent. That was in 2001 and now it's 2005 and she is still here. When she came over we got friendly. She didn't have any English but since she came here she has picked up the English language. We turned out to be very good friends and she looks after the animals - the chickens, the ducks, the geese, the turkeys and she looks after pet lambs. Indeed she's aware of anything that happens around in the area. She keeps an eye on things around the whole area. She is more careful of my place than myself! We've become good friends over the months and years and indeed she is a friend to all my family. She is a friend to my kids, my grand kids and my partner Teresa. She's a friend to us all. She always bakes lovely homemade bread and I love her cooking. She makes sure that I'm looked after, she thinks the world of me. Indeed I can say this now that she has become my second mother. I lost my mother over a year ago and I was very close to her and I still miss her. Nobody will ever replace my mother. But Elke has come to be my second mother.

She is a woman that is loved by everybody in the area. She says hello to everyone. Her daughter, Ulrike, comes over a couple of times a year and the other daughter and her son, all come to visit her a couple of times a year also. We had a lovely Christmas together and she wouldn't go back to visit her kids because she felt that I would be alone at Christmas. So she stayed and she went to see them after Christmas. During her holidays at home visiting her family, her kids, she formed a sickness and she was rushed to hospital. The first couple of weeks they couldn't operate on her. One of her daughters contacted me and told me that it was very serious. I went to the church every day and prayed for Elke. I prayed to God that he wouldn't take her away from me or her family. There were days that I was on my own that I broke down and cried when I thought that I was losing somebody that I had got close to again, like my second mother. There was a part of me that thought that my mother would never die at all, and then Elke was the next in line to her. But there wasn't much hope for her. Then after a couple of weeks they decided to operate on her. I prayed for her and I used to light candles upstairs for her. Thanks be to God they removed two tumours from her and the operation went well. She came out of it. She is ninety per cent better, indeed I think that she is one hundred per cent better. She couldn't wait to get back again to her home in Flannery's Village. After five or six weeks over there while she was recovering all she wanted was to come back to Ireland. Now she's back and she's doing marvellous. I'm delighted with that and I thank God every day for leaving Elke to us because she is a gift. Yesterday was the 24th of April and it was my birthday. There was a lot of moving going on for the past few days there. Very secretive things - like Teresa on the phone. Teresa involved in a lot of things, calling my family and I didn't know what she was at, but she was inviting them to a party, my birthday party. I was so glad and so happy. All my kids and grand kids were there, my five grand kids. The only one that was missing was my baby daughter Maria. She couldn't make it because she was working in Naas, in the bank. But she sent a card and she called me and I know that she would be there if she could. It was a lovely party, my brothers and their wives all showed up and there were fourteen cars outside my door at about half four/five o'clock yesterday evening. I was so proud and so happy to have such a nice family thing going on. That is all I wanted to have the whole family there and watch the kids enjoying themselves and the grand kids. It was very nice. It's another happy memory of family life. Elke was there and of course she had baked the beautiful bread. I got a lot of cards, fourteen cards and there was a request on Mid West Radio for me. I felt so important, it was lovely. I thank God for giving me a life with my family all around me. My brother was taking pictures outside and it was such a beautiful day. I just thought of my mother through it all as everyone was chatting, eating and drinking and cutting the cake. The cake was made beautifully with the Irish flag on each end of it. Teresa knows, and everybody in my family knows, that I am a very proud Irish man. The Irish flag means a lot to me. I always fly the Irish flag, fifty two weeks of the year that Irish flag flies. When the bad weather tears it down I put it back up again. So to see the flag on my cake, for my birthday was very special. And it was very good to see everybody happy. And that's what is all about, families around each other and enjoying the gift of food that God gives us and the gift of happiness. Elke had put together an album of pictures that she had taken over the years that she has been here. Pictures of me, working with my animals and the sheep, each page had a picture of me and the animals. It was a lovely gift to get and made me smile and that's what I am, I am always a happy person. I'm very happy about the little things in life, the important things in life. I'm glad to see Elke around and seeing her well again. Indeed Teresa, a couple of months ago as well, had a cancerous tumour removed from her eye, but it is healing up good. She was with us and happy as well. It's good to see it, as the saying goes, your health is your wealth. So yesterday was an experience of a lifetime for me to see all the happiness. My family made me very happy and very proud.

Yesterday as well Teresa did all the work with the food, making the teas and calling my family. I didn't know that she had called them up to invite them to my party. My sisters and brothers and I are very close. We are a very close family with a good bond. My father and mother left a good gift to us in our up bringing. It was great then last night when my son and his partner invited myself and Teresa out for a Chinese in Belmullet, which we did. We had a beautiful meal and sat around and talked. I'm so proud of my son, he is a good lad and he has a good partner. He's a family man. It was great to see it and it's a gift I suppose that I carried on from seeing me because I was very close to him growing up too when he was a kid. The grand kids all love me and I see them every day and I always bring them something, either ice cream or chocolates. My son and daughter say that I have the grand kids spoiled but they are only kids once. Every morning they are waiting for me to go down to feed the animals so they can come out chatting to me while I'm feeding the animals. The thing that breaks my heart then is that they start crying when I'm leaving, especially Mark, my son's little fella. He's only two years of age and he tries to hang onto my clothes when I'm leaving and cries and this breaks my heart. But I know when I'm gone for ten or fifteen minutes that he's alright again.

My life is about my kids and my grand kids and Teresa gets on very well with them and the grand kids enjoy Teresa as well. She is very good to them, very thoughtful and it means an awful lot. Her own son was there as well yesterday showing my brothers how to play golf because we were never into golf. He was taking shots and one of my brothers who never took a shot in his life, took a great shot in the golfing. So it was all enjoyment, these things are very important to me. I was just so taken aback by it all. I stayed quiet and watched everybody and enjoyed everything. It was marvellous. And to see the animals in the field, the baby lambs, nature and nature is wonderful. I love nature and Elke also has grown to the nature and indeed everybody that is around me is fond of nature. I'm glad that I have the farm with all the chickens and the ducks and the geese and the turkeys and then laying eggs. I never buy eggs. I've always had animals and chickens and all that since my kids were young so that they could see where the eggs were coming from and they are healthier. Nature is a wonderful thing and it's good for the grand kids growing up here, to see that. It's an education for them that they will never forget. They'll always think of these things and it's so important to make sure that we show our kids the wonders of nature, because it carries with them for the rest of their lives.

Last night was the 1st of May and I was going out to an AA meeting in Belmullet. A friend in Crossmolina called me and he said that his shop was overtaken by people, travellers that were going into the shop and stealing things from him. He asked me would I come out to help him because he was frightened. He was on his own except for his wife and their two little kids. The travellers were very cheeky with him. I got into my car and I brought a weapon with me. There was a lot of them in it and I figured that if they were going to fight that they would have me and I wouldn't go down without a fight. So I took my weapon with me and I headed off to Crossmolina. When I got there, they were in the shop. We managed to get them out of the shop anyhow and he was able to close the shop. The town was forced to close down when they heard that these travellers had come in. They were there for a wedding in the hotel in Crossmolina. The pubs were closed and the other shops were closed. My friend had kept his shop open to show respect for the travelling community but some of them didn't respect him in return. They stole some goods from his shop. I went there to protect him and his family in case there was violence and I stood at the door of the shop. I saw that the police were there but they kept well back. There was about ten squad cars there. Early in the evening there was no violence. It was kept quiet. But then some of them moved on, there was about fifty of them left at this stage, and then the police knew that there was three hundred people at this wedding so the police then came into town but they kept well back from these people. There was one lady and she was on the street with two young kids. They were about five and two years of age. She had them in a pushchair and she was crying and screaming and shouting for the guards to come in where there was a dispute between some of her friends and her husband inside. I seen how the kids were dragged around the streets so I spoke to her. I told her to go in the van and that everything would be alright, and just to look after her kids. She didn't. She stayed on the street roaring and shouting. Finally a couple of the police came up around, but still stayed well back from her. One of them then came up to her and advised her to go in the van and her brother was going taking her home. At this stage you could see that there was a lot of drink involved. The police told them to get into their vans and drive away home and I couldn't believe what my eyes were seeing. This is the police that we have in Ireland today. They close down on people for drink and driving and now they were telling these people to drive and they were hardly able to stand up. They were going in the vans driving and the kids, babies, with them. I felt so sorry for the kids. I thought that the police would not let them drive. Maybe try to take them away to sober them up or even arrest them for drink and driving, because I thought that that was the law. But it seemed to me that the police didn't care because they were travellers and they didn't care what happened to these kids. The next thing one of them came up and started shouting at the lady that was roaring and shouting in the van. They were still shouting at each other across the street, and she walked up to her and made for her by the hair on her head and stuck a bottle through her face. To see that woman with the two young kids bleeding all over the place was so sad. Then there was another fella with a bottle, another traveller, so the police had a hold of him in one hand and I took the bottle off him. I was there to protect Joe's premises and the police didn't care about Joe's premises and they didn't care about the traveller's kids. I felt so sorry for these kids. They were all put into the vans and they all drove away and they weren't able to drive. They were drink driving but the police didn't care as long they didn't cause any problems for them. I stayed there until about one o'clock to protect my friend and his shop. Finally, one of them came over to me and he wanted to go into the shop and I told him that the shop was closed. I learned one thing about travellers, you don't show fear. He said "Well fucking open it". When I heard that I knew that he was violent. I told him to back away from the door or he wouldn't be able to go back to the hotel, that I would burst his brains all over the wall if he didn't fucking leave. So when I put my strength up against him he backed down and he went back to the hotel. He came over then again and shook my hand. It was just sad to see how the police didn't give a damn about these people as long as they got out of their town, and how they didn't force the law of drink driving on these travellers, because most of them weren't fit to drive them vans and jeeps. They just left the town and the police were just laughing and chatting, looking down on these people and I don't like to see that. I thought that we had a better police force than that and from listening to the television or the radio how they are enforcing the law in this country. The law in this country is so corrupt and getting worse. To see them then going around catching people, normal people that wouldn't break the law, but maybe would take two pints and they'd do them for drink and driving. So definitely I saw that the law was very much broken last night. My friend's shop was alright. He called me this morning and thanked me for coming to his rescue to help him. I was there and I have no fear in a thing like that. If somebody wanted to break up my friend's shop or anything to do with my friends, I'm not afraid of taking his side. I have no fear of getting beaten either. I can handle myself, fear of fighting wouldn't excite me. I don't go out to look for fights, but I can stick up for myself. That was my story last night. Just so sad to see the young kids and them shivering in the van and the police letting them go with drink driving.

I suppose travellers have been treated badly over the years, with hundreds of years. They feel that way too that people don't want them. That people don't like them and I suppose the way the police treat them, I suppose that's the way that they are gone. The traveller knows that he is on his own. It's like as if he is not part of society, that he feels that he's left out of society and it's sad that the travellers are treated that way. They feel like nobody wants them, and when you are left out like that, you begin to stick up for yourself, and there could be violence because you know that you are not accepted in society. I always respected them, for their culture of travelling. I remember being in Castlebar where there was a traveller's group meeting where they were trying to set up a Traveller's Group. I remember Eamon Ó Cuiv, the minister, was there and I was there to support the travelling community. I always respected them for the way that they are. It is a very hard life, our country is so rich today, and yet these travellers are left out along the road to fend for themselves. Then if the neighbours don't like them, they are moved on, and moved all over the country. Yet they are our true Irish people. Back hundreds of years they were treated very badly. When the Irish people got a bit of land and a home after the English landlord, they were put out on the road. They didn't get anything and they stayed on the road travelling and begging. They had to beg. I remember when we were kids, they used to come around with the wagons that time. My mother would always give them tea, sugar, bread and give them whatever we could afford to give them at the time. It's sad now a days that society has closed it's doors on them. The government hasn't recognised these people as Irish people which they are. They should house them and if they didn't want to be housed that there would be proper halting places set up for them where they could pull up their wagons, or their caravans. They should have schooling for their kids and encourage more schools and education for their kids. I believe a traveller gets a short life that they don't live as long as a settler because they are always on the move and cold weather conditions. I feel sorry for them sometimes, but I do always respect them and their culture.

I remember one time I was in a pub down in Killala where there was a traveller's wedding in this pub. The bride and groom came in and they had their party and their food and the drink and they had everything in the pub, and their dancing and the Irish music. I remember the way they treated myself and a friend of mine, we didn't have to buy a drink for the day, they were buying the drinks for us. They treated us very well. It was a travellers wedding and I think that it was one of the best weddings that I was ever at. I was drinking at that time. It was very good and interesting and they showed good respect. I think that when humans are not accepted in society and pushed aside, they feel like they have to come back and fight their way back. I think that the travellers do feel that they have to do that today to be recognised. I think there should be more respect shown to them and more encouragement to education and proper schools put up for these people. I know that there were some homes built for some of these travellers. But they were putting some of them up here and spreading the families out. These families have travelled all their lives on the road together and the government should respect them and listen to them as to where they want to settle down. There should be land bought for them and there should be houses put up for them. They always had a great culture with the horses and the donkeys. There should be land that the government should be able to give to them, to start their lives with their kids and their families, because I think that this country owes them that.

The 2nd of May I was taken into court again by my ex wife. She got a court order against me and a jail sentence for not honouring an agreement. I'm just tired and burnt out at going into court since 1999 by my ex wife and she's bringing me into court for the least thing. I sacked the old solicitor that I had that messed everything up for me. He seemed to be more on my ex wife's side and my ex wife's solicitor's side than he was for me. I have a new solicitor now, Michael McDervy, and at least I can talk to him, and explain my case. When I got to the court, his daughter that was representing me, Kathy, and she had a barrister there and another solicitor. Five minutes before the court was to start, which I didn't know, my solicitor came out and told me that it was serious this time. They had a jail sentence taken out against me for not honouring the agreement. The solicitors were saying to me that the Judge was very bad. The solicitors and the barristers looked nervous going into the court, going up before this Judge. We went into the court and we sat down. My ex wife's barrister stated the case. The reason for us being there was that a court order was taken out against me, and that I didn't honour any agreement, especially one agreement. The Judge listened to the case. My barrister didn't say much but he said that he wanted time for me to sort out my finance with one bank in particular. The Judge asked me how much time I would need. And I said "Your honour, if I got until August I will have it sorted out". He said that he would give me until the following morning at ten o'clock. I would have to come up with fifty five thousand euros, to clear what I owed, or else that I should bring my bag with me because I was going to jail. This is the justice I have got since my ex wife has brought me into court. I came out of the court and I was disgusted to see the smile on my ex wife's face. I never imagined that anyone could be so unreasonable, that I was married to such an unreasonable woman. A woman who dragged this through the courts, never caring about anyone. It doesn't make any difference to her that she is hurting the family, the kids, or who she hurts. How could any woman go putting the father of her three kids to jail? She has done this twice before. I have been overnight in jail, twice over my ex wife's lies in court. She lies to the police, makes statements against me and it's all lies. In this case I got no justice. There are days that I feel broken and it gets to me that I was treated so badly. There are days that I curse them to hell. Days that I wish that they will never have a day's luck after what they've done to me, to my business and to everything that I've ever worked hard for. I just made one phone call to a friend, a very close friend, and I told him what had happened. He told me that he wouldn't see that happen. He helped me out. He was there the next morning with a bank draft for fifty five thousand which saved me from doing seven months in jail. That's what I call a friend to. In this case I have very few friends that would have helped me out like this man. I don't think anyone else would have done what he done. He knows that I will pay him back and I will be grateful for the rest of my life to him. I will pay him back on the double, because that is the type of person I am. If someone does anything for me, I feel that I owe them for the rest of my life, even though I would have them paid back for it. About a week later, I was up in the hospital for a check up on a sickness that I have arising from the stress of the courts and what was done to me. But thank God I don't have to go back again for another nine months. Then when I came home, I went over to my shop and there was letters there. I asked my partner Teresa to read them to me. The first thing that she said was "Oh, she is bringing you to court again, the 24th". I just lost it. I went berserk. So then I studied the letter and indeed it was going back into court again on the 24th. Her solicitor had send me out papers on land that I had signed over to her, that was given to her on the settlement. Her solicitor and engineer were out here measuring up the lands that I signed over to her, and he had measured up my neighbour's land instead of my land, and go back into court again. Then I had to go to that engineer again to sort that out. The next day, and I wasn't supposed to do it, but I called up her solicitor. I asked him why he had sent me out a map of someone else's land. Why the engineer had drawn up these plans in such a stupid way, land that doesn't belong to me. The solicitor didn't want to talk to me and she told me to talk to my own solicitor. And I said "I'm sick and tired listening to you and my ex wife since 1999 and dragging this through the courts for years, I'm sick and tired of you". She said "I don't have to listen to you". I said "when this case is over, you will listen to me". I intend to follow this up. I intend to take my ex wife into court for lying in court and for lying under oath. She took the Bible several times in her hands, and lied under oath, to destroy me or to try and destroy me, my place and my family and everything. There's a part of me that will never forgive her.

Interview 2 Mid-West Radio

<u>Winning Farm Development Farmer of the Year Award</u>

The Flannery's Knitwear from Pullathomas scooped a major National Farm Award last night. The couple won the Farm Development Farmer of the Year Award and it was the first time ever that a Mayo entry won the category. The National event was held in County Down yesterday evening and a cheque for five thousand pounds with a trophy was presented to Flannery's. The competition is sponsored by the Irish Farmer's Journal, Teagasc and the Northern Ireland Ministry for Agriculture. Today our reporter, Teresa O'Malley, managed to make contact with Patrick Flannery in County Down and she congratulated him and his wife on their achievement.

Patrick
Oh, it's great! The Farm Development Award of the Year - and that's developing the farm, the knitwear factory we have and the self catering cottages in an area out in Graughill, Pullathomas, which is known now as Flannery's Village.

Teresa
So I'm sure they'll be great celebrations there today when they realise that you have taken the National title but in other words then, it's not just for one thing that you do, it's for the combination of your lifestyle.

Patrick
Yeah, that's right Teresa, it's for, as I said, the farm, the knitwear factory and the self catering cottages and all the work that has been done there with the last two years.

Teresa
Well now you actually have twenty local people employed in your knitwear factory?

Patrick
That's right, there's twelve and there's eight going on, there's twenty hand knitters around the coast there as well that are employed with us. So it's great, I'm all excited.

Teresa

Well now it was with tough competition. There were six finalists there last night. Did it come as a surprise to both of you?

Patrick

Yeah it did, it did, you know I was shocked when my name was called out for the award and delighted but with the effort that we put into it paid off.

Teresa

Well I don't know if this particular award was ever won before by a Mayo entry, do you know that?

Patrick

No it wasn't. I was told last night now by Seamus O Mongain from Teagasc who is with me. It was him that advised me on the farm and the work that has been carried out on it. No it's one of the first I'm been told.

Teresa

Well that makes it all the sweeter I'm sure. Well you were presented with your cheque and a trophy by the Ministry for Agriculture for Northern Ireland, Lord Dubbs. That in itself must have been quite a big occasion?

Patrick

Oh, yes it was. I was all excited! I didn't sleep too well last night with all the celebrations that was going on here last night, a big meal and it's going on again today. We are going to be taken out and shown around the people's places around here that did development in farming as well. So we are been taken out on a bus tour so it's all celebrations and I can't wait to get home.

Teresa

Do you know who was on the adjudicating panel?

Patrick

Seamus has them in a list there now but I haven't got it off by heart.

Teresa

However the competition itself is run jointly by the Northern Ireland Agricultural Ministry by the Farmer's Journal and there are others involved but it's quite a prestigious farming award.

Patrick
That's right Teresa. There were some judges from Galway too and Dublin that were involved in the Northern Ireland judging as well. I don't know many of them altogether.

Teresa
Ok well look we appreciate it, it's an exciting morning for both yourself and your wife. Congratulation, well done and I'm sure Pullathomas will all be celebrating today.

Patrick
Well I hope so, I am looking forward to getting home tonight, I don't know what time I will be getting home at so thanks Teresa.

<u>End of Interview</u>

That was an interview after winning an award by Teresa O'Malley of Mid West Radio and that was in 1997 that I won the All Ireland Development Award. It was a big achievement at the time and yes, we had a big do over in McGrath's. I put on a do over in McGrath's two nights after that. There was a big crowd that did show up but there was a lot that didn't show up. Jealousy a lot of it, awards are won by hard work and good staff and positive thinking like what I had at the time. I was going ahead to build this area as a tourist attraction to the area. But it was very hard that time to get anyone to move with you or to be for you or to be supporting you. The problem with Erris is the jealousy that is there and jealousy anywhere always holds things back instead of moving things forward. People who are jealous of each other don't move forward and it's a thing that I never had. I love to see people achieving things and winning like I did with that award, and achieving that award in 1997. I was proud that I had done it and that Teagasc had put me forward for it - they had seen the work that I had put into the development of the farm and the knitwear and the holiday homes, that I was a good target for this All-Ireland award and it was good to do it and to win it.

I seen at the time, my wife at the time, a lot of jealousy set into the marriage, I seen a lot of changes in the marriage. She really was jealous of me being recognised even though she should have known herself was being recognised as well by this award. That was September 1997 when I won the award and that Christmas the rows started getting worse and she went off and left me for Christmas and left the kids with me. She went out home to her family and spent the whole Christmas abroad at her mother's home. It was a lonely 1997 for me, to think how well I had done in one sense and I hadn't the support that you would expect from a partner. It was terrible. It was a very lonely Christmas, I didn't go out at all for that Christmas in 1997. When Christmas was over, when she had her nights out with her sisters and brothers that were home from England and enjoyment, she came back. Then I knew that it was over anyway. The marriage was over then, because, whatever way it was before 1997, it was all downhill after that. The people that you think that should be more understanding and stick by you, like your partner or your wife, and you can see them going the other way. I could never talk to her about it, even if I tried it would cause a row. When I look back on it now, she was jealous of me, someone like me that could do things and achieve things. She couldn't accept that she was apart of these things for the family. I realise today that she didn't want a husband she wanted a prisoner. When I started getting recognised and getting out there and getting recognised for the work that I was putting into the area and hard work and when I was entered for this award I expected more from her, that she would have more understanding, that she was a part of it. But no, if it wasn't her that did it all, it wasn't recognised. Jealousy played a part with my wife at the time and she didn't support me the way she went on and carried on.

I lived in an area out here in Erris where they didn't like to see you going up. If you were doing well, they tried to pull you down and they would rather see you going down rather than going up because there is a lot of jealousy, for a person that starts a business out here, especially if you are from the local area. If you are a stranger coming in, they would accept you as a business person, but if you are from the local area they wouldn't accept you. That's the way it was and that's the way it is today. There's a lot of jealousy among people. So you don't expect it, it's bad enough to have neighbours jealous of you or your area jealous of you, indeed there was some good people in the area too.

Chapter 12

<u>My Daughter Maria – Queen of Punschestown</u>

Maria / Queen of Punches town / Races
Wolfe Tones organised to play in Teach Iorrais
Missing my parents
Another friend with a problem
Mother in Belfast - son has problem
Fishing with Teresa, Alan, Elke and Ulrike - memories of
fishing
My mother's anniversary
Landslide in Glengad / Pullathomas

It's the 30th of April and I went to Naas again to see my daughter at the Punchestown Races, where she was participating in the Queen of Punchestown. I was picked up by John Green who won thirteen All Ireland Championships in Car Racing. It was the fastest time ever that I was in a car, at one hundred and forty miles per hour, that's what he was doing every place he brought me. We got into the Racecourse to see my daughter Maria all dressed up. She was brought there by limo, it made me a very proud man to be there to support my daughter on that day. We placed some bets but we lost, four or five bets but we had a great day at the races. There was myself and Teresa and my friend Mr. Green. Then we went off down to Naas that night and we went into all of the pubs. Mr. Green was so well known, it was fifteen euros to get in to the hotel night club, but we were just let in because Mr. Green knows all the bosses. We met some more famous racers and we spoke with them as well. We met this fella when we were parking our car and he came up to us and he started showing us how to park. Mr. Green was kind of smart with him but I just thanked him for being so kind. During the night we bumped into him three times, and the last time, he sat down and started talking to me. Within ten minutes, he was pouring his life story out to me where he had a butcher shop in Naas and he was doing good business. He was married with three kids. He told me what happened to him. He developed a gambling problem and he lost the shop and his wife. She left him and he suffered through gambling and his brother came to his rescue and sent him to a Gambling Anonymous meeting. That didn't work too well for him so he went to this Heal and Prayer priest. This priest helped him out and within six weeks he had beaten his gambling habit. Then a new life started for him. He has never looked back since, it was like he was re born again.` The healing priest left his hand on his head and at each session he felt that the gambling habit was leaving him. He was the happiest man that I saw there that night in Naas. He told me his whole story and his father told him to be a fisherman one time. Of course I was a fisherman so I could identify with him on the fishing. But it is nice that people come to me - people that I have never met before in my life - and they share their problems with me. I hear people's life stories that will go to the grave with me. People really trust me to tell me their life stories. I think the answers that I give them gives them encouragement to move on as well. So I'm lucky to be able to do that for people. It gives me a great feeling in my life. After that we went back to the hotel again and then we visited Wolfe Tone's grave, he was one of the great Irish Republicans. And across from the grave is the beautiful Stone Building, where we stayed. He was a friend of Mr. Green's that I got to know as well. He is also a Mercedes dealer. We had such a great day. The next morning I took the train, on the first of May, to come home and travelling through Ireland makes me so proud to be Irish in my country. To see the beautiful homes and the people in Naas and all over in Ireland so friendly. It's great to see it. So I'm going to call Maria now, the Queen of Naas.

Today is the 1ˢᵗ of May and I organised a dance with the Wolfe Tones to come into Erris, to play in Teach Iorrais. There are people ringing me all the time for tickets so I expect a big crowd as usual. The fundraising that I am doing tonight is for the football pitch. The profits will go to the pitch in Pullathomas to help the young people in the area. They will have their own changing rooms, toilets, meeting rooms. They want to upgrade the pitch in Pullathomas that Paddy McGuire donated to the youngsters of Pullathomas. He donated the field for them. That's what I will be doing tonight. I'm ready here now to go out my door and to be on the door collecting the tickets. This is not the only one, I do a lot of fundraising in the area. I have raised funds for Sinn Féin for years, for their campaigns. At Christmas, I also had a big fundraiser with the Wolfe Tones for the Columbian Three and we raised about five thousand euros profit on the night. The majority of the money went towards the Columbian Three. I'm after hearing a couple of nights ago that they are free of all the charges, and I am glad. Except the charges for the licences that they were travelling with. They were guilty of that. I'm proud of that. I made a speech on behalf of them at Christmas.

Today is the May 2, and I left home to go down to Porturlin to pick up a fresh salmon, a fourteen pound salmon, from my brother. Now that my mother is not in Porturlin any more I don't go there that often. There's just too many memories of my mother and my father there for me. They were the happiest times when I used to be going down to Porturlin. I always knew that the door was open for me and the lights were on, and the salmon was cooked by my mother. It's half nine at night and I am visiting my mother's grave and heart broken. Sometimes I think that when you love somebody like I love my mother, that it would be easier if I was gone. It just crosses me now and again how much I appreciated her and respected her and when I visit the grave at least it gives me a bit of comfort. I talk to my father and mother at the grave and thank them. I couldn't have wished for a better mother or a better father. They showed such kindness to me and goodness and strength and education of life. I knew that I could never read and I remember one time, just myself and my mother alone in the house, sitting by the fire and my mother saying to me "Patrick, as long as you have a tongue in your head, you will never go astray". And that is true. That education that she gave me always carried me. I'm looking at the beautiful flowers that myself, my sisters and brothers keep on the graves. It's so hard to let go of them. Even though I know that they are gone but it's just so hard. It's like there's a part of me that's dead and I can never replace. I get strength when I come to the grave, just to thank them and the goodness they are doing for me up there. So I love them both and I'll finish for now. At least I can always come to where they are resting and buried and I know that they are happy in Heaven. God bless both of them.

This evening is the 15th May and I'm leaving my home to go to a friend that has a problem. Himself and his wife are not agreeing and he needs somebody to talk to. They had an argument, they haven't spoken for two years. They had an argument over something in the house and he wouldn't be violent. He would argue his point but he wouldn't be the type of a person to hit his wife. But she called the guards. They came out to the house and he's taking it very badly. When I was talking to him this evening, giving him advice over the phone, it's a sad story when the homes break up and couples tear each other apart. With the experience that I had I'm able to give him something back and send him down the right road. To get him to try and come to some agreement with her and not to be so bitter or tear themselves apart and to take advice from solicitors, which I think is the road that it's heading now. But I didn't like to hear him saying that he would kill her and he would drown himself. I'm glad to say that with talking to him over the phone for ten minutes I told him that that was the wrong road. But I don't think that he would do that, I think that he would kill himself before he would kill her. I'm honoured to be able to go out and talk to people with problems like break up of marriages and he's drinking today over this. He turns to drink when pain is in his life. I know what that is like too. So I'm going as far as Porturlin now to talk to him and give him some advice and hope that he will listen to me and take some of the good advice that I will give him.

Well I'm just after arriving home after spending five hours with the lad that I went out to see there. Where himself and his wife were going through a bad time. While I was with him he wanted to go to the pub to have a few drinks. I talked to him before he went to the pub and I realised that the only way to calm him down was to take him to the pub. So I took him to the pub anyway as he started talking to me about it. I tried to take away the bitterness and the sadness from him, and the temper, to cool him down. I said "You might not even think this, but what you are going through right now, she is going through much the same". He didn't agree with me at first but finally he started to agree with it. But he said that the marriage was over, once the police came to the house, and neighbours finding out about it. I told him that his marriage wasn't about his neighbours. That it was about himself and the woman that he is married to, and it was up to them to sort it, not the neighbours. But I'm glad to see that he's calmed down. I left him at home and he told me that he would go to bed. I told him that I would call him in the morning to check on him and to see how he is getting on. I will be contacting his wife as well. I'm happy tonight that I've done a good job. I like helping people if I can and leave them in the hands of God and pray to God that he will guide them for both of them. They could go on with their own lives or stay together. I thank God for the help that I can give people.

It's half one in the night, sometimes it takes hours to get through to people when I am trying to get a message through to them.

It's the 17th of May and it's about eleven o'clock at night and I am just after getting a call from a mother from Belfast, who wants to talk to me about her son. He is thirty three years old and he's married with four young kids. The youngest is about a year old, and the wife has threatened to put them out of the home if he doesn't do something about his drinking. The mother doesn't know how her son could develop a drinking problem. She wanted to know what would have caused it. I told her on the phone that nothing causes it, it's a disease, a sickness. In most cases that her son wouldn't be able to face life without drink, once he passed that fine line, of alcohol. So I talked to her for about half an hour and I told her that the best thing she could do for the son was to bring him into a treatment centre. He will be there for six weeks where they will have AA meetings there, and when he comes out of AA to call me (the son). He will have to go to meetings to stay sober, one day at a time. She was more content then when she realised that it is a sickness and it's nothing to be ashamed about. He is not on his own. There's millions of people all over the world with the same sickness of alcohol abuse. As she explained to me about what was happening with his wife, and it's very hard for his wife with four young kids, where he spend all day in the pub. But she said that when he was working then he worked hard. I explained that when you are an alcoholic you have to work harder than an ordinary person because to feed the drink habit you need a lot of money. I'm glad that I was able to help her out and put her mind at ease. I told her to keep in touch with me and I will talk to her son over the phone and help him through the problem. The main thing that he has done is that he is admitting that he is an alcoholic. That he has a drinking problem. That's half the battle that he realises that he is an alcoholic. The next step is to do something about it. I'm lucky to be able to carry that message to his mother and to him and explain about alcohol, it's a sickness and it's a very serious disease and it's a killer disease. He'll be ok. So that's my job tonight, to talk to them and carry the message to a suffering alcoholic. I'm delighted to do that.

Today is the 30th May 2004 and I went back down to Porturlin to go fishing with my brother, Alan. He told me to take the boat out and I was out with Elke, her daughter Ulrike and Teresa, my partner. We brought some deep sea fishing lines with us and it was great to be able to go out again from Porturlin. We went out and we fished off the Pig Island. We got fresh mackerel and Alan gave us some lobsters. It just brought back all the memories to me since I was a kid back out there fishing in Porturlin. How lucky we were to be brought up in such an environment and to be able to go out there and make a living out of the sea. I'm watching all the fishing boats in Porturlin this evening coming in - some of them are fishing salmon. It brought back memories to me when I would be out fishing with my father from eleven years old and all the good training he gave me of surviving in the sea. It was great to be out at sea again catching some fish and to look at the beautiful rocks from the ocean and the cliffs at Porturlin. It reminded me of one time when we were down in Porturlin fishing mackerel and we used to be salting boxes and boxes and barrels and barrels of mackerel. My mother would be many a time down at the pier, and two or three with her, cutting mackerel. We were fishing them, my father salting them in barrels and it brought back memories to me. It was also great to see a man that grew up with me, Tony O'Donnell, who had a by pass three months ago and was on his death bed, down there at the pier this evening and him taking a rowing boat out to where the boats were anchored. It was great to see it. And all the old people that I used to know in Porturlin - the older ones aren't around anymore. And the youngsters down at the pier and them telling me where to get the fish off the pier, it brought back all the memories to me. It was a great trip to be out on the ocean again. I miss it, I miss the people that I fished with. I miss my father who taught me to fish the sea, to learn about the sea, to challenge the sea but never defy the sea, and respect it. Being out there this evening brings all the memories back to me of my father and mother. I'm lucky to have my brothers who are still fishing and are carrying on the tradition for what we were brought up with. God bless the fishermen.

I'm looking across at Ballyglass Lighthouse and looking out on Broadhaven Bay such a beautiful evening and the sun just going down at the butt of the sky. And watching the fishing trawlers going across the bay, some of them going into Ballyglass, and the beautiful ocean. I know that I could never go away from the sea, it's a part of me. Every time I look out I see the beauty of the sea and the peace and quietness and sometimes to listen to the sea hitting against the rocks, down in Graughill. All my holiday homes, my holiday village is looking right out on that beautiful setting.

I was asked there lately would I go back to the sea again. There's a part of me that will always go back to the sea, I think I would. There's a part of me that can never go away from the sea. It's like I am the sea. Right now I am looking at a fishing trawler all lit up going across from Broadhaven Bay heading towards the Kid Island, heading down towards Porturlin, that's the way she's heading. It's so peaceful, there's nobody around - it's absolutely Heaven. When I see the fishermen being abused by governments, by the rights for their fishing, neglected and sold out, parts of it sold out, it makes me angry that governments would do such a thing. That is the ocean that fed us when we were kids growing up and a lot of other kids like us, like the Flannery kids and all the kids in Porturlin. That was our harvest, the finest of fish, the great lifestyle that we had, and we all came home safely. Thank God of all the years that I fished in Porturlin, nobody was ever lost at sea and God was with us. It's true, it's no man's land out there, it's God's world when you are out in the sea. I know that every time I go out on the water, I can feel it. I spent bad nights out in the sea fishing with the sixty five foot trawler that I had, in storm force ten touching eleven, hurricanes. Sometimes I gave my life to God, I was in God's hands and we made it home. God saved us at sea. I would say that I find God in the sea and the water and I'm lucky to have found that. It was such a great honour to go out again to the sea.

It's the 5th of July and I'm here again with my father and mother and my uncle's graves down in Rinroe. I was on my way to a meeting in Ballycastle, an AA meeting and I just felt that I should go to the grave. I started thinking about them and how much I missed them so I came to the grave instead. I feel at peace when I come to the grave and I say a few prayers and pray for my family as well to guide them along. It's only a week ago or ten days ago that it was my mother's anniversary. There was mass in Cornboy church. The church was almost full with all the relations and friends that came. Some of them came over from England and it was nice to see the big crowd of people and it was sad too. There was a load on my heart thinking about my mother. All the family are finding it just as difficult to let go. It's like we all scattered and we come to the grave to pray to my parents and I think that helps an awful lot. I know now of the pain of other people who lost their fathers and mothers. I have to let go of my parents with love but I don't forget them, I never will. They seemed to be a part of me as I was making my way to Ballycastle tonight and I think it was the right thing to do. I pulled a few flowers along the road and brought them to the grave.

That night after the anniversary mass, we all went back to the grave first and then we went back down to our parents house. It was like old times again with all the food and teas for everyone. That's the way that my mother used to have the house and my father. The door is always open for people to come in and no matter what food was on the table my mother shared it. She often took the back seat herself and made sure everyone else got fed before her. It was just like the way it used to be except there were two special people missing, my parents. But I'm sure that they would be proud to see what was going on in the home place that night. In the church it was sad, there was a lot of crying. I felt an awful load on my chest and was holding back the tears. I come always to the grave to give me comfort. I'm always praying and I feel very close to them all the time, and I'll never let them go in that since. I know that they are happy in Heaven now. I'm sure my father would be happy watching the site that I am here before me. And I'm looking over at Glengad and Pullathomas where the landslide was. Where I nearly lost my life and Teresa and Siobhan and Anthony, and a lot more people with us. It was so bad on the roads and the mountain and to look at it this evening it's amazing, how God and nature are wonderful things, nobody can hold back nature. Even the grass has grown back on the hills again, it has left it's mark on the mountains and the people. It's certainly made it's mark on some people with greed for money, wanting as much money as they could get out of it. I was just talking to Bridgie and Paddy this evening and how there was a meeting and how the people were arguing and fighting about how much money they could get out of it. There's a lot of people like that in the Pullathomas and Glengad areas after the landslide. And then on the other side, there are a lot of people that are not like that, they are just happy to be alive, like myself, and to move on with life. Everybody gets enough money at the end of the day anyway. So it's nice that God didn't take anybody's life that night and that people can still live in the area. I see all the new houses going up and it's lovely to see it. I'm looking from the grave yard here and I'm sure my parents were with us on that night. I know I certainly asked them for their help that night and my prayers were answered. They were both up there helping us that night. But it's a beautiful evening and it's relaxing, there's nobody around but myself. I like that, the peace and the quietness. I'm leaving the grave yard now and I'm saying God bless Mom and Dad and my uncle Peter, and I always love them.

Well now I'm back down in Porturlin - the village that I was brought up in and the village that I fished out of since I was eleven years old with my father.

<u>Conclusion</u>

I did not write this book to hurt anyone's feelings but I know that sometimes the truth does hurt. I hope this book will help somebody in their own lives. Today I have a good relationship with my kids and all my grandchildren who I often get to baby-sit. I love my kids and grandkids dearly.

Patrick Flannery